FL

HOUSES

of

FOUR

SEASONS

FLAWED
HOUSES
of
FOUR
SEASONS

A Memoir

JAMES MORRIS

atmosphere press

Contents

Preface

Mrs. Lawrence with her distinctive tone of annoyance and her usual deep southern drawl peered directly at me, *"Morris, shut your mouth!"* – words I heard more than once in eighth-grade English. Annoying my teachers was not characteristic behavior. I typically worked hardest at attempting to be liked by the teacher in order to veil academic inadequacies. Unfortunately for me, I had been exposed in eighth-grade English. My first real attempt at fiction writing a disaster. Mrs. Lawrence knew something I didn't know at the time – if I'd just *shut my mouth* and concentrate long enough on writing, I might have produced something more legible than what I submitted. No wonder she was annoyed with my talking. My first serious attempt at fiction titled, *The Spiders* – a sloppy mess of rambling, incoherent sentences full of red circled misspellings. The worst offense, *"t-h-a-y"* – throughout the faulty manuscript spelled *they* with an a. She must have thought, *good grief, he's in eighth grade.* I share my eighth-grade writing experience to illustrate two critical points. First, Mrs. Lawrence was the only teacher in my twelve years of education to require a lengthy fictional story that I recall – she forced us to write against our natural inclinations to avoid it. I'm certain other teachers assigned writing, but not as she did. Second, I was not prepared to write anything based on an organizational writing format and lacked a basic knowledge of proper sentence structure and general word usage – likely didn't even know the difference between fiction and nonfiction.

A love for writing may have sprouted in eighth grade, but didn't blossom until freshman English in college – a pivotal moment for certain. In adulthood, writing served as an outlet for expressing unconventional thoughts and concerns on a number of issues primarily in education. My Master's program required intensive reading and writing – prized every moment of sharing my views. Worked closely with a board of directors at a private institution fourteen years where I sharpened my persuasive writing skills. Purposely provoked the status quo because several closed minds needed a jolt – a cautious use and avoidance of certain trigger words also necessary. My writing at this point flowed rather naturally, allowing my quarterly board reports to illuminate what I perceived as failing policies and fading traditions.

The book didn't start as a memoir, publishing the furthest thing from my mind – never gave it a thought. I simply desired a family history for my daughter. My focused writing started after a detailed account of my mother's last day on earth. When a second profound discovery changed the family history narrative, the story began to slowly shift and take on a life of its own. I decided more must be shared – origins, reasons for choices, why certain life events played out as they did. Additional ancestry details were unearthed, I began to fit pieces together, see patterns not seen before, suddenly sensed a deeper story developing. Tentacles appeared to reach far and wide – life changing choices and decisions – people of influence – but most intriguing, people of little importance or authority began to fit into the overall narrative.

Once the serious writing process was underway, inspiration streamed into each chapter. My story, soon to become a memoir, had to be written for more than one because people sometimes start on the lowest academic rung and find pathways to success. People are often strapped with layers of deviation from the norms of proper socially acceptable behavior but discover ways to bypass, not settle for a future of perpetual dysfunction. Some people do not allow the past to determine the future – a worn out cliché but true. My stream of consciousness, verbose sentences sprinkled with dashes, episodes not chronologically ordered, are intended to entertain – evoke past memories and especially for the quotidian particulars of life – a copious amount is shared. I don't believe people herald ordinariness enough – it calms, soothes, forces reflection – ordinariness leads me to deeper understandings and more level-headed choices.

Concluding an extensive self-study of memoir writing, reading memoirs and poring over numerous selections from a variety of published works, I cautiously accepted the self-assigned task. The title changed six times as I transferred remembrances onto a fast-growing manuscript – words and paragraphs deleted; sentences restructured more times than I remember. Debated a malaise of disorder and whether to include or exclude certain people and situations. Questioned how best to communicate my deepest hurts and sorrows. Authentic honesty and truthfulness felt right after dumping the first white-washed version. The restart needed true-life language, *choice words,* words used often during my rearing by a portion of family and friends – words that may offend the most sensitive readers. To put it bluntly, decided candor is the best route. But determining how to connect a childhood story to an adulthood story seemed my greatest challenge. Memoir writing typically covers a portion of one's life, but I finally ironed out that wrinkle to my satisfaction and spent the next few months self-editing. Mrs. Lawrence would be proud I finally shut my mouth long enough to concentrate and permitted a memoir to be born and completed. And for the record, I've always been a poor speller but finally mastered the word *they*.

Introduction

Trials and persecution lasted twenty-five lengthy years and once released he didn't know how to appreciate the fullness of life that was lavishly bequeathed upon him – he believed he was well prepared – aliveness was strikingly different. He'd been conditioned to react with suspicion, partial to no trust for anyone showing any type of loving gesture toward him, this now included his wife – his love veiled by natural lust and desire for the flesh. He didn't know how to enjoy this new found freedom – still a captive of his own damaged nature he stealthily protected himself from further harm and sadness. He pretended with expert precision – hiding behind facades he loathed was his game and he played it well. He was *fortunate* to have been surrounded by *excellent mentors* twenty-five years.

Very slowly another person began to emerge from the cocoon of protection, although he still found solace within the aging and ripped space that was all his own. As life moved forward all around, he became more fully engaged at times, taking more risks – realizing daily routines of ordinariness kept his life more manageable. He began to sense there was so much more to discover, appreciate, truly love and accomplish. He did not comprehend those lessons until well after each episode, hindsight is always 20/20. Perhaps his incarceration had served a deliberate purpose – deeper meanings rested behind each episode that would eventually fuel future endeavors. He did not recognize how he was being prepared, molded, refined and wrought into what he was created to accomplish.

He sometimes fought tooth and nail against the goads attempting to push him forward into unfamiliar territory – but it was territory he needed to explore and embrace. He despises coercion from any source and has resisted conventional wisdom on many levels – it had to be done his way or no way. Those battles primarily raged within his head. He gradually began to give in and relinquish his will to a higher Will. Although battles still existed within – each subsequent battle lessened the wrangling.

His discovered submission to a greater Will is the consummate struggle for him. He still questions everything, ask his wife. His questions come in many different forms, but there is a constant refrain – how is all this possible as he gazes across the short span of his existence? How has he accomplished anything when he has allowed himself so often to be marred in an overabundance of trivial pursuits? So much of what he sees around him, even in the smartest of people, seems a waste of precious time on useless issues – an expenditure on garbage. Someone far beyond his decrepit and feeble capabilities must be guiding him, leading him, directing him onto correct pathways. But he still questions, how can this be?

He knows learning must never end or he ends. He knows everyone that has crossed his path has taught him an abundance of valuable lessons – both negative and positive. He knows brevity of life and his longing to experience one more precious moment with a few souls, but knows it will never come. He knows he must deal in reality, although difficult for him. He knows he has no other option in the face of all that has been lavished upon him after the first quarter. He knows life can be tough and life can be easy – his life perfectly displays both. He knows that at many junctures critical decisions determined his fate. He knows he was loved on some strange level as a child but never understood his parent's manner of expressing that love. He knows he was short-changed emotionally and fights to overcome that deficit. Would his life have taken a different course had he been given an alternative path? He knows eliminating any significant or insignificant occurrence in his life might have drastically altered outcomes – possibly in dangerous and destructive directions. But he cannot seem to fully release the *what ifs*.

Rudyard Kipling's poem *IF* provides inspiration about how to live despite challenges. Had it been ingrained as a child by affectionate, attentive parents, perhaps he would have been spared – he will never know. Or perhaps, he would have ignored advice as so many do when parents attempt to intentionally guide children on true and worthwhile paths. Again, he will never know. Kipling's *IF* has potential to be universally impactful when spoken by well-meaning parents or caregivers fashioned by their own personal interpretation and style of language. Kipling believed it was possible for young vulnerable listeners to be positively turned forever in a right direction...

IF
If you can keep your head when all about you
Are losing theirs and blaming it on you,
If you can trust yourself when all men doubt you,
But make allowance for their doubting too;
If you can wait and not be tired by waiting,
Or being lied about, don't deal in lies,
Or being hated, don't give way to hating,
And yet don't look too good, nor talk too wise:

If you can dream—and not make dreams your master;
If you can think—and not make thoughts your aim;
If you can meet with Triumph and Disaster
And treat those two impostors just the same;
If you can bear to hear the truth you've spoken
Twisted by knaves to make a trap for fools,
Or watch the things you gave your life to, broken,
And stoop and build 'em up with worn-out tools:

If you can make one heap of all your winnings
And risk it on one turn of pitch-and-toss,
And lose, and start again at your beginnings
And never breathe a word about your loss;
If you can force your heart and nerve and sinew
To serve your turn long after they are gone,
And so hold on when there is nothing in you
Except the Will which says to them: 'Hold on!'

If you can talk with crowds and keep your virtue,
Or walk with Kings—nor lose the common touch,
If neither foes nor loving friends can hurt you,
If all men count with you, but none too much;
If you can fill the unforgiving minute
With sixty seconds' worth of distance run,
Yours is the Earth and everything that's in it,
And—which is more—you'll be a Man, my son!

–Rudyard Kipling

One can only hope children without these words of guidance and encouragement, in some form, will encounter thoughtful and caring individuals as he did, and will one way or another discover alternate paths that ultimately lead to a life of fulfillment.

Spilling

"That's a hell of a story," he mused with a seemingly curious, confirming nod and slenderest of grin. Fifty-eight years after childhood innocence first began to gradually erode, we awkwardly met at the rear entrance. He checked my temperature – traditional handshake banned. We ascended the concrete stairs to his private corner space with a sunny view. He asked if it was okay, we could remove our masks – made it clear he was not politically correct – that eased a bit of my apprehension. He and I both sat on couches, his dark brown leather and mine grayish olive green, soft puffy cushions enveloped me, we sat opposite one another. He appeared totally comfortable nestled onto leather after pulling one leg across the other, dangled foot slightly shaking just beyond a fixed knee – one hand holding his ankle he rested a booklet for notes on the makeshift bureau. He asked what I was seeking. My mind swirled with initial responses – nothing seemed like the right opening, but everything needed full disclosure – my chance to confide in another male without constraint – but could I remove the *real mask*?

Allowing my body posture to relax a bit more, tension eased into my seated position. He appeared to exude masculine confidence I don't naturally possess – estimated he was early forties with his updated taper-fade cut and scruffy short beard. The first ever *spilling my guts* – don't hold back. His space a minimalist style – a large framed print of shelved record albums titled *Vinyl* above his couch – a guitar mounted on the wall, he must love music, small computer desk, credentials framed and hung above, a few personal items mixed with neatly arranged books on a sparsely filled book shelf. Above my couch a framed cartoon satire and politically incorrect statement regarding addictions – I wasn't offended. Time flew. I didn't want the time to end. My verbal stream of consciousness overflowed. Validated – I departed and prepared to resume *spilling* until emptied because he only knew a portion. Told myself six weeks and pondered his *"hell of a story"* musing on the drive home.

Yearning validation and acceptance in the sixth decade are honestly no different than sixth grade – desperately needed it then – desire it now. Fascinating how simple words penetrate each synapse regardless of age and how choices lead to succeeding or failing. Thankfully, remarkable discoveries and revelations are born of failure, the lightbulb, telephone, Ford Motor Company, liquid-fueled rockets – sometimes people like me. Since the beginning of time, we've desired more and more, we are perpetually unsatisfied – a natural human strength and weakness. Human destinies set in motion by choices often create royal messes or, a *hell of a story,* as I was told. We are afforded choices, and choices good or bad alter circumstances. Two fates born of Eden shaped by choices led to malfeasance before God, *"Am I my brother's keeper?"* – a declaration of natural human denial. Funny how little has changed since then.

A strongminded desire to overcome external choices ruled my existence even though I continually struggled. That's life on earth in a nutshell unless pathways lead one back to a remnant of *Eden* – aren't we all searching for it in some form? I'm not attempting to paint a miserable portrait of life, but simply stating truth as I once knew it. Nothing I've created has altered the world, although life events around age six and beyond altered my world. A number of significant choices and what most would consider insignificant moments remain deeply imbedded, vibrant within my conscious – profound because adults around me either botched it or got it right, botched seemingly more highly favored. The first twenty-five was generally shitty with a few exceptions. How did I manage to overcome all the shit thrown at me? Did I learn to dodge and appropriately respond? My story is nothing earth shaking except for the fact my ordinariness of life is exclusive – it's my story of life altering choices. My life, though, is no more distinct or favored than anyone's. This is the true story of how I reckoned with everything thrown at me, how a legion of human complexities, failures, triumphs and Divine coexisted to shape my fate.

In order to communicate a true story requires one to be a little risky, telling mine with full disclosure and honesty, I believe, is the only way, (at least to the closest degree possible). Men typically struggle to be completely open and honest with feelings and thoughts. Why is that true of the human male species? Why are men rarely transparent when telling a story? As little information as possible is the characteristic norm. Men seldom share their deepest emotions unless there in a close-knit support group or safe setting they completely trust – I had finally discovered my safe setting. Transparency does open one up to judgment and ridicule, but that's okay with me. I've been judged wrongly and ridiculed by many individuals. My concern, though, is always how transparent should I be? In certain social settings I've attempted to step ever so slowly into the transparent realm but would sometimes sense an uneasiness from my hearers. In those moments I retreated to a safer physical space or simply back-tracked with a statement to redirect conversation and ease tension.

Literary proficiency and general knowledge for me were severely hindered and stifled by a common characteristic of poverty – my parents didn't take the time or spend money to expose me to classic children's literature – they were too immersed in their own shit show. My exposure to literature in general occurred at school by a few well-intentioned teachers. I knew basic fairytales and loved L. Frank Baum's, *The Wonderful Wizard of Oz* – that's the extent of my childhood exposure. Which explains why I write in a stream of consciousness – my adopted and highly preferred style because I often speak in the same manner, jumping from one stream to another, or over-explaining as my wife likes to tell me. I have literary precedence for writing as I do because several phenomenal authors employ the same unique style.

Speaking of transparency, one interesting aspect of my unconventional character is a desire to project masculinity – this is primarily due to battling natural inclinations I've had since early childhood. I feel the manliest during intimacy with my life partner and during the limited dating encounters before marriage. I only dated three other females before marriage and even though I desired deeper intimacy on several occasions and wanted everything to go in that direction, a damn restraint mechanism I possess was activated and ruined the moment. It's the same with people in general, restraint has controlled my impulse to overreact. I've never been an impulsive type and to this very day consider potential negative consequences. Where in the hell did my impulse control come from? My parents certainly didn't have it.

Before I delve too deeply, this *spilling* is not about seeking manliness but instead about my fight to navigate family dysfunction and attempts to insert maleness within the confines of my natural inclinations. My propensity toward female oriented activities and natural talents in female dominated areas confused me and created inner conflicts. Of course, my generation held to strict boundaries in defining male and female roles and I rarely breached those publicly – thankfully those boundaries no longer exist. I did not desire to be female – embraced my maleness and sought to accentuate those characteristics through many forms beyond those natural inclinations. Hiding talents for the most part was a challenge as I fought to hold my own with male peers. I was always the last person chosen for kickball or football, struggled to throw a baseball properly and didn't dribble a basketball very well – things I wanted desperately to do but simply didn't have the skill level to perform as I desired.

I've always been very comfortable talking with women and my sexual desires are for the opposite sex. However, during my physical development from about ten to sixteen, my natural propensities were viewed negatively by male counterparts, which led to all the gross misinterpretations and typical reactions that occur for so many like me. My social/emotional development suffered greatly during those critical years and home life did nothing to counter the barrage of unsolicited attacks on my character and general person-hood. I was accepted by a small band of outsiders like me and a few male friends, but I was extremely prudent in maintaining protective barriers at all times. I simply couldn't risk letting my guard down for fear of being discovered and not understood for what I knew in my heart was actually okay.

How did I develop into the person I am today? I suspect the answer may be choices. Throughout those turbulent years circumstances led me to make critical choices. My choices allowed me to see why others in my life made the choices they did, and without any doubt, I recognize now all those choices prepared me to receive everything torpedoing in my direction. Thoughtful choices clearly altered my circumstances. I ponder sometimes why so many individuals do not seem to grasp how every choice has a consequence. Perhaps Nelson Mandela said it best, *"May your choices reflect your hopes not your fears."* Wouldn't life as a whole work better that way? Unless, of course, the person is riddled by a sense of hopelessness.

Imagined

Without full custody of a vivid imagined world around me I would not have successfully maneuvered reality. My imagined world invented coping mechanisms. I self-talked and counseled myself enough to know this to be true. From the real world sprang the fantasized world, a world I fashioned – seeing what could be – what I knew was within the realm of opportunity kept me attentive to an array of possibilities. Possibilities that protected me from destructive choices that could have shriveled hope, or at least delayed the journey significantly. I dreamt big, fantasized big, idealized big, planned big – all with slightest direction or coaching, scant words of encouragement reached earshot. Life as a child was a lonely existence, perpetually desiring more from adults charged with my care, but they failed on many levels. In the darkest, gloomiest moments I longed for stability – saneness – not chaotic – or crazy.

Religion at an early age became a refuge – begging God for salvation and release. My imagined world coexisted with Divine. In my early twenties I mustered enough courage to tackle a portion of the real world and pursue college. Launched into a new reality I didn't know how to navigate – an uphill battle academically, learning in traditional methods my struggle – until discovering how systems worked for people like me. More frightening was the financial burden real college brought to bear. Again, begging God and he answered with an affirmative. Partial desire to fully engage this new world seemed less intimidating because I was skilled at pretending to be someone I wasn't – a maternal influence. I was absorbed in raw, immature, unsophisticated faith – but that obviously doesn't matter to God. I expressed open, honest, utterances from deep recesses within my heart. At this stage of life, my only way of approaching God was innocently conveying total dependence upon a Divine power I barely knew.

I endured a lot of shitty conduct in the fissures and valleys during the first twenty-five – clinging to hope fueled by idealism and fantasy, no clue what *idealism* meant until college or what truly drove a resolve to look beyond meager means and circumstances. Somehow, there was something better awaiting me, instinctively knew circumstances were not the whole of my future – a craving deep within my gut. My fantasy world like any other child was typical but turning away from childlike play, new fantasies developed to fill emotional gaps. Enter amusement park rides, high fashion, and cheerleaders, three primary fantasies – perhaps obsessions. An odd combination at best but before I'm dismissed, none of these weird obsessions qualified as addictions – nothing that ever led to more than typical mind games or a plethora of artistic endeavors. I drew, drew and drew – was drawn, no pun intended, to all three fantasies but at different times for different purposes.

Fascination for amusement park rides began at an early age. Any time a traveling carnival visited I was intrigued beyond measure by the lights and fanciful colors. I wasn't always allowed to attend, although I begged. I held on to hope of at least seeing and admiring the uniqueness of each thrilling ride. State Fair time was the best ever. Every day I couldn't wait to peruse the newspaper for photos of the fair – and deeply disappointed if I didn't find snapshots of the midway. The State Fair developed into a *religious* experience for me. I drew the rides from memory, and as I got older my drawings advanced in greater detail – even perfected to the large generators and attached electrical cords – sought perfection in my labor. I knew how amusement rides looked after being packed and readied for the next town. These were drawn in every phase from setup to take down – hours upon hours of devotion to my insane craft. Imagining the aroma of deep-fried funnel cakes wafting, "Wooly Bully" blasting as the Scrambler and Tempest twirled captives into dizziness increased the craving. I'm certain it's true this passion was based in fantasy escapism, which shielded me from the surrounding reality. One year we didn't attend the State Fair, I considered it a *crime* – shouted at my father I hated him – sat crying uncontrollably on the patio trying to process reality. He instead allowed my mother to purchase floor length draperies for the wood paneled living room – contented wife – irritated son. My stint as an artistic *carny* lasted several years. I do a double take when I see an amusement park or traveling carnival – my childlike mind space.

Hillbilly Day, another yearly ritual that fueled amusement park fascination and imagination was an event sponsored by Madison Chamber of Commerce – drew thousands every October dressed in hillbilly garb for a day of corn cob pipes, overalls, straw hats and robust *"howdies!"* My favorite, the amusement park rides – a Ferris wheel, paratrooper, bullet, and scrambler mesmerized my senses. The festive day ended with a grand parade – marching bands, clowns, homemade floats. I treasured every moment, but the long-held tradition eventually died a slow death. A few community leaders attempted to resurrect the dead event but at best it was on life support. I was teaching sixth grade at Neely's Bend Elementary, and we dressed in hillbilly garb on Friday to fully support the shallow breathing Saturday event – this time held at Madison Park. The original charm long ago faded – lost forever. The local newspaper visited my classroom that Friday and highlighted us on the front page – surrounded by sixth graders I sat front and center in denim overalls. Madison Hillbilly Day took a final breath that Saturday and is now resting in peace.

A peculiar love for high fashion was again grounded in total fantasy. Cher and Diana Ross perfectly captured my imagination and creativity simply overflowed. I drew and drew and drew. In my mind I was as talented as Hollywood costume designer Bob Mackie, but I was the only one that knew it. I could sit for hours creating and designing magnificent show stopping outfits for Cher and Diana Ross. I had the audacity to mail a package of original designs to both singers. Driven by innocent adolescent illusion, I believed those reached the direct source – waited months to hear a response – I was naive. Innocent efforts instilled hope, kept me moving forward, made me feel alive, created anticipation for a brighter future. I never received any responses, but the dream persisted and continually whispered desire.

The cheerleader fantasy centered around teenage infatuation and a one-sided love affair with cheerleaders in general and especially for one particular female. What guy didn't want to date a cheerleader? Reality check, not one cheerleader I knew was more than a casual acquaintance. My artistic ability did afford me opportunity to work for the cheerleader's creating ballgame run through signs and painting megaphones. My fantasy side job was that – pure fantasy which led me to draw and design cheerleading outfits for imaginary schools. Like my other artistic endeavors, always highly precise and detailed. I never crossed the boundary of drawing actual cheerleaders. That would've seemed too weird, although what I've described may fit the category. What I knew, my adolescent fantasies regarding real cheerleaders were no different than any other guy, but I wasn't any other guy when the banter turned into crude, locker room talk – wasn't comfortable sharing my fantasies – mine remained private. I didn't circulate among popular circles; those relationships were nonexistent – artistic flare allowed a front and center position with cheerleaders – just not with real people. Reflecting on the three primary worlds of fantasy, each seemingly harmless but all three served me well when I needed hollow spaces of worthlessness filled with meaning and empty vacuums of emotion occupied with connection.

During the first twenty-five I perceived myself a loser, someone to loathe most days – surely that wasn't my fate. A mother unintentionally taught me to pretend, ignore reality, deny, and I did that with precision when those characteristics worked to my advantage. Twenty-five lengthy years of forced circumstances are difficult to overcome. An imagined world is never too far away that it doesn't occasionally creep in and take me away momentarily – to a good place, sometimes not a good place. However, no more amusement parks, high fashion, or cheerleaders – instead, normal day-to-day life. I share to release an overflow of thoughts and remembrances that overwhelm at times – these must go somewhere. And I share to express a surplus of tightly held emotions – anger, resentment, joy and grief, quiet moments of somberness and reflection, doubts, guilt, love and hate, passions, dreams and hopes, obsessions – safer sharing vivid remembrances within my head and those hidden deep inside my heart while on a couch.

A major portion of my story is familiar to countless others who are, as I was, shaken by a remarkable, yet commonplace revelation. Mine shocked the core of my existence late in the fourth decade and I wondered how I didn't know? Then a second shock wave of reality several years later. But the only sane response was maturity and disciplined calmness of reaction because I needed to move forward attempting to explore and discover wonders of the unknown newest parts of my world. Nothing imagined this time, pure gut reality – refused to deny, pretend or ignore as I was faithfully taught. In the midst of my quest for truth, I've collided into some impenetrable walls – unable to fully conquer. Numerous secrets and suspicions lead me to ask two simple, yet significant questions: Who am I? What's my real name?

Secrets

Eighteen months before me, he was born to an unmarried, thirty-four-year-old. His birth mother named him Jack. He was immediately adopted by a wealthy family from a swanky southwest Nashville neighborhood – they renamed him. Forty-seven years later an uncle revealed a long-held secret. He drove his older sister to a Catholic convent in Kentucky to give birth and eliminate family shame. A multi-layered concealed plan unraveling – exposed without warning and confirming lies and half-truths. Countless situations constantly questioned throughout a young life into early adulthood – little truth experienced time and again over insignificant circumstances when truth would have been easier. I believe the inability to consistently state truth was learned behavior that falsely protected a wounded and suffering soul. Simply stated, untruths appeared easier than truth and the lifelong consequences never contemplated. He listened well, jotted remembrances as I articulated context for the perplexing lack of truth I sought.

Discovered my parent's marriage certificate at the bottom of a heap of junk in a storage bin – they were never good at hiding things. Dated July 1957, I counted forward by months – born November 15, 1957 – something didn't add up because I knew a woman carries a baby nine months before birth. I asked my mother why the marriage certificate was dated July 1957, but I was born in November. Her answer was quick, perhaps pre-planned and without hesitation. *"They made a mistake and got that wrong!"* She paused, looked away, lips pursed, nervously washing the plate more than necessary in the small stainless-steel sink encased with cheap yellow speckled Formica. I paused, waited for more, restated my question. She turned to me with repugnance and blurted, *"Oh Jim, he's your father!"* What did that response mean? How did her response relate to the initial question? I didn't verbalize a question about my father but certainly pondered her retort now. I chose not to ask anything else regarding the marriage certificate *mistake* but remained curious about the unknown. I recently reconnected with a childhood best friend, he and his family lived a few lots away from where I resided nine pernicious years. He remembered being there the day I discovered the marriage certificate date and asking my mother. He chuckled recalling her response and said I yelled at her, but I didn't remember yelling or his presence. Sometime later I randomly asked my mother why I couldn't have a brother like my friends. She again nervously answered with a short meaningless, somewhat agitated response I didn't understand – decided it was best never to ask about a brother, at least not until many years later and for different reasons.

In the brief moments after the big reveal, I peered at my aging uncle across a table at Shoney's, my life of half-truths and lies flashing before me as he spilled truth. Inhaled a putrid odor from soured cleaning cloths at our table – wiped quickly, wet then smeared dry. My uncle sipped coffee, I ate and drank nothing, my world was colliding with revelation – news that was somewhat of a surprise but not entirely. An intuitive feeling always told me something wasn't right, but I couldn't explain it until now. Nearly all my suspicions unexpectedly becoming tangible, but nothing I pondered ever included what

I was told. What else could be a lie? Who's the father? Perhaps the man that raised me was not my father? Could he be the father? How would I ever really know truth? My father died at age fifty-five. How would I convince my mother to state truth regarding many unknowns? I desperately needed answers but knew fully well how difficult navigating this unraveling would be – could not have been more precisely correct.

Born in 1921, my mother's destined role became the classic ill-fated protagonist. The third child of ten, her name, Velma Tenpenny – no middle name. Graduated from high school but didn't pursue any type of professional career. She worked several years as a nursing assistant at the VA and in a nursing home in Murfreesboro, Tennessee, her hometown. At times she would live with an elderly person providing domestic care. I remember thinking my mother was a nurse – not true, but I shared she was a nurse numerous times to school friends and teachers. The thought of her being a nurse made me feel proud, even though I knew truth – one of many denial habits I reaped but eventually rejected.

She married Charles Sneed shortly after graduating from high school. He was deployed to serve at the end of World War II in the south Pacific. He lost his life on one of the remote islands and was posthumously awarded a Purple Heart by President Roosevelt. His remains were returned after ten years and buried in the Murfreesboro, Veterans Cemetery. My mother said his parents wanted to see the remains, but she refused their request – not certain that's true. Perhaps there's another side to that story I'll never know. His recorded death date is November 14th – my mother's same death date almost seventy years later. By beauty standards of the time period my mother was considered very attractive, shaped well from head to toe, high cheek bones, shoulder length wavy hair, posed in photos as if she was mimicking aspiring Hollywood stars.

Dotting high cheek bones with cheap red lipstick, rounding mouth and elongating her face, she smoothed red dots into beautiful olive skin – a daily ritual along with a distinct habit of slow flutter blinking. She cared deeply about her image and how others perceived her – I hate that trait in myself.

My mother lived a little on the *wild side* of life during her years of widowhood before a second marriage to the man I called father. Raised in a devout, Southern Baptist family – she rejected those principles and chose differently – perhaps she rejected the family's disguise of perfection. Based on my mother's account, her mother experienced an emotional breakdown during the time frame she returned home and lived with her parents – another one-sided story. I visited my mother's ninety-one-year-old brother, Jay Thurman, in his hospital room in the Fall of 2019 – he was the only sibling to attend my mother's graveside memorial. I questioned him – he confirmed his older sister was considered the *black sheep* in the Tenpenny clan. He chuckled feebly as he thought about my question and repeated what he'd just told me – Aunt Linda, his wife, said he does that a lot – but he plainly remembered that particular reality about his older sister Velma and said, *"but we loved her anyway."* I loved her too, but numerous secrets, suspicions and a few odd habits with no clear path for determining truth or why was forever frustrating.

In our collection of tattered bath towels we possessed a few white towels with an orange stripe down the middle, towels that originated from a Holiday Inn. We also possessed a few unmatched eating utensils, primarily different shaped spoons from various restaurants like Cracker Barrel and Shoney's. My cousin Janice told me she admired a cookie jar that was in a rental cabin, at Trails End on Kentucky Lake. This particular cookie jar, a ceramic jar decorated with bright red apples, was to be used by occupants during their stay. The Holiday Inn towels, eating utensils, and apple decorated cookie jar all had something in common – my mother's *sticky fingers*. She had developed a habit of helping herself, feeling entitled to items such as these because in her manner of misguided reasoning she had paid for these with the normal charges for lodging or eating. It was the same in a grocery store – she often helped herself to grapes – something she could easily grab and consume unnoticed – I didn't understand nor did I mimic her odd habit. My cousin had no intention of taking the cookie jar, she merely expressed her liking of it, but it was bequeathed upon her by my mother – she wanted her niece to have it – why not? My mother believed she was entitled – all fees had been paid and settled.

I always knew this was flat out stealing but never confronted my mother. Janice's mother, my mother's sister, did confront her letting her know she shouldn't have taken the cookie jar. My mother offered a simple reply, *"Oh Lora, it's okay because we paid for it."* Of course, the irony is she never funded any visits to Kentucky Lake, Holiday Inn's or restaurant dining – she was totally dependent on the meager wages of her husband or the generosity of others. Janice said she kept the cookie jar until it was accidentally broken. I used orange striped towels until threadbare and full of holes; the pilfered eating utensils remained with my mother until she broke her hip and was forced to abandon her tiny government subsidized apartment. A host of faulty reasoning triggered her lifetime of misfortune. I simply didn't understand what appeared to be defective cognition and was often embarrassed but had no power to alter or control her choices. Somehow, I managed enough fortitude and avoided repeating what I witnessed. Her *sticky fingers* secret remained securely concealed in my heart.

Hidden Dysfunction

Throughout childhood and adolescence, I struggled with the family where I found myself trapped – at times feeling like an outsider wondering why life had to be so crazy. Fortunately, two sets of grandparents provided much-needed calm and security I longed to embrace, although neither was perfect. My father's parents lived in the same community as we did a few miles away – my mother's parents lived in Murfreesboro, Tennessee. Both prepared delicious southern food, homemade desserts, and my father's parents bought my winter coat each year. There was a stark contrast in behavior between both sets of grandparents. My local grandmother cursed a lot, but in a funny type manner – a habit of her everyday life, and she was hilarious in many ways too. One day while I finished breakfast at their kitchen table, she stood at the sink washing dishes in her nightgown, braless. She turned to me in faux disgust with a comical tone, cupping her breasts in both hands. *"I think I'll get these things cut off because they just get in the way."* She blasted laughter and I forced a half smile of *faux* innocence without words sipping orange juice. She often told me how my parents did not manage money well – steaks for too many friends, partying all the time, but never mentioned alcohol, nor did I. She didn't drink alcohol nor did my grandfather, but he smoked. Both William and Lucy Morris never expressed a religious faith in my presence.

The Murfreesboro grandparents, on the other hand, were devout Christians. Never heard one foul word from either of them, never saw them angry – my perception was quiet-calm rhythms permeated home and life. I loved staying overnight at both homes, crisp bleached sheets, puffy pillows, comfortable beds, well-being and peace the norm. When I stayed in Murfreesboro, I loved sleeping in the front bedroom. High ceilings, decorative bed frame and tall posts, a large circle mirrored dressing table with side drawers, and grey wallpaper with pink and white flowers spoke royalty. I felt loved and well-connected with both sets, but as I grew older, began to realize something didn't connect with my local set of grandparents. My funny cursing grandmother died when I was a senior in high school. I don't remember grieving and no longer desired to visit much or stay the night. Grandfather Morris provided transportation at times to and from school – it gave him something useful to do. Shortly after graduation he drove me to a downtown interview with the phone company. I was at a loss on what to do with my life – failed the entrance test miserably – he accidently bumped a car attempting to parallel park – not a good day for either of us.

The Murfreesboro grandparents lived on a small farm at the exact geographical center of Tennessee. They claimed thirty-two grandchildren. I'm the only grandchild named after my grandfather – his first name, Vestel, my middle name. During Tenpenny gatherings my grandfather privately slipped me a dollar bill. My mother told me it was due to his name – the dollar bill helped me appreciate a middle name I didn't particularly like. Grandfather Tenpenny wore black framed glasses with thick lenses that made his eyes appear much bigger – also hard of hearing – always cupping hands behind his ears. He was the first grandparent to die, December 1973. It was Christmas break, and I stayed an extra week with my grandmother after mourners left. It was the first time I experienced a side of her personality I didn't know. The first few nights I heard weeping – hadn't seen her cry since the loss of her oldest daughter, my mother's older sister. We sat down for another meal of leftover funeral food. *"This food has been blessed enough, let's eat."* I loved the moment – she never ate a meal without first giving thanks.

An island war casualty and purple heart permitted a widowed offspring care over her mother seeking knives. Electric shock therapy removed troubling conflicts about an unplanned pregnancy restoring a sense of normalcy and peace. We lived together a week, wish she'd taken the opportunity to be honest and real about a grandson's origin. Didn't realize how she might have altered my life with truth – a troubled period she didn't wish to resurrect – a period she may have lost or didn't fully remember.

Home life was often chaotic and unsettled, especially when my father drank heavily. He was basically a quiet boozer but occasionally had violent tendencies toward my mother. My junior high years were particularly difficult – hated school, hated home life, sometimes hated parents, especially the squabbling and violence. At the time I didn't recognize the truth but later understood the source to be his own guilt and anger. During that period, he was having a *fling* with a family friend living just a few yards from us. My father was openly affectionate with her, and my mother appeared very passive about it. Never heard my mother question him – seemed odd because he often accused her of cheating. The other woman's second son Andy was a best friend – we played together every day. My father allowed him to go with us wherever we went, like the brother I never had – the brother I desperately desired. We recently reconnected and met for lunch – it was good to rekindle our relationship and reminisce. I was curious why he and his family moved abruptly without explanation. He dropped a bombshell.

Andy's mother unexpectedly got pregnant by someone other than his father and had an abortion. I fought to control my facial expression and emotions but immediately realized he didn't know. Should I tell him what I knew? I debated quickly and concluded it was best not to share what I have suspected since the long ago impromptu fast-food dinner. I wondered why it was assumed the pregnancy was not his father – had he undergone a vasectomy after four children? I clearly remember the day we were all playing together in my front yard. Andy often had to watch his three younger siblings while his mother enjoyed herself. My mother was working a part-time job at a local meat and three. My father and his mother were sitting on our patio visiting when he handed me money and said take everyone to Burger Chef – it was less than a block away at the top of the road, in clear view of our yard and patio. Andy and I walked the younger children to the restaurant. Positioned myself where I could see the front yard – suspicion consumed my thoughts. No one else noticed when my father and best friend's mother went inside. Returning, the two paramours were sitting on the front patio smoking and drinking their usual whiskey and water over ice. Curiosity apprehended my full attention, I walked inside alone – peered at crumpled bed sheets exposing adulterous lust – old enough to know but said nothing to anyone. My mother wasn't the only secret keeper and to my knowledge she never knew. Discovered Andy's uncle revealed to him everything I suspected all along – he knew we almost shared a common sibling.

Hiding family dysfunction from a few friends and extended family was commonplace – everyone to a certain degree in my generation did the same. My first secret love in school was Ruth. We met in first grade and separated at high school graduation – twelve long years and we never dated once – of course that was my stupid fault. I'll never forget the look of disgust on her face in the aftermath of receiving diplomas, donned in robes and mortarboards, Ruth's white mine bright orange – after twelve long years we exchanged a few brief awkward words. I really wanted to ask her to celebrate our accomplishments but it wouldn't come – words inside but not enunciated outside. My timorousness blocked access to every dame effort to engage her in something deeper – I completely failed – a true *Charlie Brown* moment. We separated – she's disgusted – I'm humiliated by self-inflicted defeat. Turned to a best guy friend as my default – he was alone too – no pressure to impress him. My best friend and I ate dinner at Shoney's in Madison – two losers celebrating high school graduation. I never heard from or saw Ruth again.

My after-graduation act of stupidity was not what she desired according to her lengthy message in my senior yearbook. She had hopes of us remaining friends, perhaps more. Her yearbook message to me definitely contained undertones I clearly ignored. She chronicled our time together from first grade to twelfth with a host of remembrances – some I didn't recall. She did forget one that surprised me. During eleventh grade English I executed a really dumb stunt one day that thoroughly embarrassed her. She walked to the homework basket to submit work. As she turned to back into the one-piece desk and chair, I slid it away and she fell onto the floor. A stupid high school male stunt that I immediately regretted. The teacher fussed at me and Ruth was humiliated. For a few days I got the cold shoulder and deserved it but I eventually regained her trust. Reflecting on those actions I can't explain it other than it was an impulsive testosterone fueled act for a cheap laugh – she didn't see it as funny. We rode the same school bus during junior high because she lived in a brick house on the other side of the railroad tracks in a real neighborhood. We were always in several classes together and found time in between classes to occasionally talk. We laughed a lot but she always remained more guarded and reserved. I liked her mostly because she accepted me just as I was and never asked me to be something different – nor did I of her. We found a commonality that worked well for both of us but I maintained secrecy about a troubled homelife. I hid it well – likely the deeper reason for not taking our relationship to another level.

Rebellion

Reflecting on childhood and adolescence I can honestly state I was a self-made pompous asshole. This elevated attitude of heart and mind fought against a barrage of choices forcing my fate into circumstances I did not desire. I wanted nothing of it – considered myself a prisoner within my home. I was often extremely rude toward my parents but always felt justified by self-righteousness. The true source anger – anger born from their inability to maintain any type of consistent normalcy. I was a prisoner because I had no ability to alter circumstances – stuck. These feelings were not constant day to day, hour by hour. As a younger child I simply didn't possess the cognitive maturity to understand or fully grasp my situation or see any hope beyond it. I see similar reactions in elementary children I have taught over my long career. Personal experience afforded me a level of empathy and understanding many teachers and administrators did not possess. As I matured it became demonstrably obvious, I had multiple issues to navigate in an attempt to survive many years ahead. Oddly enough, I feared the loss of life as I knew it. Although I loathed feeling like a prisoner, I didn't want it to come crashing down. I saw this trait in foster children that lived with Pam and me. They always desired to return to the *prisons* from which they had been released. I desired as they did the security of sameness – not the unknown. As I've previously alluded, my fantasy world and grandparents offered the taste of normalcy I longed to have, or my situation would have seemed hopeless. By another juvenile misinterpretation, my uncles, aunts, and cousins gave me a false sense of hope for the future because I aspired to be them – little did I know at that time. My sense of prison was primarily rooted in fear – fear of the present and uncertainty about tomorrow. Even today, fearing loss of normalcy – a reaction deeply rooted in the past and always lurking in the shadows of my reasoning.

Rebellion was not in a typical manner – a teenager with literally no rules to follow – no set standard to attain or strive toward. Both parents very passive regarding rulemaking – they simply didn't do it. I was expected to treat others with respect in their presence, but that expectation was never literally voiced. My parents displayed a giving attitude toward others with limited resources and conducted themselves properly in public but always shielded their underlying dysfunction. I instinctively knew the importance of playing their deceptive game – don't lift the veil around certain groups of people, especially the Murfreesboro household. I was never specifically told to do so. My lawless home life led me to religion and my own dysfunction of perfectionism. I created a set of compulsory rules and followed those perfectly. Cleaning and organizing my limited possessions were executed flawlessly. Maintained the pompous attitude toward the vices of my parents so I never sipped their beer or any liquor, never tried smoking – seems odd because these vices were in clear view and available at all times. I tried cursing in my parent's presence but didn't gain much attention, those words didn't seem to matter – I stopped. Once I cursed my father hurling *"fuck-you"* and he came after me – unfortunately for him, being *three sheets to the wind* caused him to stumble and he was unable to catch me. In typical fashion, he didn't remember the verbal slander in the soberness of morning. But I did, and continued to clothe myself with a form of righteous indignation clinging to a fragile faith.

When home alone, I could have easily indulged and did in another coming-of-age vice, his pornography, abundantly available – both text and images. I found it in drawers and on top of the refrigerator and in the bottom of the built-in hamper in the back bedroom. My sexual awakening was brought to bear before my physical body was prepared. The pornographic images were graphic in nature, involving male and female – sometimes all male – confusing with no context or understanding of what I observed. Some images remain crystal clear in my mind, those never seem to fade with time. I couldn't fully understand or comprehend the text but read with perfect attention – unlike at school. Mental abuse? Yes. Intentional? No. To my knowledge my parents never knew I looked and partook in this particular vice. I made sure to always return it to the same place I found it, covering my preadolescent curiosity, intuitively knowing they didn't remember how these items were stored or how much they possessed. I do know it was a lot for a preteen boy. I became the superstar of the *boy's club* when brave enough to sneak a magazine from the stash. Why didn't my parents understand the seriousness of their negligence? When I was about fourteen my father told me something about one of his bosses being a deacon in a church and he possessed various types of pornography, including films. He referred to him as a hypocrite. I didn't know how to react to this revelation and chose to remain silent. I didn't wish to have this discussion with my father, perhaps he was testing my curiosity – did he wantonly desire my participation? Perhaps he knew I indulged.

Age six is my earliest remembrance of anything remotely related to pornography or exposure to sexual anatomy. A grey, straight-edged, shingled simple house sat in the center of our small microcosm of rectangular rentals. He may have been twelve or perhaps thirteen at the time and occasionally talked to me, but I was too young to be a serious playmate or friend. I often played alone in the front and back yard of the grey house. The juvenile called me over to the back porch one day and motioned for me to crawl under the porch with him. The weathered wooden porch was open on both sides, but scrubs blocked a direct view underneath. I could easily sit upright but he bent slightly with his legs crossed. We sat on the cool dirt and rocky soil picking at rocks for some unknown reason. He suddenly told me, *"I have some black hair down here"* – pointed to his crotch. I said nothing nor did I understand what he attempted to communicate or why. He then asked if I wanted to see. There is a vague remembrance of him arching backward to lower his pants but no memory of anything beyond that action. I don't recall answering. Another time, he led me upstairs to his bedroom when I was about the same age. The solid oak staircase and planked flooring creaking beneath his feet. Another vague remembrance is the physical arrangement of his bedroom – a study desk, chair and soft, plump mattress covered with a homemade quilt – belongings I desired but didn't possess. Other than those brief memories, I have no recollection of why he brought me upstairs. At the time he was probably a seventh or eighth grader. Later exposure to pornography led me to recall the two moments with the juvenile but no additional memories of anything beyond what I described.

After spilling this story, I asked, *"Could I have blocked or erased something from my memory?"* He said it's possible. I looked to the sunny window for a moment and contemplated his comment. No additional memories immerged.

A pompous pride continued to develop within and drove unconventional rebellion because I did not wish to be like my parents. Hated their vices and what it did to our threesome. I desired normal, whatever that might be. The landlord knocked on our door often asking for overdue rent, that wasn't normal. My father offered him a drink of whiskey to hopefully distract from pleas to pay, but he always declined, was a deacon at his church – perhaps not a hypocrite. Additional creditors hounded my parents over other late payments – a monthly occurrence. In my thinking that wasn't normal. That's why we lived in a rectangular rental nine malignant years. The downward nine-year spiral started after my father lost his job as an airplane mechanic and the bank foreclosed on our new brick house with a full-size basement on Shepherd Hills Drive in a real neighborhood. I was a first grader and thought moving would be a fun thing, remember jumping up and down with excitement but quickly learned how wrong I can be. My first-grade teacher purchased our red brick house – foreclosure probably presented a fantastic deal. I've wondered what she told teacher friends about the new brick home and how she viewed me afterwards. My parents filed for bankruptcy twice that I know, perhaps three times. However, during the next nine years beer, whiskey and cigarettes never appeared in short supply. My parents had priorities – I had mine too.

Unconventional forms of rebellion continued within the family, with friends, and within church life. Within the nucleus family I craved something more than what I received – always knew I was being short-changed by parents but had no power to make it work differently – so I learned to work within that system, skilled manipulation the key. I learned early, as most children do, how to manipulate certain situations to my advantage – all children do it to some degree. I was typically free to operate as I pleased as long as those choices didn't interfere with my parents and their self-centeredness. My father ended up a full-time butcher and worked at a small independent meat packing business on the edge of downtown Nashville. We had the finest cuts of meat in the poor neighborhood by far, but I was extremely picky and never liked the manner in which he grilled steaks. He liked blood oozing from his thick T-bone when it hit the plate – his favorite – not mine. What did I do? Refused to eat – didn't like blood in my plate. After several refusals to eat bloody steak, and another mixed drink or two he eventually gave in to my desire and brought the pre-made hamburger patties from work – I requested well-done – T-bone blood for him. To this day if I order steak in a restaurant, and I rarely do, I ask for well-done and hear a voice: *"Well-done ruins the damn steak and you offend the cook!"* A preadolescent arrogance spoken within didn't give a damn and sometimes it would take full control of my actions. One particular morning when it did, I recall not liking what my mother prepared for breakfast and stood from the table and smugly walked to the trash and dumped the contents – a sober firm hand grabbed my shoulder, and I received an old-fashioned punishment. That was the last time I allowed my pompous attitude to overtake reason. I didn't know there was a rule about dumping food – after the reckoning I was clearly informed.

I was the only son he was raising; he gave in often, I believe, to my desires out of partial guilt. I also remember catching him at times staring at me in what I thought an odd, kind of creepy way – nothing sinister or evil, just odd. Did he have doubts about my paternity being a different source? I've wondered if he was pondering that issue – minus, of course, any knowledge of DNA. I'll never know if he had suspicions or knew truth. This remembrance was during the time period of my growth spurt – not suggesting his ogling was based on something perverted, but I felt uncomfortable and removed myself from those settings when it occurred. I knew his vices well and had no desire to join him.

It was easiest to rebel against my mother – she could be

convinced of almost anything until she breathed her last. She was the primary cook, other than grilling – my father's domain – where I indirectly learned grilling skills. I was very confident in the kitchen as well but didn't particularly like some of our regular menus. My mother was the typical southern country type cook – meat and potatoes, always some type of beans. She made white floor biscuits a lot – my father's favorite. I thought my mother's biscuits ranked third in her family – my aunt Pat in Spanntown made the best biscuits – flatter, buttery, flakier, slightly crispy around the edges. Grandmother Tenpenny in Murfreesboro made a very close second, small, light, and fluffy. My mother's biscuits were mid-size, dense, slightly drier – always tasting more white flour. Don't eat biscuits today because I ate so many growing up – at times I rebelled and refused to eat all the white flour before it was dubbed *bad for you*. As most families of our generation, we had monochromatic dinners; white beans, mashed potatoes, white flour biscuits, white gravy, and white pork cutlets – may have been my father's favorite dinner combination. Sometimes I protested as angry adolescents do and at other times quietly rebelled and would only eat meat – if I liked it.

As I grew older my mother cooked an early afternoon snack meal for her growing adolescent. High school dismissed at 1:30 and I was home most days before 2:00. My favorite afternoon snack was a fried hamburger with French fries and lots of ketchup – could eat that every day. As a spoiled *only child*, I never really appreciated this extra effort on her part but certainly loved eating as most starving teenagers do. Looking back, most of my rebellion had a lot to do with food, didn't like beef stew or any dish where everything was mushed together. Hated fried salmon patties; our tiny home stunk for days. Hated spam, hotdogs after my father told me how those were made, oyster pie, pig brains in scrambled eggs, and chitlins. Rebellion took on many forms but rarely the type most parents endured – wasn't my nature to practice a lot of risky behavior. Cussing, the popular term in my circles, was the norm within our small space and at the local grandparents. My pompous rebellion didn't fully adopt that norm – rarely used those words even with friends during adolescent years. Attributed to parents and local grandparents, those words rest just below the surface and occasionally rise to the occasion.

One classic form of rebellion is universally common among teenagers – choosing a music genre opposite of parents – mine was manifested in a strong attraction to Motown – the *Motor City*. The time period was not necessarily a good time for a white pre-teen boy to be drawn to Motown. My infatuation started in the late 1960's and continued throughout high school. It was tempered somewhat by college and marriage but remains my favorite music genre of all time. My parents didn't really protest much since they had so many of their own issues and infatuations like country music – Patsy Cline, Ray Price, anything Elvis, and Les Paul their favorites. On the tiny paneled wall behind the thin mattress, I taped magazine photos of the Supremes – my favorite Motown singers. My father didn't protest when I picked a magazine off the store shelf that featured Motown – not certain he really gave it much attention or thought – he had his liquor and cigarettes – all was well with him. On a few occasions I convinced him to buy the latest Supremes album. One time he actually agreed to buy the greatest hits double album at Zayre – the Wal Mart of that era. I was thrilled. My cousin Janice in Spanntown owned several Motown albums that I was not allowed to touch – just listened occasionally. I can easily say these life events were considered some of the best times for me. I never really understood my parent's silent approval because societal norms at the time expressed extreme disapproval. I never associated it with any racial issues of our time in the late sixties and early seventies. For me it was an innocent desire for something I really liked, and it also served as a distraction during the not so good times. I listened to those albums until I memorized every word. Didn't actually understand my own infatuation – not really certain what drove the desire. What I did know, I was basically alone in my infatuation for Motown and the Supremes – few people around me felt the same. The lone *white rebel* – perhaps I felt empowered because it made me different and unique.

Favorite cousins, Janice and Little Bill, moved to Selma, Alabama in the early 70's – a hotbed of racial strife. Uncle Bill transferred to Selma to work at the air force base – he was a civilian worker. They first rented a house on Alabama Avenue, an iconic red bricked street lined with picturesque southern cottages and small Victorian homes, just a few blocks from downtown Selma. What I didn't connect at the time were all the historical events that recently occurred in Selma – racial tension still fuming – but as a pre-teen I didn't connect those dots. My uncle and aunt eventually rented a little larger home on the other side of the famous Edmund Pettus Bridge – the bridge where Alabama State Troopers attacked civil-rights demonstrators on *"Bloody Sunday,"* March 7, 1965. I didn't know or remember the historical significance as I rode over a famous bridge many times. The cousin's new rental home wasn't huge but did have three small bedrooms and a spacious yard – the house located a short distance beyond the famous bridge in a small neighborhood next to a large open field – didn't compare to their spacious farmland I once knew.

I hold fond memories of my aunt's cooking – always very special. The simplest breakfast of buttered toast, bacon, and scrambled eggs firmly planted in my mind to this day – can see, smell, and taste it. My mother and I visited Selma during spring break – traveling by Greyhound Bus – big time travel for a kid like me – getting away from our confined space always a special treat. During our visit I noticed in several stores entire sections of magazines dedicated to black entertainers – especially the Motown singers. I had never seen this in Nashville. I was especially interested in the magazines with the Supremes on the cover. A white boy standing at the black magazine counter in Selma, Alabama in the early 70's – why all the glaring looks from store patrons? I finally selected the magazine I wanted and took it to the counter. The white cashier actually paused, looked at me with puzzlement and said, *"Are you certain you want to buy this?"* Without hesitation answered yes – didn't understand why she questioned the choice. She rang it up – told me the price and handed her money – her eyebrows still raised in disbelief. I walked out of the store and enjoyed my prize magazine full of The Supremes. I didn't know or understand racism.

Looking back, I'm glad I was ignorant to the racial issues all around me. Also, thankful my parents didn't make a big deal about black and white racial tensions of the age. To this day Diana Ross is my favorite nostalgic entertainer – my wife surprised me with tickets to her live performance at MTSU in the mid 80's and most recently at the Schermerhorn with the Nashville Symphony. I'm a fan of Vanessa Williams, Whitney Houston, and Anita Baker. I've seen Houston and Baker in live concerts but not Williams. A love for Motown led to my fascination for other famous black entertainers, and perhaps another manifestation of harmless unconventional rebellion that may have offered the life I desperately needed at the time.

The year was 1976, we arrived at the high school playoff game in Antioch, a suburb at the south end of our county. I rode with Jerry – his dad had given him a new Mercury Cougar as a graduation present, a really sharp looking car. I think my parents may have given me $25. How does a father buy a son a brand-new car? It's easier if your father owns a chain of local grocery stores – a butcher's salary hardly paid for a tote-your-note used car – my dad's mode of transportation. Jerry was an average guy but used his dad's money to fund a growing marijuana habit and sexual escapades – he sometimes shared too much detail. Apparently, I was missing out on life. A few other guys went that evening including my best friend from high school and church. Everything seemed fairly normal on our drive to the game. Once we arrived all the other guys started going back to car for alcohol and pot. I knew they had it but thought it would be an after-game indulgence. Instead, they all got drunk and stoned during the game – not me. Rebellion on my part. I started devising a plan to get us home safely. Upon arriving at the car to leave, I blocked the driver's door and asked Jerry for his keys – told him I had never driven a new car – demanded he let me drive. He resisted but I insisted – determined he wasn't driving. I turned out to be a designated driver before the term was coined. I was the only one not stoned or drunk – they continued their indulgences and I drove. Somehow, we all got home safely but I don't recall exactly how it all played out in the end. Perhaps I inhaled too much residual smoke. Unconventional rebellion likely saved our lives that evening.

Training for unconventional rebellion began with my father at an early age but not intentionally. After a long day or weekend at my cousin's in Spanntown, my father was typically intoxicated when he finally decided to leave – he was the only licensed driver – I was too young. Going home was usually a nightmare because I had a serious self-appointed job. I couldn't fall asleep in the backseat after a long day of play like most children. My self-appointed duty kept my father awake – liquor was in control. I intuitively knew he wasn't fit to drive because he could barely walk to the car. What was my mother thinking? She obviously wasn't. She sat on her side of the front seat and appeared totally oblivious to our impending doom –

her typical form of denial. If she didn't speak about it or acknowledge it – it didn't exist – but this did exist and was terribly frightening for a child. She may have spoken his name in a tone of disgust to get his attention but rarely said anything. I sat in the middle of the back seat on the edge so that I could push my body forward between the two front seats. Leaned forward to watch his face, watched his eyes slowly blink, noticed if his head nodded forward – my job and duty to keep us safe. As we drove slowly, he occasionally jerked the steering wheel to bring the car back within white lines – one way to spot an impaired driver. I asked my father questions – an attempt to keep him engaged and from going unconscious. His focus slightly improved when the liquor wore off a bit, but it always seemed like an eternity before we reached Monticello Drive. Thankful to be home in one piece but emotionally exhausted. My mother never spoke a word regarding those experiences – resentment and anger began to grow for what I knew was wrong.

My best friend Cliff sort of inherited a family car that looked like it wouldn't get you across the street much less a few miles. His car needed water constantly due to overheating and would quit running if it was jolted by a pot hole – probably a loose connection to the battery. Neither one of us knew much about auto mechanics – other than we could put water in the radiator and gas in the tank – another major issue that always concerned me. Cliff ran the car on fumes – suppose he didn't want to waste gas in case the car died a final death. One evening we felt brave and decided to drive around downtown Nashville. On our way out of the city as we crossed the Cumberland River Cliff was careful to dodge a few potholes. Suddenly blue lights raced up behind us and we pulled over. Panic arose in my mind then I realized we were driving the speed limit or a little under – too risky to speed in his car. The officer asked Cliff how much he had been drinking – he told the officer he had not been drinking, which was true. The officer said he had witnessed us swerving on the bridge. Cliff explained he was trying to dodge potholes to avoid the car from not working but got nervous and also said something about the lines on the road as if he couldn't see those – not good. I knew at that point we were going to jail. The officer called the breathalyzer truck. I started to imagine the scene in our jail cell – we would probably get beaten up by the other prisoners – panic arose again. Cliff got out, was escorted to the truck for his breathalyzer test. I sat patiently awaiting our sentence attempting not to have eye contact with anyone. Cliff returned to the car, and I asked what happened because he seemed overly calm – he registered double zero. Of course he did because we were not drinking. Another car adventure to share with friends but not parents.

On several occasions Cliff convinced me to attend rock concerts at a large downtown arena – Edgar Winter and Foghat to name two. He was growing very fond of pot – something I was not comfortable with or interested in. On one occasion, I walked out of the concert in downtown Nashville and sat in his old car until it was over. Inside was total bedlam, the concert venue was thick with marijuana smoke – an empty beer bottle thrown from the upper deck, I was done with it and out of there. After tolerating this downward spiral for too long I finally confronted my best friend – stood in his tiny bedroom following one of his drunken, pot smoking antics of the previous evening – told him our friendship was over if he continued his current direction. Long story short – he was the best man in my wedding, and we remain friends to this day. It was not my intention to be *holier than thou*; I certainly had many faults. But I couldn't bear to see a best friend end up like his father and mine. I honestly do not know what fueled my unconventional rebellion, but it seemed to serve a purpose in my life and in those around me.

Within the church environment I often resisted conventional wisdom – instead used unconventional rebellion to battle the status quo – so many things built on tradition created by men. Several teaching practices I implemented were considered unorthodox within a very traditional Sunday school setting, but my students always seemed highly attentive and participated. I didn't do these things to deliberately disparage anyone or create disunity. Most of my choices to push against the status quo within the church setting were subtle. One example was a long-held tradition in how communion was served. In a three-thousand seat auditorium it required a form of order to ensure that everyone was served proficiently and within a short amount of time. A tradition had developed over the years where different groups of only men stood in certain locations throughout the auditorium and then fanned out to serve communion to certain pews of people. Focusing on this process and somewhat amused by the preciseness, I noticed how the men stopped at certain locations, waited until everyone was ready then returned to a designated spot in unison. Also, how the men who stood in front of the auditorium always remained in the same order, clasped hands in front of themselves – and how they returned to the communion table with practiced precision – it captured my full attention. Why did everyone walk and step like well-trained soldiers?

When I was first asked to serve communion, I followed the plan perfectly – growing in faith, or perhaps rebellion against the status quo, I wanted to subtly buck the man-made tradition. My first attempt was to scrap the *traditional tie* – second, walk back to the communion table before everyone completed serving their designated area – sometimes standing alone. Thirdly, on a few occasions when returning to my assigned position, I purposely took another spot because in my thinking it didn't matter the position, I knew the assignment and had every intention of returning to the assigned spot to serve. I wanted to challenge what seemed a pointless tradition – crazy? Perhaps, but I delighted in attempting to shift hearts and minds to contemplate why they acted so rigid and bound by tradition. I now have a purer understanding of the sacredness surrounding *The Eucharist* – it's now about shifting my heart.

Another amusing example of unconventional rebellion is when the church's children's department started hosting a Halloween event called *Trunk or Treat* – we were informed children should dress in fun, child-friendly character type costumes – nothing scary or demonic. Our daughter was four at the time and we had already purchased a witch outfit, black hat, green make-up and long black fingernails. She was the only cute little witch at the event, and we don't think anyone suffered long-lasting trauma over the presence of a charming four-year-old witch.

A few years before our daughter was born, we were serving as supervisors of the third and fourth grade Sunday school department. It was our responsibility to make sure teachers had curriculum materials to teach, and we ordered those materials through the church offices. A former school principal was placed as overall director of the elementary children's program. At one of the initial meetings where he laid out his vision and plans for the elementary program, he stated that Sunday school lesson plans must be created for each grade level. I immediately spoke up and challenged the new mandate. I was not going to create lesson plans for the department because curriculum materials with a detailed lesson structure was in place – plus, I was a public-school teacher required to have weekly plans for my students. It wasn't necessary to add an additional burden to an already busy and hectic schedule. My comment was not challenged, and we moved forward without ever hearing about Sunday school lesson plans again. There is a bit of irony in this situation; the person I challenged was my first public school principal who had fought hard to hire me – more of those details later. I believe rebellion is not always a bad thing and especially if the rebellion is properly directed toward changing a negative status quo. I find it satisfying to challenge status quo issues when I deem it necessary and especially for a greater good – perhaps I remain slightly pompous at times but overall, unconventional rebellion continues to work well for me.

Determined

Two years after high school I purchased my grandfather's Chevrolet Impala. I obtained a small loan from the local bank – monthly payments $62.00. I proudly made each payment on time, sometimes early when I had extra cash from part-time jobs – fervently determined to never be late on a payment. I had no desire to repeat the pattern that had been faithfully modeled before me. A newly developed tenacity for bill paying felt right – gave me a level of hope for the future I had never felt before. Looking back, it could be seen by some as insignificant, but for me it was empowerment to change the hand that had been dealt. Learning I actually had the ability to do something different – chart my own course – and I did – it felt good. I am humbled and blessed by the fact I'm not forced to submit delinquent payments. Would my world end if I were late once or twice? No. For me, it's all about not repeating a pattern I loathed.

During my four-year college stint, I typically paid tuition with cash. I clearly remember the clerks at David Lipscomb College being visibly perturbed by cash payments. They obviously preferred a check from daddy or mommy. Instead, they had to count my money, sometimes loose change, pull my payment record, mark the payment card and write a receipt. Their facial expressions spoke truth. They were rude; I made their work more difficult and time consuming. Somehow, I managed to make every tuition payment on time. The same has occurred with every purchase for the span of my independent adulthood and married life. I say all this not boasting or bragging but from a place of gratefulness for the ability to do so. Determination and persistence did pay huge dividends – two traits that make life easier. I was proud and a little prideful to be doing something different than what was faithfully modeled. Is it fair to give additional credit to a self-righteous faith? Perhaps more appropriate to acknowledge Divine power and my marriage partner. Both are by far the two most influential ingredients that launched my career and steered me to achieve successes I enjoy today.

My initial religious influences were imparted by grandparents in Murfreesboro. When I was younger my mother visited her parents more often, and when we visited Sunday, we sat on a pew at Bellwood Baptist Church where my grandmother taught a ladies' Bible class. Another early religious influence was the Beacon Baptist bus ministry a few miles from our home. They scouted our underprivileged neighborhood regularly and convinced several of the unchurched heathens to ride their bus, including me. I took the opportunity very seriously by wearing a tie and what I deemed my *Sunday best*. My favorite was a purple checked shirt with a matching clip-on tie. I waited faithfully every Sunday morning and evening for the bus. I sat close to the front in church and listened intently to every word. I responded one Sunday to the call of repentance and gave my life over for a ticket to heaven. I was baptized and from that moment absorbed in Christian faith. I was now in true opposition to a forced homelife of lawlessness. I managed to maintain a wobbly faithful journey for about five years. Upon entering high school in the tenth grade my faith began to seem less important and eventually I paused my faith journey but maintained a pompous and defensive attitude toward the sins of my legal guardians.

Life for me didn't change drastically, but I grew increasingly impatient with my parents. Not once did my parents ask how I was doing in school or attempt to help with homework. Once or twice my father attempted to assist with math but was terribly impatient because whiskey had already kicked in. Having beautiful penmanship, I was able to forge their signatures on failing report cards. Why didn't they ask about my progress, report cards, homework, term papers, nothing? I believe if they had known my lack of academic progress and failure, they would have had a minimal response. Being artistically bent I loved expressing my talent in art class. I drew all the time at home and received what I perceived as half-hearted, *"that's good,"* when sharing creativity. I don't recall one conversation about how I might further pursue artistic abilities in a career or post-secondary education. For the most part, my parents remained submerged in their own dysfunctional world. I'm not certain they knew how or wanted to assist me with school work. Perhaps they relinquished the responsibility for my learning to the schools and let the chips fall as they may. I don't believe they envisioned a bright future for me. On some level I sensed their indifference and witnessed firsthand their uninvolved, *throw it to the wind* mindset. For an adolescent this mindset was a grand way to be left alone to the wiles of nascent substitutes for family, unhealthy substances, or dangerous actions to distract and ease the pain and suffering of neglect. Instead, I watched and listened for the next explosion and did what I could do to subdue those situations – often to no avail as my perfectionism thrived and didn't allow for obtuse deviations from self-imposed norms.

Perhaps my father felt a little guilty, so he started an interesting way of including me in his indulgences. As his alcohol craving increased, he developed a habit of stopping after work at a local convenience store for one can of beer and would buy a pack of small donuts for me – the type at the counter for a last-minute impulse purchase. He then stopped at *Last Chance Liquors* for his daily fifth of cheap whiskey – took one sip then opened his beer. I witnessed this routine on numerous afternoons when he allowed me to borrow our car and I was the driver. Didn't fully comprehend his craving for alcohol at the time. The afternoon sweet indulgence began to show around my waist, but I never protested. I'm certain this pattern was his way of doing something cheap to redirect attention from his boozing and inattention toward my life pursuits. Donuts before dinner for me – alcohol before, during, and after dinner for him – we both enjoyed our indulgences.

The first high school event my parents attended was graduation 1975. After high school I had no plans to attend college – no family discussions – nothing. A small business college opened in Madison the year I graduated, and I was told about a fashion merchandising program they offered. I asked my parents about the possibility because of my interest in fashion designing. They said it was up to me but made it clear no additional funds were available. I applied, completed a test I failed, but was accepted anyway – realizing later the whole operation was a business scam to loan money and profit from high interest rates. I attended one year and completed the program. Sitting in class I peered out a window watching children and teachers at the school next door – I recalled playing school as a child and loved it. Patterson, Outlaw and Ramsay – my inspiration – a long-ago dream and persistent yearning – faint voices calling.

A local Nashville fashion designer was searching for a sketch artist to draw her creations for a sales booklet. She hired me, and I worked for her about five years as one of numerous part-time jobs. I was exposed to the high fashion world through her and by the school. Two trips were built into the program to attract students: one to New York City, the other Atlanta. Both trips allowed us to see a side of the fashion business I longed for but also a side that I knew would lead to a life of dysfunction I worked hard to avoid and didn't wish to embrace. More details about post high school college experiences later.

Shortly after high school I began to experiment with social drinking – I had a lot of experience watching but never participating. It was something I never shared with parents because of the strict stance I had taken at home. Living with them I didn't wish to participate openly in their vices or discuss it. My social drinking occurred at parties, with friends, and a local night spot for young adults – the drinking age was eighteen – I was never carded. I preferred sweeter drinks and typically no more than two, three at the most – self-control prevailed. I was introduced to marijuana during this period but never participated, not one toke. I've never been drunk because I made a vow to myself not to mimic my father's choices. But a *tug-of-war* existed deep within I didn't fully comprehend – nevertheless, I remained steadfast in the effort to avoid most sinful vices. Why? Perhaps it was a little easier than I thought to keep the vow. Determined not to become the man who raised me, but wasn't able to explain why – could never put my finger on it but something was missing – a definite gulf – dormant truth patiently waiting to be freed. Although I didn't announce determination as a flag waving decree, I persisted with a steadfast boldness to conquer negative forces that could have easily become my ruination.

Life Altering

The wood-paneled rectangle shrouded in cold dimness reeked of musty tobacco. Breath visible, I fixated on a toxic cylinder trapped in murky frozen liquid, hearing words but not discerning my looming future. Barely six years old when life began to gradually erode my innocence. At that same moment, privilege of another allowed a different gaze and aroma. Two connected but separate fates allotted a thousand threads of destiny – all by choices past, present, and future. One suddenly confined in a narrow rectangle for nine long years during critical stages of growth and development become profound life altering years. Tension between past and present required me to balance a set of delicate life strategies – delicate because at any moment everything could literally go off the rails. Though I live now in totally opposite circumstances from my past, tension is present, and I have the ability to react appropriately, financial means to remedy or correct imbalances. Strangely enough, I'm not quick to jump on remedies to ease tension from the past that interfere at times with present capabilities. Much of my reactions I simply don't understand, but *spilling my guts* in the sixth decade is a good example – why the wait you might ask? Unexpected discoveries and revelations jarred the past open, freeing unknowns. Since I'm a product of my past, it's not wise to ignore revelations or attempt to strip it all away – residue remains. My past is always present; thus, tension unavoidable.

My maturity and social development lagged far behind female counterparts – I knew this to be true. Educators know it's true about males, although some argue it's psychobabble. I'm an excellent example of the slower maturing process because it was roughly four years after high school before I entered an accredited college and received a Bachelor's degree in elementary education, grades 1-8, a certificate I hold to this day – another life altering moment. Before making the decision to pursue a real degree, my natural proclivities led me to several part-time jobs all at the same time – fashion illustrator, men's clothing salesperson, florist delivery and designer, private school substitute teacher, and free-lance artist. I met my future wife during this time at the big church where I reestablished a commitment to faith and Christianity – perhaps more appropriately stated, I was married to a doctrine – a controlling type inflexible system I fully embraced outwardly but inwardly questioned.

Cliff told me about a tall, nice looking new girl attending class. He was thinking about asking her on a date – he often talked about asking several girls on dates. We eventually met in the church lobby, and he was correct, tall and attractive. The first time I saw her she was wearing a brown and burgundy plaid skirt, with what appeared to be a pale colored silk blouse under a dark burgundy velour jacket. Light brown hair fell in soft curls lightly touching her shoulders. Her skin was delicate without blemish – nothing false, a presence of purity. Kathleen, a mutual friend, introduced us and we exchanged a few timid comments – Jim and Pam finally meet. I noticed everything about her and wondered what she noticed about me. We ended up together in several social settings and got to know each other fairly well. We no longer seemed timid in conversation. A group of my friends, along with Pam, attended a college basketball game at Vol State. I sat directly in front of her on purpose – her knees brushed against my back several times – we didn't watch much of the game. When the group conversation turned to dinner plans and pizza was the choice I turned to Pam and informed her we would share a pizza – my treat. She seemed a little surprised but pleased with my impromptu aggressiveness – Cliff didn't seem impressed. My best friend continued his interest, but he never asked – I officially did and she accepted. Our first official date was at a restaurant named Ireland's. I was again bold enough and initiated a cautious kiss before we departed.

We dated roughly a year and I got very scared. My solution – RUN – I broke up with her, an idiotic, foolish choice on my part for certain, and I later learned she thought the same about my decision. We got back together a week later thanks to my Impala Chevrolet. I was at the library next to her apartment complex; my car wouldn't start when I attempted to leave – fate? It was about the time she arrived home from work, so I stood next to my dead vehicle as she zoomed by with no recognition of my dilemma – she actually did see me, but I deserved the royal snub. I walked to her apartment and asked if she could jump my battery – I knew deep in my heart she was the one I truly loved. Financially, I had nothing to offer but my love and a junky old Impala Chevrolet that would occasionally need the battery jumped. A silent *Voice* spoke into my doubting heart – *don't worry, she's the one for you.* My father's drinking continued but we had less and less confrontations because I was basically never home. I said nothing about this new person in my life. While washing the junky old car and cleaning it out one day, my dad walked outside and asked if I had a girlfriend. I questioned why he was asking. *"I've never seen you cleaning your car before and thought you must have a girlfriend."* I suppose he was more perceptive than I had given him credit for, and I admitted the truth. I now had to introduce her, but my thoughts shifted to my mother because she was very protective in an odd way of her one son – the only son she raised.

A short social drinking stint stopped – marrying into this religious family meant one thing – drinking alcohol was strictly prohibited – sinful – only for the immoral deadbeats of society. Finally, I would have the *perfect family* I always desired – I was seriously naïve. My fiancé worked full-time in engineering at Peterbilt Motors and had no concerns about our financial future – I did. Those fears were embedded deep within a dysfunctional rearing. One week before our marriage we signed for a three-bedroom brick house in Madison. I'll never forget the look on the bank lender's face when he reviewed my zero assets then reviewed hers. I knew exactly what he was thinking and how this must have looked – he must have been thinking I was taking her for everything she has – or perhaps just a lucky man. Of course, the latter is true. What he didn't know, how very proud I was of the engagement ring I bought from a small, privately owned jewelry store across the street from the college I attended. The jewelry business thrived on young college men buying rings for future mates. The owner allowed me to pay what I was able to afford weekly or monthly. The initial down payment came from my father because he generously offered five-hundred dollars from the small estate settlement after his father's death – providential timing? I graciously accepted his gift knowing he fully approved of the person I loved – one of those rare memories that help cover the many mistakes and character flaws of his sad life. He was a generous man with limited funds. His drinking often interfered with his generosity, but that time it didn't.

One such time when his addiction interfered was the start of my freshman year at Volunteer State Community College. He promised to pay the first quarter's tuition but when the time arrived, he didn't have extra money – it upset me tremendously to say the least. Luckily, I saw an ad in the newspaper where I could sell gold and receive cash – sold my high school ring and covered the first tuition payment. I'm not clear how I was able to pay the remaining payments but by the grace of God. My fiancé assisted and eventually paid the tuition in full once we married. My sister-in-law secretly paid an installment, didn't tell me until many years later, and a lovely older couple, the Bryan's, did the same. We married August 12, 1983 and started our honeymoon at the Music City Sheraton then headed to Gatlinburg in east Tennessee for a week. My first time to visit Gatlinburg. My parents rarely vacationed except for Kentucky Lake and Florida twice with my favorite aunt and uncle, more about them later. After our honeymoon we started life together in a new brick home – life was good – emotional baggage and all.

On Father's Day, 1985, my father's only brother phoned about 3:30 pm, informed me Willie, my father's nickname his brother and the locals called him, had been taken to the hospital and we should get there quickly. We arrived and were ushered into a small waiting room, my mother, my dad's brother, my wife and I were alone. After waiting several minutes, a doctor walked in, and I noticed his detached somber look and emotionless tone as he addressed my mother. *"Mrs. Morris, I'm sorry but we were unable to revive Mr. Morris. He has passed away."* Those words penetrated deep – all my senses hit the floor with a heavy thud – a surreal moment. Immediately sucked grief into my gut and turned to comfort a twice widow – this time she wouldn't wait ten years for a body – she needed me now more than ever before. Collecting our emotions, we were handed a clear bag – billfold, keys, glasses never to be used again – we stepped warily while processing shock. Sorrowfulness knocked loudly – I refused to respond – instead, comforted a grieving widow with words offering little comfort – a profound life altering moment.

Sudden Death

The man who raised me died on Father's Day – he was fifty-five years old. How did this happen? What was my mother going to do? She didn't drive, she had never written a check in her life, didn't have a checking account in her name, nor a savings account, didn't work outside the home, she was totally dependent on my father for support in every way. Grief stopped for me, and my focus suddenly changed to her immediate needs. My thoughts flashed back to earlier in the day. My wife and I visited after church to give him a Father's Day gift. I recall him opening the box slowly, seemed difficult to tear the paper off. He had a grey, ashen look to his skin. We didn't know he was suffering signs of heart failure – blood wasn't flowing properly. My mother noticed nothing unusual – perhaps she had gone into her typical denial mode. Obviously, many years of self-inflicted abuse upon his body finally caught up with him – he was slowly dying, and we didn't recognize it during the brief visit. In the car we did mention he didn't seem to be feeling well – dismissed slow movements to alcohol. Buried in the only suit coat and tie he owned, ten short months earlier he wore the exact combination on our wedding day. Twenty-six years later buried my mother in the same dress she wore on our wedding day. A framed wedding photo of my parents sits on a table in a room we dubbed the parlor – both in their wedding and burial clothes.

She struggled greatly the first year after my father's death – depression, loss of appetite, became a recluse, hiding behind pulled shades and locked doors. I recommended we sell the house and she move to a high-rise for retired people. Thankfully, turning sixty-five in September she started drawing my father's social security – financially secure – not exactly – but a wonderful blessing. We made a quick sale of the house and moved her to a high-rise, a one-bedroom apartment on the seventh floor – a government subsidized complex. Slowly but surely my mother regained her footing and began to venture out into her second tour of widowhood – this time would be totally different. She made a few friends, complained a lot about the *busy-bodied* neighbors, but eventually settled into a new normal. She often monopolized my time away from work because she didn't drive and refused to use the free bus services provided by the complex. She eventually gave in and used the daily bus service when needed. During this same period of time, we purchased land in a rural part of a neighboring community and made plans to sell our home in Madison and build in the woods among the tall trees. I never really knew what my mother thought about our lifestyle compared to her simple life. I managed her finances because she couldn't, and we often supplemented her accounts. A few weeks after moving into our new home we discovered my mother would have her first grandchild – at least that's what we believed.

Sudden death created a fight for life – a life that couldn't fight for herself. The fight was not a tied game but an impasse for me – somewhat emotionally defeated, I knew what life was about to become because my mother was totally dependent on her husband for everything except cooking and house cleaning. I foolishly trusted she could handle her personal finances after a brief tutorial – my thought was she must learn how to write a check because she would soon be sixty-five. Once everything was finalized and settled, some financial relief was on the way in the form of $10,000 – thanks to an insurance policy death benefit. Once the money arrived, I quickly deposited it in the bank under her name – another big mistake. My mother visited some *so-called friends*, and I'm convinced she bragged about the death benefit money. In her view she was a wealthy widow and wanted others to know – a poor choice on her part.

Within a few weeks, unknown to me, an acquaintance of the *friends* befriended her, and she was lonely. Within another few weeks I attempted to transfer a small amount of the money for a necessary purchase she needed for the house and discovered to my surprise $7000 missing from the account. I immediately went to my mother, and she told me she loaned money to a new friend to have his truck repaired – she assured me he was planning to pay her back. He drove her to the bank, wrote the check and she signed. The low-life man knew exactly what he was doing. He took advantage of a grieving widow – he seized upon her emotional weakness, loneliness, and vulnerability – she was a perfect target for his scam.

Emotions overwhelmed me, and I yelled at the top of my voice, *"Mother, you will never see a penny of that money ever again. It was a scam; he stole the money from you!"* I knew the money was gone forever and major changes had to occur immediately. It was like my father's sudden death all over again – another thud – this time coated with anger and rage. Sure enough, she never saw or heard from him again, but I was determined to conquer this terrible situation and win. I didn't seek to locate him – may have ended up in jail I was so troubled – my impulse control mechanism served me well. I transferred her limited assets to my name but left her name on the account and set up a new checking account – the checkbook my sole possession. She never held another check in her hand unless it was written and signed by me. I no longer cared if she ever mastered how to write a check. I managed the account and supplemented her insufficient funds until the end. She was never left alone again to manage the struggles of daily life. Turning sixty-five in September was a blessing because she now received my father's monthly social security benefit as long as she didn't remarry. And that was another stipulation I made perfectly clear – she could not remarry or she would lose the monthly benefit. Boyfriend? Yes. Remarry? NO. Sudden death taught me a lot about life, trust, and decision making. I had no other choice but to play the *game* strategically well. Sudden death did not defeat me – I was unyielding.

First Grandchild?

Audrey Caroline Morris, born at 3:03 pm, April 1989, Memorial Hospital in Madison. My wife's parents were there, Pam's sister, a few close friends, but my mother was at home not feeling well – convenient stomach pain again. I guilted her into visiting the next day – she seemed nervous about it. She held her grandchild as if she might break and barely voiced any words and asked no questions. I didn't understand her reluctance toward welcoming her *first* grandchild, but I put aside those concerns and allowed our new joyfulness to overpower stomach pain and averseness. My mother-in-law couldn't be happier and remained with us a week to assist with our new tiny bundle. I spoke daily with my mother to keep her informed but always carried the conversation – couldn't pinpoint the issue, but something didn't seem right. Resented competing issues, desired my full attention to rest solely on my child, but my mother's emotional manipulation demanded a portion. Thankfully, everything slowly fell into place as it does for a growing family – all the usual ups and downs, mostly joy and fun times surrounding a new baby.

My mother eventually adapted to her status as grand-mother but always needed positive affirmation to stay focused on her new role – she appeared so uncertain. She had smoked since she was about twenty years old – hid it from her family for all those years as if they didn't know. I didn't like it and especially now that my child would be in her presence – I'm sure she sensed a disdain – knew it from my childhood. Knowing eventually my mother would babysit – perhaps our house where no one smoked. She never babysat at our house – easier at her apartment because she didn't drive. I tolerated her smoking just as I did for twenty-five years but asked that she limit it around Caroline, although, I could still smell it on her clothes after every visit. My mother was terrified of storms, tornadoes, or anything that might bring any type of destruction or possibly disrupt her life. She was fearful of everything. I discovered cigarette ashes that had fallen on her carpet and burned a tiny spot. I expressed she might catch the apartment on fire if she wasn't careful with her smoking – *"You could get trapped inside with no way out!"* The suggestion frightened her so much she quit smoking that day and never smoked again.

Caroline ratted on her grandmother one evening after a babysitting stay on the seventh floor. Pam and I had gone on a date night and returned to my mother's apartment around 9:00 pm. Everything appeared calm, not much said; Caroline was especially quiet, and my mother's friend Doris was visiting, and she barely spoke. While driving home, Caroline volunteered some information: *"A police officer visited Me-maw and talked with her."* Pam and I looked at each other with puzzlement, wondering if we heard her correctly. We asked her to repeat what she just said, and she repeated the exact same statement. I then asked for more details. Caroline told us Me-maw got in an argument with a lady in the hallway and started yelling. We suspected someone likely called the police because they felt threatened by the verbal altercation between my mother and the other lady. A rage of disgust enveloped me – thoughts of arguments between my parents surfaced. I was not going to tolerate this type of behavior ever again and especially if it involved my daughter. I phoned my mother once we arrived at home and, as usual, only a mild version of half-truths – my rage didn't subside. I made it perfectly clear this type of behavior in front of Caroline must never occur again or she would not see her grandchild. Yes, I was harsh – my *perfect life* disrupted – my hippocampus fired on all cylinders sending my shitty past back to the present. I was consumed. To my knowledge my mother complied with the stern directive and my rage subsided.

I recognized my mother as a fragile soul, vulnerable to any suggestions, innuendo, or gossip. I know she allowed fear to direct her life most days. She possessed many good qualities too. When at her best, she could cook a southern country meal that would rival any great cook. She loved growing flowers, especially giant zinnias, marigolds, petunias, and snap dragons. She worked the soil diligently, watered religiously, and always took great pride in people noticing the beauty of her floral genius. My mother loved Caroline dearly – I never doubted it. My relationship with her began to slowly improve because I slowly matured. Letting go of years of resentment and occasional rage was emotionally freeing. I began to see her as not only fragile but deeply wounded with no one but me to assist. As she aged and grew feebler, I washed and trimmed her hair, clipped her nails, soaked her feet, did all of her grocery shopping. My wife cleaned her apartment, washed her clothes and secretly threw away years of collected useless junk. I think she finally felt appreciated for the first time being treated with dignity and respect she had never experienced.

My mother didn't fit in, marginalized by eight obedient siblings – one sister the exception. Why? My mother walked a different path, chose sensual and reckless love leading to unacceptable consequences. She never sensed forgiveness or unconditional love from siblings but the one. I knew there was talk behind the scenes; my mother's family likely thought I didn't have a *rat's chance in hell*. Nine fairly successful siblings she couldn't compete with – seven never visited our home – nine years in a trailer park, two of the three visited once or twice. The one sibling my mother counted on was sister Lora and her family, a unique bond occurred between the two. The others had some understanding what our home life was like and simply chose to avoid it. Her siblings didn't believe their sister when she made excuses for her inebriated husband at home – *"too tired, he needs his rest"* and so on. Most of her siblings knew more than she thought they knew because those things were discussed in private whisper groups – that's how it worked in *dutiful families* before social media. Perhaps that explains why three of her siblings and spouses didn't bother visiting a sister when meeting for lunch less than five miles from her government subsidized apartment on the seventh floor – a lonely sister – not even a phone call to my knowledge. Perhaps there are deeper reasons. One local sibling attended her graveside service, six living at the time of her death, some declining in health, others lived a long distance away. I chose graveside only with no visitation – loathed the thought of people visiting the dead if they didn't visit the living.

During the two years of teaching at a private school I completed a Master's Degree, then Caroline and I moved to Southeastern Christian Academy for my first school administration job. Caroline entered third grade – she rode with her father and principal every day. This is the time frame I began to experience a greater empathy for my mother. My mother was proud of my professional success and enjoyed bragging to her few friends. She frequently told others of my professional work as an educator and principal. During my stint as President, head of school at SCA, she especially loved dropping that title. Her one granddaughter Caroline graduated in 2007. I was on stage as an administrator when she walked across to receive a diploma – a unique moment for father and daughter because we were together at the same school for ten years. My mother didn't attend. I returned to public education a few years later as principal of a large, urban elementary school in Madison, the city of my childhood, only two blocks from the first home I purchased with my wife, more details about career later. My mother died one day before my birthday, before the official return to public education, before another secret was unraveled and exposed.

Truth Dies

Chronicling a detailed narrative of our mother's peaceful departure from a lifetime of disadvantage and conflict is important for sons and brothers to remember. She unselfishly chose to protect her first born by giving him the greatest gift she could give – a family of privilege adopted a son. A birth mother's coverup and denial unwittingly set-in motion a path of prosperity for one and unforeseen poverty for another. Our mother was admitted to Skyline hospital early Saturday morning, my birthday two days away – November 2010. My wife and I visited, and she was resting comfortably when we left. We told her I would stop in before church Sunday morning. I arrived at the hospital a little before 8:00 am. She was tired and worn out from poking and constant checking from techs and nurses. She appeared weaker than the day before, but she knew who I was and responded to questions. She was no longer cold as she was the day before and actually complained of being hot.

Adjusted the bed and fluffed the pillow as she took another sip of water. Nurse Michelle asked how long I would be there; said she needed to get my mother's medical history – information taken on the computer attached to the wall. Told her my plan was to be there until 8:45. She seemed rushed as most nurses do but said that would work. The food service person walked back in with a tray a few minutes after leaving. She brought grits, milk, and a small cup of vanilla pudding. I thanked her and she said to let her know if we needed anything else. I recognized her considerate attitude and eager willingness to serve – a sweet blessing.

Michelle prepared medicine at the counter with her back to us. She turned and requested I try to get her to eat as much as possible. I prepared the grits by adding butter. Opened milk and placed a straw in it. She actually took a couple of long drinks using the straw, which surprised me. Michelle crushed a couple of pills in a small cup. She took a spoon full of the grits and mixed them with the medicine and gave it to her. I also fed her a few bites; in all she may have eaten three or four bites of grits and four drinks of milk. I told her about the pudding on the tray and she uttered, *"pudding"* with a perplexed tenor. Assured her it was okay to eat pudding for breakfast. She agreed to have a bite – ate about three bites of pudding. As she was eating, I reminded her that I probably swiped a few cookies from the cookie jar before breakfast when I was younger of which she never knew. It caused me to think of Caroline and what she would ask my mother when she stayed with her. I asked if she remembered, she held up one bent, weak finger and said, *"One more cookie Me-maw?"* The fond remembrance seemed to delight her for a moment. Michelle took a quick glance, smiled and said she would be back in a few minutes. Experienced nurses like Michelle know – I didn't.

Helped her get comfortable after eating and sat next to her bed on the right. Told her about open house at school and that I would come back late afternoon. Michelle returned to the room after ten minutes and walked to the computer. She started asking all the same questions we had been asked back in July. Many of those were still in the system from that brief stay. The GI doctor walked in and introduced himself. He spoke to my mom then gently pressed her stomach – she said it hurt. He looked to me and said we really need to do a colonoscopy in order to know exactly what we are dealing with. He sensed my hesitation, but my mother didn't seem engaged with our conversation. Michelle waited by the computer. He said it may be something really simple that can be fixed, or it may be something serious. He asked what I wanted to do. I reluctantly agreed it was best to go ahead but was concerned and wanted nothing done if it were something serious – he nodded. He used the term *"mass"* but never said cancer. He said she would need to be given a special liquid prior to the test through a tube in her nose. Thankfully my mother wasn't clued in to what he said. Michelle didn't ask any more questions – she knew.

After open house, called my wife before arriving at the hospital and she told me about her visit – she was now back home. Said my mother was very uncomfortable with pain. She asked for more pain medicine and Michelle got permission from a doctor. Michelle administered the additional meds through her IV. She was getting more comfortable before my wife left. Late Saturday during my wife's visit, she and my mother watched two Andy Griffith shows on her favorite channel 59 (TV Land). She remembered watching one of the shows about a goat being kept in the jail cell. Both tried to think of the name of the *"town drunk"* but couldn't. She asked for the TV to be left on so it would be on the same channel the next morning. When I arrived, she seemed lethargic – TV still on. His name was Otis.

My wife said Michelle asked if I was returning to the hospital, she had some papers for me to sign. When I arrived, Michelle sat at the nurse's station but said nothing – she knew. As I approached the room a young lady stepped out; she appeared to be a technician. I spoke and she said they were completing x-rays. I waited a moment at the door. The tech re-entered the room then said I could step in a few seconds later. Another tech was in the room pulling the large x-ray machine away from my mom's bed. The tech in the room looked down as if to prevent eye contact. She said nothing. I thought it seemed a bit odd but dismissed my concern. Both techs quietly slipped out of the room. My mother seemed uncomfortable but quiet. She was almost upright in the bed because they had it raised quite a bit. I concluded it was for the x-ray – my mother appeared less focused than earlier. She did not complain about the bed being up as she usually did.

I asked several questions attempting to engage her in conversation. She responded but with few words and seemed especially feeble. The time a little after 4:00 pm, so I decided to turn the TV off. It seemed she was beginning to feel more uncomfortable. She asked for help and medicine a few times, and I told her she had been given medicine to ease pain. I noticed she had a lot of congestion in her throat. Said she needed to spit. I gave her a small plastic dish, but she couldn't hold it. I held it at her mouth; she tried but was too weak. Encouraged her to try again – no success. I suggested she close her mouth and breathe through her nose. She did for a few moments then went back to mouth breathing. She repeated this pattern a few more times after my suggestions to try again. The gargling sound in her throat increased as did her overall discomfort level. She did not seem to be doing very well overall.

I sat quietly on the right side of her bed as she continued to become more uncomfortable. She started reaching for the left side of the bed and also pulling herself to the left. I shifted her back to the center of the bed a couple of times and asked her what was hurting. She mumbled something I didn't understand and appeared extremely uncomfortable. I went out of the room for a moment to the nurse. Michelle was sitting at the nurse's station on the computer. I told her what was happening, and she said she needs to try to spit as much as she can. I said she was having trouble doing so because she was so weak. Michelle nodded her head slightly in agreement but offered no other suggestions. I turned and walked back to the room. Michelle knew what was happening. My mother remained uncomfortable and continued to move toward the left side of the bed. She did not have her head on a pillow since she was sitting upright. I decided to move to the left side of the bed and attempt to make her comfortable again.

I took the pillow and positioned it against the railing where she seemed to be migrating. She slightly turned her whole body sideways, pulled her legs up and moved both of her hands over to the left of the railing. Suddenly I realized something different beginning to occur. It's difficult to describe the actual feeling I experienced in clear terms, but I wanted to make her as comfortable as possible. She rested her head against the pillow, and I placed her hands in mine. A sudden rush of emotion swept over me, and tears flooded my eyes. I prayed that if this was her time it would be peaceful. I started to talk – her eyes were open and seemed somewhat fixed. She appeared to be looking beyond the bed, slightly up – the room extremely quiet as was the hallway. It had just become dusk outside. I noticed her breathing pattern had changed – breathing through her nose and unexpectedly very comfortable.

With a few slow dribbling tears, I gripped aged bruised speckled hands in mine, expressed how much I loved her, how she had been a wonderful mother to me, and it was okay if she needed to go – assured her I would be okay. I then noticed her breathing pattern again and started counting seconds between breaths – five, then six, seven, then eight. I stopped to wipe drool from one side of her mouth – did that twice. Occasionally she had a small puff of breath that slipped out – ten seconds then twelve. She was suddenly so peaceful and calm. Wrinkled weak hands in mine, bluer than before. The realization of what was happening now crystal clear – I was at peace – she was at peace – the moment deeply spiritual.

Michelle walked in and said her heart rate dropped very low on the monitor and she called a code, checked her heartbeat with the stethoscope. I continued to hold her hands in mine. Michelle spoke softly, *"I'm not getting a beat."* Two additional nurses walked in quickly with code equipment. Michelle looked at me and asked if I wanted to cancel the code – no hesitation – yes. No thud this time. I beheld my mother, tranquility and rest – all pain, fears, struggles erased, no more need for denial. Eighty-nine years of life on earth – I held her hands; it was 5:15 pm. Behind waterlogged eyes I told the nurses about the last several moments. They stood in respectful silence – listened sympathetically. Michelle responded with a tender voice and said she was sorry for my loss. As she unhooked the heart monitor and turned off the IV another nurse walked over and put her arm around my shoulder and gently patted. They told me I could stay in the room as long as I needed – still clasping her hands. One older tech said in a kind and compassionate tone, *"Let's put the bed down, she didn't like to sit up like this."* She was correct. I stood up and turned toward the window – desired to call my wife but waited – reflected as I peered across the serene darkness beyond the glass where life continued without pause for my sacred moment.

Michelle said, *"We will make her all beautiful and will be cleaning her up in a few minutes."* She also said they would fix her in the bed so that I could be alone. Turned away and called my wife – told her what had occurred. She cried, listened intently as I shared my experiences. After ending the conversation, I turned back around, my mother was covered up with only her head exposed. She looked especially peaceful, no more pain or sorrow, no tests, no more needles or health issues. Michelle walked over and extended a timid hug, said she was leaving the room, for me to stay as long as I wanted. I walked to the bed and thought of my grandmother Tenpenny – my mother looked much like her mother – my devout Christian grandmother. Gently kissed her forehead, stroked her hair, tried to call Caroline but forced to leave a generic message to call back. I now knew what Michelle had known all along.

My mother often proclaimed, *"I'm going to live to be one-hundred"* – she didn't make it. I'm extremely grateful for my mother. She loved me deeply in peculiar ways and couldn't share truth. In spite of it all, it was my privilege and desire to see to her needs for twenty-six years after the untimely death of my father. Enormously close in heart and constantly in my thoughts – now only memories to cherish. I am satisfied with everything I was able to do for her with no regrets. Yes, unanswered questions persist – in time a new DNA blood line will reveal another long-held hidden story my mother buried. *"What is truth?"*

Raphael

My mother's brother called unexpectedly and asked if we could meet, had something to discuss. I wondered what it could be? Did he call my mother first and talk with her? We had never spoken in a one-on-one conversation. He was a successful business owner in Murfreesboro – a man of few words. He didn't mention my mother, so I didn't think it had anything to do with her – little did I know. We met at a Shoney's, shook hands and sat down. *"Jim, you have a brother. I'm the one that took Velma to Kentucky to have the baby."* Smacked with a few simple words – life tersely altered again – my brain needed a moment to process this mammoth revelation – did my best to refocus. As he talked, I began to realize it all seemed possible – made some sense – shards of a disjointed past fitting together. Raphael Lewis is his name. His birth name Jack Tenpenny, not really a name fitting for high society, growing up on the rich side of town. I grew up in a Madison trailer park; bet he lived in a spacious brick home on an expansive lot. I lived in a wood paneled rectangle next to railroad tracks; bet his family drove new luxury vehicles. My father drove junk vehicles bought at tote-your-note lots – choices shaped two fates. Poor and rich – deprived and privileged – perhaps I was cheated. Did I get the short end of this deal?

My uncle said Raphael hired a private investigator to search for his birth parents – of course he did, I thought. His search hit a roadblock until he came across a name plate at the law firm in Memphis that handles his business affairs. Law firm, business affairs, what in the world are we talking about here? My cousin's wife worked there as a legal secretary. Her last name is Tenpenny. Raphael told her he was searching for a Tenpenny family with origins in Murfreesboro. He had stumbled upon his *holy grail* – it all opened up at that point – fate? He found his mother's brother – was given phone numbers and addresses. My uncle shared Raphael's contact information and urged me to contact him. I clearly remember my uncle stating, *"Velma can't deny it. It's true. I drove her, I know."* He remembered his sister's bad habit – not very good at truth telling. But how would I do this? When would I do this? Will this destroy our fragile relationship? Will this unearthed secret destroy her? So many unanswered questions to ponder – so many unknowns. But one thing I knew – I have a brother and there was something exciting about this news.

I scheduled an appointment with my mother's doctor to ask if this news could make her sick or potentially cause any heart complications. The doctor thought she would be fine. I made the decision to wait until after Christmas in case it created an awkwardness or tarnished our holiday family time. Shortly after the holidays I visited my mother prepared to ask her about my brother, her first born. I first told her I had something fairly serious to discuss. I then went straight to the core of the matter. *"I've discovered I have a half or full brother. He was born in Kentucky eighteen months before me and you named him Jack. Is this true mother?"* She immediately hung her head in silence and didn't look at me – she confirmed truth without words – obviously a difficult thing for her to do and admit. I reassured her nothing about our relationship would ever change. *"Nothing at this point is worth destroying our relationship over. I will always take care of you and love you – you can count on that!"* I asked again if this was true. She said nothing, but I had to hear the words. I told her about my meeting with Nile and that the adoption birth records in Kentucky had recently been released. His name and original certificate number matched. She looked up and glanced at me – a look I remembered so many years ago when I first asked about a brother. *"Yes, it's true."* Hushed words shrouded in tones of shame, but this time I finally heard truth.

She shared no other details – nothing, absolutely nothing. I wanted more, just like I did the day I found the marriage certificate – lots more, but it wasn't coming. I stopped pressing, sensed shame and anguish in her body language. Unexpectedly wounded all over again – her past reared its ugly head – shards are painful. I'm certain she wanted me to leave – unlike other times when I visited. She bravely crossed a great divide she never thought she would have to cross. I recognized her pain and embarrassment. I was thankful for *"yes, it's true"* – satisfied? No. Perhaps more would come later on another day – never happened. Yes, I brought this major development to her attention a few more times over the next several months – she shared nothing more. Denial reigned. It was time to meet my brother face-to-face.

My immediate thought after opening the front door – his body shape is like my father's – we must be full brothers. Is that what I wanted, was I creating that image in my mind? We shook hands and I invited him in – could barely comprehend it – my brother, is he really my brother? We were alone so that our conversation would focus just on the two of us getting to know each other. My wife graciously agreed to go out for a few hours to give us time alone. The conversation started with a lot of small talk then gradually to family. He has four children. Immediately I thought about my mother having five grandchildren instead of one. Would she ever know them, hug them? As men typically do, our professional work was discussed first. He graduated from Duke University with an engineering degree. Didn't like it so he convinced his father to let him attend MSU and major in culinary arts. He is a trained chef. He worked in and owned fine food restaurants in New Orleans for over twenty years. Next, he described something somewhat unfamiliar to me – in his exact words, *"I sign a lot of papers at a law firm in Memphis. They handle my business of loaning to small businesses to expand or start up."* He didn't use the words *venture capitalist* but instead said, *"my children's friends think I'm in the Mafia because I'm always home."* He laughed.

I shared my professional career as a teacher and principal then I brought out family photo albums. I wanted him to see his Tenpenny family – he appeared to study the photos with intensity. I asked if he would like to take a few albums with him to share with his family and he did. The conversation never lagged; didn't want the moment to end – not certain what he thought. As he departed, noticed his body shape and recognized my father again. Thick fingers, also like my father's. He was dressed very nicely, perfectly shined shoes. His wrist watch noticeably expensive and could smell his overpriced cologne. He told me they have a beach home in Florida, and own Lewis Cove in Gatlinburg – *"Just let me know if you want to visit and stay there."* *Poor* and *rich* finally meet – two upbringings so different. I was excited to have a brother, know my brother. What did our future hold? How would we navigate this new found relationship? Is it possible for two very different DNA attached lives to develop a strong bond? Only time will reveal more – so much more I didn't know.

Raphael spoke clearly. He did not wish to surprise my mother with a visit but would like to speak with her if she was willing. He sat in the parking lot of her complex hoping to see someone he thought might be her – that surprised me. I asked my mother about meeting Raphael or speaking to him by phone. She chose to speak with him by phone. I looked forward to hearing the details of their conversation. It apparently didn't go well. My mother shared nothing – even after pressing her a bit – Raphael didn't share details. He returned the photo albums by mail, and we basically ended our brotherly reunion. We received photo Christmas cards for three years with the children and family dog Rollin casually posed. Based on photos I can see strong resemblances in his oldest and my father. His third child smiles like my mother. The other two favor Tenpenny family in obvious ways. Perhaps I'm creating comparisons because that's what I desire. A few weeks after my mother's graveside memorial Raphael called to extend condolences for the loss – I thanked him; we talked a few moments – an odd conversation. That was our last conversation for a long period. I attempted to contact him a few times since with no response. My mother took her secrets to the grave and my newly discovered adventure ended – until a DNA shocker.

Poor meets rich, I know one side of the story well – only slightly familiar with the other. Existing within one side for twenty-five years with all the ups and downs afforded me unique perspectives. Likewise, Raphael has his side with ups and downs – his side is framed very differently but nonetheless, his side shaped character and perspective on life as mine did. My story is what I know, but just beneath the exterior is the nine-year trailer park kid, age six to fourteen rolled up into one fairly high-functioning adult. I make a powerful effort to appear well put together, an individual living the good life. That's a fairly precise account with the exception of the usual hang-ups and neuroses we all possess in a variety of forms. Mine surface occasionally, sometimes more often, usually in negative forms. My wife knows those moments well because she's the one on the front lines –

experiencing my moments more than others. Perfectionism typically the culprit – my view of the way something should be as opposed to her view – we clash. These moments are never anything serious but do cause emotions to flare at times – she's especially more tolerant. I've tried to explain my self-diagnosed OCD imperfections but usually to no benefit. It's simply not possible for me to be completely free and unaffected by past experiences. Those experiences are deeply engrained and shaped me – it's simply not easy to contain or terminate all compulsions.

Eventually a few conversations occurred with Raphael via mobile phone and texting. I decided he needed to know what I discovered, so I sent a brief text stating what my search with AncestryDNA revealed – a new family connection – he was obviously intrigued because I received a reply within the hour – it was December 4, 2019. He asked if we could talk soon – I replied yes. I hesitated several times before calling because of my deep-seated fear of more rejection – understanding the source for that feeling forces a straight forward look at the remnants of my screwed-up childhood. I'm skilled at protecting myself from more emotional hurt even when it's not necessary. Though Raphael's text did intrigue me – he stated, *"I'm at a loss for words in my research. I discovered what you now know, and it made things very uncomfortable. In my quest all things pointed to Murfreesboro, and I found the man who knew the whole story and he would not talk. I think out of respect to family and circumstances."*

I finally reconnected voice to voice – an immediate calm rushed over me. Nothing seemed awkward as I spoke to my brother, a vibrant awareness that felt good and true. The man he was speaking of is Lloyd Campbell. A distant relative by marriage to a Tenpenny second cousin. His name was somewhat familiar because many years ago I received a letter from someone asking for information about my father after his death – the writer knew a lot about him, his military service and offered to give me additional information, but I never followed up. It may have been Campbell during the time he was researching family history – but not certain. Campbell has since died, but his research was mentioned on a new Facebook page dedicated to the Tenpenny family – thus far it has only traced ancestors I've never heard anyone mention. Raphael told me during our conversation he believes we may be full brothers. It is also his belief Lloyd Campbell didn't share any details because whatever he knew was a prickly issue and very disturbing for the family. I responded to the person hosting the Facebook page and revealed several details regarding my paternity search. I never received a response and within two weeks someone scratched the entire page – another mysterious occurrence and potential coverup.

I shared with Raphael the name of a recent connection that popped up on Ancestry – the last name is Shaufler. He immediately recognized the name – said his father had a good friend by the same last name. It's not a common name, and he said the friend lived in Murfreesboro – coincidence? This person has a high enough connecting number to be a second cousin of mine, and they appear to be connected to the family I do not know, but we share DNA – so many perplexing knots to untie. As we concluded our conversation Raphael said he was working on a big project in Louisiana, probably his last before retiring. He and his wife were planning to buy a new home in the Gulf or restore an older home they own and move there – said it might be eighteen months or so before moving. He and his wife Mitzi currently are located in southeastern Tennessee, outside of Chattanooga. He said one of his four children is living with them again as he transitions into another career. They have grandchildren now that keep them busy – that was good to hear, and I congratulated him. He was planning to come through Nashville soon. I suggested we meet for lunch or dinner – he agreed, and that was shortly before Christmas 2019. I texted him March 20, 2020, to check on his family on how they endured the tornados that hit the state and COVID19 becoming a growing issue. He responded that same evening, *"Tornado, China flu, what else? Things are good here so far."* We never met for lunch or dinner – I'm disappointed but still hopeful. My last text was September 21, 2020, asked if his beach house survived hurricane Sally. He said they experienced some trees down and a little beach erosion. His boat floated away and hasn't been found. He ended with, *"This may be a blessing in disguise, nothing money and time can't fix."* As he typically responds, it was within minutes, obviously money will replace his boat – thus far, time hasn't fully united two brothers.

Trailer Park Trash

My father, mother and I walked in, barely six years old and bitterly cold outside, not much better inside. Our first time to see inside the tobacco saturated trailer we ended up living in nine long years. My impressions as a young child very different than if I had been a pre-teen or teenager. My parents were lucky that I thought it was a good idea to move from a new, spacious brick home on Shepherd Hills Drive, where we lived only one year. The first and only Christmas tree we bought at the red brick house was a white flocked tree – floor to ceiling with blue lights. For the next nine years our trees were four feet tall or shorter – sat on a window table and purchased at a grocery store. We walked through the dimly lit, eight-foot-wide tin rectangle by Magnolia Homes. My father later told me Magnolia was the finest made mobile home one could buy – believed him because I was a child.

The inside covered throughout in light brown wood paneling – I was assured a mark of quality. The washing machine a Bendix – *"finest washing machine made."* I heard my mother repeat those words many times, to me and to others. The layout was simple, directly inside the front door a living room – this particular trailer had an expanded, pullout space which offered the living room additional footage on the opposite side. The kitchen was small but had the necessary appliances – my mother would be the dishwasher. The strange part, which I didn't recognize as a young child, the layout of bedrooms and one bathroom. Immediately after the kitchen the first bedroom, a pocket door separated the two but there was no hallway, access to the bathroom was directly through the first bedroom, then a tiny bathroom, sink, toilet, tub, and the finest made washing machine. Another pocket door separated a back bedroom. The first bedroom had a thin stained mattress on top of a built-in wooden shelf platform with two storage bins below. A slender closet on each side of a built-in chest of drawers, and the narrow-shared hallway separated the bed from the closets and chest. That was my bedroom for the next several years.

When I was twelve, in a gesture I didn't understand, my parents gave up the back bedroom for me after I begged for the *larger* space – the only difference was no one walked through my room, granting a sliver of privacy. The back door positioned in that bedroom was never used. The inside handle didn't seem firm and eventually broke. My father wired it shut with a coat hanger, thankfully we never had to make a quick escape. Our trailer was often cold in winter and hot in the summer. We had heat and air in the form of two space heaters and one window air conditioner. I remember sitting in front of the space heater, turning my body to warm the other side, and standing in front of the air conditioner capturing cooler air. The most vivid memory that frigid night of the first walkthrough is the opened toilet – a memory firmly chiseled in my brain. I paused and fixated on the faux porcelain bowl full of yellow liquid and a half-smoked cigarette trapped in frozen sewage – thus the stench. My six-year-old intellect didn't comprehend how life as I knew it was about to become what eyes beheld. I unknowingly faced nine long years literally stuck in the middle of a narrow tin rectangle – the exterior dull yellow and white with silver pin stripes. When I look at the old photo of my mother standing next to the trailer in the snow, I'm saddened even though she's smiling. I know that smile – layered complexities of hurt and pain behind it. For some strange reason I remember the stiffness and scent of her plaid coat too.

I did feel stuck as I grew older and the narrow rectangle grew smaller. Events good and bad, relationships, family dynamics, and numerous conflicts shaped my fate for nine years. Frequently exposed to a lot of *trailer park trash* behaviors and situations, but pleasurable moments occurred too, and those aided in buffering the negative. Mrs. Patterson, a retired school teacher, invited all the little *heathens* to her porch for story time. She evidently saved all her old school materials and enjoyed sharing with the neighbor children. I remember being captivated by her stories and especially a record album of different song birds. Very animated in her approach, a grey braid encircled her head, wrinkled jowls shook as she spoke. A tiny set of delicate eye glasses sat on the end of her nose for reading. My parents never read a book to me, but a retired school teacher did. One day she invited us inside to see Fluffy – once alive, now her stuffed pet rabbit. On the hottest days of summer, she shared frozen fruit juice ice cube treats with a toothpick. In December she placed in her window a cardboard cutout of a Christmas tree covered in faded green paper with holes for lights at the end of each point – something else she used in her classroom. Mrs. Patterson contributed to my earliest interest in teaching. My mother and I rode with the Patterson's once to a funeral for a relative of a trailer park friend. We sat in the back seat. Mrs. Patterson pointed to numerous sites along the way, distracting Mr. Patterson from driving as he looked away a lot. My mother became extremely nervous and fearful. I wondered why she seemed overly concerned about Mr. Paterson's distracted driving but hardly noticed my father's intoxicated driving – he was old but not drunk. We never rode anywhere with them again. In addition to Mrs. Patterson, I was drawn to teaching by several excellent teachers at Gateway Elementary where I walked to school every day for six years.

Third grade teacher Mrs. Outlaw, and sixth grade teacher Ms. Ramsay, were two of my favorites. Both inspired me in different ways because I believed both intuitively cared for my well-being and appeared to understand the complexities of trailer park life and the potential pitfalls. At least I felt they did and that was enough for me. Mrs. Outlaw, tall, big bosomed, dyed black unruly hair, crooked teeth and she smoked, a *character* to say the least. Slightly disorganized and haphazard, her classroom enthralled me because the entire room was decorated with lots of teacher made materials. Cardboard cardinals, blue jays, and robins hung from the metal ceiling frames. Her Christmas bulletin board an absolute favorite. She draped sheets of white cotton from the middle of the flat winter scene across a table to represent a snow-covered slope. Underneath the fake snow she placed boxes to hold ceramic winter homes and formed a blanket of white around each home. The scene appeared as a winter village on a snow-covered hill side. A highly impressed third grader couldn't keep his eyes off of it. But my all-time favorite item in her classroom had to be a record album of the musical soundtrack *The Wonderful Wizard of Oz*. My all-time favorite movie televised on Sunday evenings one time a year. Mrs. Outlaw played different musicals as we worked independently. I mustered enough courage to ask if I could borrow the Oz album for a weekend – she surprisingly said yes. I couldn't believe she allowed me to do this. I remember walking home that day clutching my prize securely under one arm – listened to it all weekend until we lost electricity. I was bold enough to ask linemen if they'd have the power back on before my favorite movie – looking up, yelling my important question toward the elevated bucket – to my pleasure they yelled a robust yes.

Mrs. Outlaw, of course, was *old school* and ran a fairly tight ship. To my knowledge we experienced one negative moment when she forced me to stay in the cafeteria and eat slaw – I hated slaw. At that time, we still ate on thick white glass plates with a gray ring around the edge, but the best part for me that day was the cavity under the plate. I deposited all the slaw in a neat circle under the plate and gently pressed – slaw disappeared. Upon second inspection, Mrs. Outlaw looked at the empty plate and allowed me to return to the classroom – my deception succeeded. Sixth grade teacher Ms. Ramsay remains my all-time favorite because she touched my deepest emotional core with her thoughtful spirit when I needed it most during a hellish period of homelife. Details of my sixth-grade story I'll share later. Unfortunately, school was always a difficult place for me for many reasons. Mrs. Outlaw and Ms. Ramsay both possessed a unique ability of recognizing me as a person worthy of their caring – both possessed innate ability to connect the heart to their teaching craft, and I loved them because of it.

At the same time on the south side of Nashville, a different fate occurred for my brother attending private school, wearing school uniforms. My parents typically bought me two new pants and two shirts for school, and I alternated those. Raphael probably had a closet full of clothes he didn't wear – as I do now. He graduated from Catholic school in 1974, one year before my graduation at a public school that is no longer a high school. Our upbringings so different – one privileged; one trapped in poverty. One in spacious rooms; one in cramped spaces. Same city, same birth mother, but we had very different lives and experiences. I've often wondered if our paths ever crossed during those developing years? How often did my mother think about the child she named Jack? Did she ever wonder about his growth and well-being? Did she ever regret her decision to give him up? In an uncanny way, our life successes are similar. I hoped for an ongoing, brotherly relationship, but it hasn't come to fruition – it may never become the relationship I desperately desire.

The common phrase I spoke of earlier to describe folks like my family and the way we lived for over nine years – *trailer trash* – not a pleasant description and certainly not true of all people choosing to live life in a mobile home. The phrase in many ways may have accurately described many events I experienced as a child and adolescent. People of privilege in higher socioeconomic segments of town like Raphael's probably used the term among themselves not knowing how their lives might one day intersect. I have vivid remembrances of several experiences that illustrate my trailer park life. My utmost concern as a young child was, of course, the same as any child – playing and having fun. When we first moved into the trailer it was winter as I detailed earlier. Directly behind our trailer were railroad tracks without a crossing bar where the road met the tracks – only flashing lights. Every few hours our trailer trembled as a train stormed through – sometimes slowing down or coming to a complete stop. Rail rectangles jerked and reverberated in unison after resting – sometimes a line of vehicles trapped and waiting impatiently. Early on I was fearful of the brash noises but still curious – a fence blocked direct access to the railroad tracks. As I grew older a realization became clear if a train ever derailed our tiny rectangle home would be smashed. Those fears soon subsided but remained in distant thought. During the upper elementary years some of the trailer park heathens, including myself, grew less fearful, so playing on and around the railroad tracks turned into a pastime. As a train approached, blowing warning signals, we would always clear the tracks but many times just below the wooden ties and onto the graveled slope – too close for children, but that's what heathens do. It was also fun to place coins on the track to see what would happen, finding those afterwards not always an easy task. Actually, it was not my nature to be a *dare devil* type kid – a trait that probably saved me from several potential calamities.

Next door to the trailer park was a large vehicle junkyard – a thrilling place for curious boys. We climbed in and out of wrecked vehicles and imagined what happened to the person who once owned it. When we were younger our fantasies led us to search for body parts – morbid but exhilarating. After a few years the junkyard owners bought *junkyard dogs* for security purposes – German Shepherds – seeing dogs and hearing vicious barks padlocked access to junkyard adventures. Several friends and one best friend within the span of nine long years moved in and out of my life. Karen, a cute blond and my first *love* was a little younger than me, but we played together daily for about two years – she moved abruptly as most did. Kerry, a total thug – *"rough as a cob"* my mother often proclaimed. He cursed like a sailor, would do anything on a dare – but I liked playing with him because he was audacious and fun. His father was Guy Drake, a country music song writer, one hit sensation, of *"Welfare Cadillac"* – also an alcoholic – no doubt. His one album and one hit may still exist somewhere in a vintage music store – it's on Google. The Drakes made enough money to build a big deck on the other side of their trailer – I thought they were rich because he also drove a long white Cadillac. I occasionally spent the night with Kerry – he had access to a stash of magazines too – we looked and wondered. He pretended to act out what he saw, I only watched.

His older high school brother was already well versed in *adult life*, and don't suppose he was as interested in the magazines because he had Rosemary. Rosemary, her younger sister Teresa and their older obese sister Darlene lived in a trailer that backed up to the junkyard. I have no memory of their parents – perhaps the reason for the promiscuousness.

Kerry's older brother frequented their trailer – often had his arms wrapped around Rosemary. She was a beautiful girl but looked very tired all the time and didn't appear physically clean, and of course she started smoking at an early age. Her sister Teresa was very funny and seemed a little less concerned about having someone's arms wrapped around her – we got along very well. All three girls had several brownish scabby type sores on their legs and a few on their arms. I never asked about those but knew it was probably best to maintain a *hands-off* policy – obviously Kerry's older brother didn't have the same policy.

Paul was my age and a friend, but his parents were extreme religious fundamentalists. Although they attended a regular southern Baptist church, their strict personal interpretation was to avoid as much of *worldly life* as possible – strictness also required of Paul. They didn't believe in owning a television and celebrated no holidays – dried their own fruits and vegetables in their small front yard. Paul was a big guy and often played rougher than the other boys. He would sit on our little wooden porch and press his head against the screen door to see what was on television – felt sorry for him in this way but he wasn't allowed to come inside. I wondered why television was banned? He likely rebelled against all fundamentalism as he aged – seemed overly strict to me, but an odd feeling of privilege gripped me when I compared.

Ralph was another friend but seemingly an odd type of perfectionist – so was I, but not in his exact ways. Ralph's shirts were always tucked, pants high on his waist and always with a belt – he had a northern accent. We played often as long as it was by his rules and what he wanted to play. His father was a really strange, nerdy type guy – never felt comfortable around him. Sometimes his father would attempt to show us complicated mathematical formulas when I occasionally spent the night. I was polite but hated every moment of the impromptu tutorials – useless information for boys. Ralph's mother once accused my mother of flirting with her nerdy husband – my mother could give that impression at times. The two got into a yelling match that lasted several minutes – that's what *trailer park trash* parents do sometimes. Ralph's sister was a few years younger and often smelled of urine – pulled at her private area and also very odd – I didn't understand it all at the time. During the time of our friendship, I had a very scary dream about a black gargoyle type demon that flew up during the night and landed on top of their trailer toward the back – a threatening image that truly frightened me. I'm not even certain where such an image came from in my mind. Ralph's sister eventually ran away from their home when she was in her mid-teens. Reflecting as a young adult about this situation, it's likely she was sexually abused by someone – a disturbing thought, but explains a lot about the dynamics of their home life. I knew in my gut something wasn't right within their mobile home. The terrifying dream had now taken on a deeper meaning – a strange creepiness I wanted to erase but often pondered.

On the other side of Ralph lived Ricky and his family – their trailer was a total mess of clothes, toys, empty beer bottles and junk scattered everywhere. Everything was disorganized and chaotic inside and outside his trailer. I never spent the night with him because there was nowhere to sleep unless on a pile of dirty clothes. Ricky was fun though, one of my diverse friends, and we shared a common bond. His dad was addicted too – witnessed Ricky's dad stumbling drunk on many occasions. He and my father shared a common bond of alcoholism. I never remember seeing Ricky's father without him appearing intoxicated. Ricky seemed to be a child headed in the very same reckless direction as his father – how did I know?

Donna was a year older than me and a good friend during my early high school days. We were never interested in each other beyond being friends, but we had a special bond. She was from a broken home, but her mother had recently remarried. During a couple of summers when we had nothing much to do, we played monopoly and other board games endlessly and loved baking cakes. Donna then met Gerald, the younger brother of the bus driver at Beacon Baptist. Gerald was a country talking, tobacco chewing, high school dropout – but he had a car. Donna was suddenly taken by his country charm, and I tagged along – except for those moments when I knew they were behaving like Kerry's older brother – knew it was my time to exit the scene. Several months after unofficially dating Gerald, she told me some shocking news – she was pregnant – first time a friend of mine had become pregnant. She confessed it happened in her trailer and he forced her – neither of us ever used the word rape. I believe they married, but it only lasted less than a year until both basically hated each other. I was sad for Donna, but she was now a mother and our friendship basically ended. I've often wondered and questioned how I came out of these experiences intact? My best explanation, I wasn't a big risk taker – considered consequences – a bit fearful thanks to my mother. My best friend of all time in the trailer park, Andy. He substituted as the brother I didn't have – at least that was the simple truth of my life during our brief years of brotherhood friendship.

Fascinated by the monstrosity slowly wobbling into our trailer park, I watched every moment as the skilled driver carefully backed the white rectangle with rust trim onto thin concrete lanes – six tires supporting the massive structure – dwarfed my yellow and white rectangle. On the front appeared to be an upstairs room – intriguing – something I had never seen. I eventually learned the higher space in the front was a small bedroom – basically a few steps up to a loft bed and small closet. The oldest sibling occupied this room. I met the second oldest, Andy, shortly after he moved in, and our friendship immediately blossomed. We liked many of the same things, same foods, played in similar ways and just got along perfectly, although I was always in charge. One day we were playing on the asphalt drive, he was on his skateboard and accidently fell. His face hit the curb and chipped a front tooth. The dentist fixed his tooth but couldn't save the broken part – he had a fake piece attached to the tooth, and I could see the line where it had broken. As friends do, we had our typical boyhood disagreements. A few times I sent him home, mad over something and threw all of his toys onto the asphalt drive – probably challenged my self-appointed lead role. We were best friends again by dinner. He owned a bicycle before me, and I was a bit jealous, but he always allowed me to ride his. Once I finally got a bicycle, we were *hot stuff* on wheels.

Admittedly, Kerry was the coolest though – he skillfully converted a regular bicycle into a chopper – he popped wheelies too – I simply couldn't compete but still loved riding my bike. Our motley crew peddled with confidence to the gas station a block from the trailer park to get air for our tires – I overfilled a tire once and it exploded. Of course, my father didn't immediately go out and purchase a new bike tire – seemed like an eternity because adult priorities always came first. We enjoyed pretending our bikes were school busses and we created bus routes. Pretended we held the door handle and opened the door with all the bus sounds as we picked up passengers. For some reason I remember asking God to save me one day as I paused on my bicycle – perhaps I was pondering a phrase I heard at the Baptist church or felt guilty about boy sins. And as all boys of our generation would do, we attached playing cards to the spokes of our bike tires to create a loud muffler sound. We were also expert dam engineers when we put aside the bus route and our Tonka trucks, the real metal, heavy type that occupied truck driving fantasies for hours upon hours. We honestly prized all those times of riding bicycles, building dams and pretending with real metal Tonka toys – always totally serious – always without restraint – always big-time fun.

Childhood fantasy and innocence is something I lost too quickly – memories almost *sacred* to me now. Growing up in the sixties had many advantages I didn't understand then. Most children of that time period can remember the soles of their feet being black from playing outside all day because barefooted play was the preferred choice. Didn't worry about cutting our feet, stubbing toes, breaking a toenail, or getting a splinter. In fact, the soles of our feet became a protective cover of leather after several days of outside play. My greatest concern as a child regarding outside play was it ending at dark, or having to come inside to take care of *number two*. Holding off the urge probably caused more problems, including constipation, but not interrupting play was worth momentary discomfort. As boys we never concerned ourselves about *number one* unless a girl joined the crew – that was usually rare. Even then we could slip behind a tree or someone's trailer for a quick pee break.

A favorite outside fantasy was playing with real metal Tonka trucks. Andy and I dug roads and transformed the Tonka trailer, originally designed to carry cars, into a mobile home. We were experts at mobile home life. We knew how to properly pull our Tonka mobile home around sharp dirt road curves, back it into the desired living space, and level it just like the real mobile homes we lived in and among. I was a keen observer of everything relating to mobile home life. I became so sophisticated that I added landscaping all around my pretend mobile home. In my fantasy world it was my home and it had to be perfect – that's what I desired. After a day or two Andy and I would get restless and bored with our location and decide to move. We never literally picked up our mobile home by hand and moved it – absolutely against our rules. We slowly prepared our move just like real people did in the real trailer park. It was so much fun to talk through all the steps, experience similar difficulties as the real folks, then move to a whole new location. I clearly remember one of the exact locations in the small strip of green grass behind my real mobile home. I stretched out across the grass to keep my head close to the pretend trailer, carefully removing tiny blocks and slivers of wood that were precisely placed to level the converted Tonka trailer on the sloped lot. I remember Andy watching and listening, taking my lead and doing the very same to his pretend home. Being a little younger than me, I figured he needed expert guidance. We were both very serious about the slightest motion. Unfortunately, my mother, the *overseeing government bureaucracy*, would occasionally hinder progress because she didn't like us sequestering new land and building additional roads. We attempted to minimize damage to the landscape, but boys had to do what boys do. So, we often defied *government mandates* and moved forward with building additional roads. We didn't worry too much about punishment – we knew the overseer was somewhat weak and wouldn't enforce rules. We operated unhindered – pushed forward all in the name of innocent boyhood fantasy.

Interesting when I reflect on my actions and capabilities around the larger group of trailer park peers, all within the microcosm I inhabited nine long years. I was able to hold my own and was accepted by male peers – stand up to any aggression and actually lead when it was necessary. In fact, I remember dominating most of those relationships – especially with Andy. We played countless hours away from our tiny spaces, underneath trailers when we were younger, in the stream building dams, all along the railroad tracks, in an abandoned hole in the ground created by the electric service – a secret hideout for more nefarious escapades, the vehicle junkyard, and bike riding when I finally obtained my own bicycle around age nine or ten. Kick the Can a favorite game of mine after dark, but war games ranked high probably because I was smarter at strategizing – often sneaking up on the enemy totally unaware. As a whole we were basically a band of heathen thugs on a mission to have as much fun as we could, but I separated from the heathen crew when our activities involved purposely damaging someone's personal property or indulging in more adolescent like behaviors with the exception of pornography. I might have earned the title, *trailer park pimp* – supplier for our immature lust, but only when brave enough to steal from my father's plentiful stash. The guys appreciated the impromptu anatomy lessons. We huddled around as guys do breathlessly peering at exposed human forms – all trying to jockey for the best view – sometimes not understanding what met our eyes and sometimes silence permeated the private club as we processed our newfound knowledge. Curious boys being boys – my *supplier* never mentioned missing anything.

As a pre-teen, surrounded by a myriad of heathen behaviors, my reckless choices though, were far and few between. I remember pretending to wreck our bicycles in the ditch next to the main road. One of us flipped our bicycle upside down, one-wheel spinning. We stretched out on the side of the ditch as if hurt and injured. We did this on the slope below the railroad tracks so the approaching driver couldn't see us until they topped the rise. Someone stood at the top of the slope to alert us a car was coming. Without fail people slowed and most stopped to check on the kid laid out in the ditch. As soon as they opened the car door or rolled down a window to ask if we were okay, we jumped up and ran like hell. I'm certain most people just rolled their eyes and realized they were duped by trailer park thugs. It was fun. On another occasion during winter, I noticed a sheet of ice formed in the slope of our asphalt drive against the curb. The ice had formed a perfect sheet I could lift and hold like a large piece of glass. I calculated a sinister but harmless plan – sent a friend to the top of the rise to watch for the next car. When he announced a car coming, I went into action – stood at the edge of the road and as the car approached in full view of the sheet of ice, I threw it into the road shattering it like glass. The driver slammed the brakes and a very angry man got out and started yelling a lot of curse words at the heathen running from the *crime scene*. I looked back and yelled, *"It's just ice!"* He stopped yelling, got back in his car and sped off. We laughed and talked about the ingenious stunt for hours. Aside from stealing Playboy or nudist camp magazines from my father's mass collection, that's about the extent of my public recklessness.

Bonanza Mobile Homes built a sales lot on the other side of our creek boarder facing the main road. The lot was stocked full of new, fully furnished mobile homes for sale. I'm truly surprised the owners allowed us to look inside the new mobile homes. I recall dreaming of living in one of the spacious new rectangles. New fresh scents, new furniture, new fixtures, nothing old, scratched or damaged, nothing dusty or dirty captured my full attention – fantasied about picking my favorite – believed my parents might actually buy a new mobile home since it was so convenient. I didn't possess a true concept of how financially strapped they must have been. What's interesting, we never thought about vandalizing anything within the new mobile homes. I marveled at the bow-legged Bonanza cowboy sign as tall as a telephone pole. The sign appeared to project total confidence over the new homes on wheels I desired – opposite my fragile confidence which coexisted with fantasies making our tiny microcosm seem more tolerable. I possessed zero confidence at school in the ability to hold my own – didn't do it, and therefore, became a target for undeserved bulling – never bullied in the trailer park. Within our microcosm away from school, my fragile confidence stemmed from the fact we were all in the *same boat*. A cautious level of trailer park male dominance created a control I desired and embraced, though, diminished within the confines of my tin rectangle. Of course, I had no power to alter home or school life, so a typical default was to shrink into worthlessness or a state of discontent when situations were less than desirable.

It was a big deal in our trailer park to secure one of the back spaces away from the main road and railroad. Perhaps it was a little more private – not really sure, but the prize spot was at the bottom of the sloped driveway with a large front yard and stream we coveted as its boarder – we called it a *creek*. Our pretend play life became reality when Andy's family moved their oversized mobile home to a back space about half way down the slope – then the prize spot became available – my parents got it. We moved our small, eight-foot-wide Magnolia home, *finest mobile home ever made*, to the last space. I now had the best yard, the most privacy, the coveted creek directly in front of me – everything a growing boy needed. As I described earlier, my friendship with Andy was deeply bonded by the fact we were together a lot. Andy ate dinner with us often and spent the night to get away from his younger siblings and rebellious older brother Roman – a perfect name matching his rebellious, abrasive nature.

Andy's older brother Roman, a true rebel without a cause and too cool to play with anyone younger, he basically ignored us unless he felt like cussing at us for no reason. I'm sure he occasionally beat up on Andy. One day when we were all on the school bus going home it was time for his uninhibited girlfriend to exit at her stop. She looked like a cross between Janice Joplin and Carly Simon. As she stepped with her commanding stride toward the exit in her skin tight, hip-hugger jeans and extra wide belt, she looked back at everyone and used her middle finger to send us all a clear message, then motioned to Roman, without words, she wanted something requiring his presence. When we got off at our stop Roman promptly lit a cigarette and headed back to his girlfriend's house on the opposite side of the tracks from the trailer park. He eventually dropped out of school and left home – Andy inherited the isolated upstairs bedroom – three younger siblings remained in their home. My father allowed Andy to go everywhere with us – felt like I actually had a real brother. I'm sure it also released my parents of having to be attentive to my needs, although that was never high priority anyway. During short visits to Kentucky lake or wherever they might go when I had to tag along, I begged for Andy to go – everything seemed more tolerable when Andy was by my side. My mother may have thought about Jack as we played for hours without interruption. Perhaps our relationship offered her a glimpse into what raising two boys would have been like.

I liked Andy's family as a whole and enjoyed assisting him as he watched younger siblings. He was often left alone with his siblings, but when I was present it afforded me another opportunity to be the dominate figure since I was the oldest. Andy's father worked two jobs to make ends meet – his mother didn't work outside the home. His mother loved partying with my parents, but his father wasn't as interested. Andy's mother grew very fond of my father, and he likewise grew fond of her. When Andy's family moved abruptly, breaking our long-cherished bond, I was truly saddened and missed him tremendously. I never associated their exodus with an affair between my father and his mother. Although I didn't know exact facts, I now recognize poor adult choices, once again, altered boyhood circumstances and ended the brotherhood closeness I cherished. Fortunately, Andy chose a similar path as mine, opted for order, calm, family unity, and focus on Divine power for life guidance – perhaps the reason we developed a close bond during our formative years. My heart is delighted to know Andy is a successful family-oriented man.

Hell on Earth

Junior high and high school brought about a whole new set of friends – one particular situation in high school stretched my small circle far beyond approved social boundaries at the time. I'll begin with junior high in order to set the stage – a battle ground of pubescent testosterone, hormonal dysfunction, and sheer cruelty for basically everyone in that age category. Emotional scars from that time frame in one's life often deeply wound an individual and can literally shape someone's future creating many negative outcomes. Today, that particular school setting is known as middle school, but it's all the same with regards to its general function – middle schoolers remain basically *crazy* most of the time. During my time in junior high the cruelty played out primarily behind the scenes, but I believe educators were well aware of the dreadful circumstances and most chose to ignore it.

The absolute worse place on earth for a budding pubescent boy was the junior high locker room – for me a form of *hell on earth*. Dreaded gym class every day without exception – often forgot gym clothes on purpose. In the concrete dressing room, a rank odor permeated the entire space – a mixture of body sweat, putrid socks, and jock straps. The grey painted slabs were cold and often wet with humidity from the showers – the school was occupied by high schoolers, and they used the same locker room. I honestly felt like we were in an underground holding chamber for hardened criminals. The overcrowded space gave us hardly any room to dress. I recall one instructor's office where he could easily have a clear view of the dressing area but instead chose to ignore chaos and cruelty behind his back. When it was time to dress out the budding juveniles who were proud of their growing bodies strutted around so that those of us who were *little boys* cringed at the thought of taking our clothes off in this public setting. What did we do? We gravitated to more private areas which actually made us clearer targets for the cruelty that flourished. Once I quickly dressed, I made my way to a relatively safer spot sometimes close to the coach's office, but at times I was unable to dodge the onslaught of testosterone rage. What primarily befell my boy allies and me was a harsh, mocking type bullying language. I believed the threats, but those mostly ended up hollow intimidations. No one ever really roughed me up – but being pushed around a bit was normal. Timid body language and the fact I looked like a younger boy placed a target on my back.

My nemesis Jeff added to the gloominess of the concrete dungeon looming before me each day. He was lean but firm, pale with dark circles under his eyes, smoked, and walked with a wide cowboy type gait. Due of his crude intimidation tactics, his actions forced hatred from me with a passion. What I didn't understand at the time, Jeff hated his miserable life too because it was probably much worse than mine. When he approached me with his crude language and aggressive threats, I likely beheld the abusive behavior of the adult male in his life. What I did know, I wanted to kick him where it would really hurt. In my mind I was a street fighter – a trailer park fighter. I knew his type of nasty language well and knew I could go toe to toe, but didn't. If I had released my rage upon Jeff, it would have ended the bullying. Instead, Charlie actually took up for me once – not sure why because he was cool, high on the popularity scale and very proud of his budding adolescence. He stepped in between the bully and me – firmly shoved Jeff away and stated, *"Leave him alone!"* – he glared at Jeff with feigned disgust, I heard under his breath a muted *"damn-it."* I said nothing to Charlie. He turned away and said nothing to me – we were not friends. What a relief to have the aid of an impromptu bodyguard. Crude bully Jeff walked away – I wanted to yell, *"Yeah, leave me alone like he said!"* I smartly remained silent.

Those of us who were still *boys* were not always targets. One day a member of the football team became the target. He appeared normal to me – red headed and freckled may have been his downfall. The stronger jocks picked on him often, but it was particularly horrendous this day. He was wrangled into the middle of the locker room, gym shorts and underwear unwillingly pulled off as he fought the cruelty, but he finally relinquished resistance. The bully jocks forcefully turned him upside down, spread his legs in what appeared to be a coordinated hazing. He was completely naked. A riotous crowd quickly gathered close, cheering, clapping, laughing, yelling. Someone holding him yelled, *"Look, he has syphilis"* – I didn't know the meaning of the word. What I did know, he was totally humiliated by what looked to be a rash. I was completely shaken by the entire demonstration and felt tremendously sorrowful for this victim of callous brutality. Those of us who were less aggressive and timid knew it could be one of us at any moment – we kept our distance and didn't join the riot. Where were the instructors and coaches? Feckless men placed in charge of all those vulnerable junior high boys should have been severely reprimanded for what they allowed. Sadly, they instead chose to act as though nothing was happening in the stinky concrete hell hole. I'm certain this situation and more occurred often, and the adults in charge rarely intervened. Every time I saw the red headed freckled boy my heart hurt, but I never spoke a word to him.

A student teacher for physical education was assigned to our junior high class. He was tall, dark headed, perfectly tanned – he looked like what every guy secretly wanted to be. I don't recall any significant impact he made on our physical development, but I do remember a strange behavior – at least I believed it to be. Following class on days when we were more physically active, we were required to shower. On more than one occasion the student teacher joined us in the community shower room. His actions made the awkwardness of showering more awkward for me – an adult naked man, white butt-cheeks accentuated his tanned physique. To my knowledge he never said or did anything other than walk among us completely unclothed – fully present and conveying masculinity. Perhaps he was just another dumb college jock who wasn't thinking how his actions might force uncomfortable feelings in some of us. No one ever spoke about it, but we all interpreted his actions in our own personal way. Perhaps my uneasiness was tied to an unhealthy introduction to adult anatomy and my own personal insecurities. In a strange twist I ended up teaching his sixth-grade son several years later while substituting at a private school. I recognized the last name due to its uniqueness and asked about his father's time in college – it was him. I said nothing more. Discovered years later the naked student teacher founded the scam Fuller's Business College in Madison. Amazing how life is continually spattered with unexpected coincidences.

Hell taught me the purpose of deodorant – my parents didn't. Some guys regularly used it; aerosol wafting through the concrete dungeon aided in covering the overall adolescent male stench. I ignored its use until I assisted someone reaching for a chin-up bar – I couldn't do one chin-up. He jumped with my assistance; exposed arm pits released a repulsing scent – I suffered in silence. My brain, though, established a quick connection – perhaps he needs deodorant – perhaps I did too. Embarrassed to ask parents, from that day forward I secretly used my father's – until I wafted my own aerosol.

Sometimes though, a light will break through and is not afraid to shine among excruciating insanity. That person was Rand, my hallway locker mate. He was tall, athletic, very popular, full of self-confidence, totally opposite of me. We were assigned the same locker because the school was over-crowded – the hallways total grid-lock every class change. When I finally made it close enough but still couldn't reach the locker, Rand would yell asking what I needed and retrieve it – his height allowed him to reach over most of the craziness. He was super friendly and never once looked down on my inferior junior high status. Rand was elected student council president and probably held that honor throughout his school career. Regrettably, I never told him how much I appreciated his kindness toward me. Those words do not come easy in junior high – usually never. We parted ways the next school year and someone else had the privilege of knowing light amid darkness. Junior high experiences taught me a lot – most important, treat people with respect and kindness. As a professional teacher and administrator, I never forgot the unfortunate locker room incident involving a red-headed freckled boy or my locker mate Rand. I learned my responsibility is not only to teach and lead, but equally important is the task of protecting those who are most vulnerable to ridicule and bullying – be light amid never-ending darkness and insanity.

Twelve years in public schools taught me a lot about humanity in general, as it does everyone, but failed me by not intervening or teaching me what I really needed to fully succeed academically. Unfortunately, I started school too young – only five years old in first grade, didn't turn six until mid-November. I desperately needed another year to grow and mature, but it never happened until I made it happen. My real growth, maturity and academic development occurred after high school, the years I stayed out of school before returning to a real college. Throughout the twelve years I was basically a poor academic student – only accelerating in areas I either liked well or had no issues learning. Reflecting, I could have easily been targeted for academic support services, but those were not available during my public-school years. No one ever sought to intervene in my academic struggles or provide my family with social services I was in urgent need of – school counseling didn't exist for elementary, beyond a focus on class scheduling. The repeated phrase I heard, *"I need to work harder"* – but that didn't do it – it simply wasn't enough.

A profound example was seventh grade social studies. The teacher implemented one method week after long, boring week. She didn't teach but instead relied on our ability to memorize. Monday, chapter reading assigned – Tuesday, vocabulary words assigned – Wednesday, questions assigned – Thursday, all previously assigned work was checked and orally reviewed without any interesting discussions – Friday, the chapter test. I failed seventh grade social studies, not because I didn't like social studies. In fact, I loved social studies until seventh grade. I now hated social studies and sort of hated the teacher because she didn't understand me, but I had no control over my predicament. No one at home seriously cared either. I've wondered if I had a specific learning disability that interfered with overall academic development.

Compensating became a mentor – learning to work around obstacles that presented roadblocks. Finding alternative paths is actually a highly intelligent enterprise – so, I began to self-teach. Once I got a taste of academic success, I craved learning what I missed and didn't let go of the yearning and hunger to succeed. People like me know exactly what I'm illustrating. They understand the excruciating mental pain of learning differently, how certain skill sets come easy for those who passed seventh grade social studies. But for me it was a constant struggle. Academic *systems* for numerous years were not designed for people who learn differently. Those systems may have claimed to serve students – but I beg to differ. I'm a witness because I sat in a front row seat – knew the truth behind feeble efforts implemented inconsistently. I'm not demeaning today's dedicated teachers working tireless hours assisting struggling students, their work is absolutely necessary, and they are making good things happen daily. But it's not how it worked for me, even though I'm certain I sat under several highly proficient teachers who were well intentioned.

In countless circumstances, perfectionism served as a positive, allowing me to present final, well-polished products without anyone knowing the agonizing struggle which brought me to a perfect end. After landing in real college, I quickly learned it's about working the system to my advantage – learning to play their *game* but according to my approach. The biggest difference in college, as opposed to secondary education, was a newly attained maturity, a focus and determination to reach specific goals. I knew learning was a highly complex endeavor, at least it was for me. The best-case scenario was to be distinct, get to know my professors, display high interest, be self-guided, but I needed stimulation by well-trained facilitators to bring about the best possible outcomes.

My best learning occurred when I was inspired to push beyond the confines of personal limitations, what I incorrectly setup many years prior. When teachers inspired me to think deeply about ideas and simultaneously integrated fundamental tenants of essential knowledge, I learned the greatest. My college freshman English professor is a perfect example. She inspired me to push myself far beyond what I thought capable. The first assignment was to write a detailed paragraph teaching someone to walk. She then acted out our directives before the class which ingeniously verified the absurdity of our limited writing skills. My first paper was massacred with a red pen, sliced and diced until it bled from top to bottom. But from that point she recognized potential and methodically guided the class in writing fundamentals while at the same time inspiring the hidden writer in each of us to emerge. Learning for me never occurred by writing answers in blanks, copying vocabulary, penciling in circles, or answering questions at the end of a chapter.

Pre-college education for me was entrenched in a model of learning solidly stuck in archaic methods and practices. I've often thought about the unfortunate number of highly intelligent people that may be aimlessly wasting away in prison cells because obsolete education models failed them. Somehow, I chose to challenge systems where I landed, work around those, and sought to beat odds supposedly stacked against me. In the deepest caverns of my soul, I believed it was possible to commandeer my own success. Sometimes I'm baffled by and somewhat mystified how certain successes occurred.

At Vol State Community College, I managed a required pre-teacher mathematics course because I'm not certain the young professor new a lot about what he was attempting to impart. A big problem arose at the end. We were required to meet a certain requirement before progressing to a mathematics education class specifically related to teaching. I completed the test knowing I did poorly unless I made a lot of lucky guesses. My score arrived – a perfect score. What? How was that possible? Shocked and dumbfounded. A very smart classmate told me she scored below the required cutoff and would need a retake – she was shocked like me but for opposite reasons. I immediately thought our scores may have been mixed up somehow. Or was Divine intervention the only explanation? The four-year college I transferred to accepted a perfect math score – just not sure whose score.

I avoided all upper-level math courses in high school and college because I feared failure and because I knew my foundation was extremely weak. I knew and understood the basics and could easily squeak by but didn't like risking potential failure – at times equating math classes with the hellish junior high locker room. At moments during the test when I had nothing – nothing to adequately solve a complex problem – when there was no other way but to guess – I was at the mercy of God or a faulty scoring system. Something happened. I'm not suggesting God mixed up test scores – I don't really know. Somehow, I made it to the next level and eventually succeeded in spite of it all. The smart classmate with a failing score made it too because she was smart enough to do it again and pass. During my teaching career I was determined to demonstrate deep empathy for academically struggling students. I knew their pain well – I could seriously relate. It's ironic I loved teaching sixth grade mathematics, and especially when I was able to facilitate struggling students to turn on the light of understanding. All teachers know those are the special moments of greatest achievement and delight – it's why we teach. I worked hard to create alternative paths to learning. I didn't need a training or a seminar to teach me how to identify and work with struggling students. I learned firsthand.

The Artist

High school was a much safer space for me than junior high, other than Jimmy and Mike who insisted on maintaining their asshole form of verbal bullying. As luck would have it, I always ended up with one or both of them in a class but chose to ignore their ignorant banter. I found solace and relief in art classes where Jimmy and Mike never walked. Artistic ability allowed me to rub shoulders with the elite – the popular. But truth be told, I was never considered a rightful member of the so-called *in crowd*, but at least I had a skill they could use to their benefit. I made certain art classes were a part of my high school schedule each year – Art II, III, and IV elevated me. Mrs. Ardella Thompson was the art teacher – her uniqueness made an indelible impression upon me. A small circle of unpopular peers knew my artistic abilities, some of them budding artists like myself.

Most of my ability was self-taught, but Mrs. Thompson helped to refine and enhance natural skills. Many non-artistic people think one can learn to draw, paint, or create a work of art by simply being taught – not really true. A true artist is someone with natural ability to create what is within – without being taught – and it's deeply connected to emotion. A true artist is naturally visual, can see it all in the mind before a work of art becomes reality. Skilled and passionate art teachers do what Thompson did – help one with techniques, broaden understanding of mediums, expose one to a variety of artistic styles as one develops a personal style. I recognized her skilled ability to identify a person's unique style and then help students develop it through a variety of art mediums. I discovered my favorite art mediums were pen and ink, watercolor, and pastels – those mediums remain favorites.

My artistic abilities were confined within the art class until we held a school-wide art show. The showing occurred in the late spring after basketball season so that the upper levels of the gym could be used while bleachers are folded away. The timing was also for the purpose of allowing everyone in art class to create throughout the school year and collect several art pieces for showing. For the spring show I entered several original pieces of art – to my surprise and delight I won a first-place ribbon, second-place, third-place, and a fourth-place ribbon – several ribbons were awarded for a variety of different categories. As the non-artistic throngs of disinterested high schoolers walked through the gymnasium art gallery, my name and ribbons were seen by anyone curious enough to notice. I didn't get a rush of invitations to parties with all the popular kids, except for one, nor did people stop me in the hallway to offer congratulations on a successful showing of artistic genius. It's not like Monday morning following the big game Friday evening, *great use of color Jim* or *hey dude, that last brush stroke won it all!* I did, however, gain a personal satisfaction in knowing I had established myself as a true artist among certain high school peers. I'm certain Jimmy, Mike and their band of assholes never gave my artwork a glance.

My one invitation was to a sign painting party for a candidate running for student council president. I drew and painted several campaign signs which met the approval of the *in crowd* – several in attendance that evening illegally drank and smoked pot including the candidate running for president. I didn't allow it to hinder my detailed sign making. As I walked the halls over the next two weeks, I admired my artistic campaign renderings. The alcohol drinking pot smoker won – artistic propagandist talent at its very best.

Shelia was the cheerleader captain during my senior year and sat in front of me in Mr. Forehand's junior psychology class when we officially met. We did not run in the same circles, but she did notice my artwork in the gallery showing. I don't remember why we eventually talked, but we did, and I immediately fell head over hills in love and fast. Our fleeting conversations always occurred during class – never in the hallway when she was with boyfriend Wayne – his family owned the local pharmacy – how would I compete? But she was all mine in junior psychology, and it was time to make my move. I offered to do artwork for the cheerleaders like spirit signs and Shelia mentioned they were buying new megaphones. *"Would I be interested in painting those?"* I said yes without having a clue how I would manage such a task. But of course, love will drive a young man to do crazy things. I clearly remember Shelia and some of the other cheerleaders coming to me with ideas, and I drew up the plans – she loved my plan, and I loved her for loving my plan. My infatuation was growing deeper, but I had a job to do – had to keep my focus because I couldn't disappoint her. I don't remember what I charged for painting each megaphone. Probably not enough because I had no understanding of how much money upper-class families paid for their daughters to be cheerleaders – I later discovered a lot.

The megaphones were the large type about three feet tall – there were nine cheerleaders – but I only cared about pleasing one. On each megaphone I painted the head of a ram, our mascot, with bright orange horns. Above the head a collegiate type capital M for Madison and on each side an orange stripe that started small and gradually widened at the bottom. At the upper rim I painted a solid orange triangle shape connected to the two orange side stripes – the design formed another M – an artistic touch that only I truly appreciated. I painted each cheerleader's first name in bold black letters across the bottom. Shelia was thrilled – I was thrilled Shelia was thrilled.

My love obsession continued to grow with one minor obstacle, Shelia still dated the pharmacy owner's son. In the fall I painted several run-through signs for home football games. I didn't care that my stunning artwork was destroyed and crumpled by a mass of football pads, cleats, and testosterone infused sweat. What mattered most was the fact Shelia was pleased with my work. One day as I painted in silence on the upper deck of the gym, a serious discussion ensued between cheerleaders Shelia, Talisa, and their friend Susan – Shelia appeared upset. Susan introduced herself and complimented my work – immediately sensed a kindness that wasn't typical of the *in crowd*. Shelia later told me she and Wayne broke up – I was stunned – barely contained my unbecoming delight. Shelia was elected senior homecoming attendant and she needed an escort – Wayne had been her sophomore and junior escort for the past two years. I thought she should have been elected homecoming queen. In my thinking she was the queen and so much more. I fantasied about the potential of being asked – thought we had grown so close – at least in my fantasy world – I was her artist. She instead selected David – a really cool looking guy with long hair, long sideburns and he smoked – he was a member of the *in crowd* – I wasn't. We continued our friendship from a distance, occasionally talking, and I continued cheerleader artwork during football season in silence.

After graduation a mutual friend was getting married – the friend was madly in love with her wedding, not the guy she was marrying. I was invited, so was Shelia. I worked up enough courage to ask her to dinner afterwards, and she actually said yes with a perceived hesitancy – I couldn't believe it was happening. I borrowed my grandfather's Impala, bought a velvet grey clip-on bow tie to wear with my unstarched white dress shirt, and attempted to hide my pimples. After the wedding I waited and waited thinking she was helping with gifts at the reception downstairs – everyone was almost gone. Finally, someone found me waiting and kindly told me Shelia was not feeling well and needed to go home – I was crushed – another *Charlie Brown* moment – *good grief!* It was the last time I ever saw her – the one-sided love affair ended that evening and the marriage vows both of us witnessed ended one year later.

Tony Girl

Ardella Thompson was a tiny bundle of vigor and passion for high school artistic endeavors. She could see something unique in the slightest creative effort. When a student shared an artistic creation, she would step back, tilt her head, drop her mouth open, and sigh with enthusiasm – sometimes both hands pressed against her face – she was truthfully captivated and absorbed – always seriously dramatic in her critiques. *"Marvelous"* was her favorite one-word description. This is not an overstatement, and I loved it. Ms. Thompson provided the attention I longed for regarding my artwork. Classroom management was a different story – she struggled to maintain order, but we also loved that aspect about her – it afforded us lots of freedom to have fun and create. Obviously, she knew her subject well – if we had all been Jackson Pollock type artists, we could have just thrown paint onto canvases all year and she would have been overjoyed. A small collection of imaginative minds began to band together and form a group – we seemed to have a lot in common – friendships formed – some I still have to this day. Ms. Thompson was happy if you appeared to be creating something or preparing to draw, paint, or create a colorful pastel expression. One day a classmate made use of a few colored markers after returning from the restroom with a long strip of unused toilet tissue. He drew several uneven lines in different colors straight down the fragile tissue paper, in her typical manner Ms. Thompson was ecstatic – his creative endeavor was apparently worthy of the Metropolitan Museum of Art.

If Tony had only figured out how to appease her in that way – instead, he chose to sit alone and do nothing. Tony was definitely a loner – rarely looked directly at anyone or spoke a word. One day our group decided to invite him to join us. At first, he was reluctant and getting to know Tony was a slow process but we all quickly learned he was a very unique person. As he grew more comfortable, he opened up a bit and seemed pleased to be sitting with our group. He started dabbling with different art mediums but nothing of any significance. As we got to know him, we encouraged him to share more about himself. He shared a photo of a female dressed in a beautiful long-sleeved yellow flowing chiffon dress – full Hollywood type makeup, false eyelashes and all. Upon closer inspection we realized it was Tony – we were a little stunned, a little shocked, and somewhat speechless. Our group went silent for a few moments – he sat in silence seemingly testing us, waiting for reactions. I don't remember who broke the silence, it may have been me. I know we all began to laugh nervously – but not at him. I remember asking if he had dressed like this for a costume party – it seemed like a reasonable possibility. He said no. Then with a jerk of his arm and a snap of his finger he enlightened us by stating he was a drag queen. A *drag* what? The whole group erupted into hysterical laughter and total skepticism – we truly thought he was trying to get an easy laugh. We honestly didn't fully know what he was talking about but pretended we did. He shared additional photos of each stage of dress, including his stuffed bra over his hairy chest. Another eruption of laughter occurred until we finally calmed to face our new reality. We had a hairy chested drag queen in our midst – a male who dressed as a female. Once the truth was unleashed, he wasn't shy anymore.

How were we supposed to navigate this new discovery? We all had questions that needed to be answered, but time was always a factor and class ended – we continued each new day with some caution but also with a newfangled curiosity for Tony's frankness and willingness to share his secret life. As Tony began to describe his lifestyle it was apparent: he was emotionally involved with a number of men. I do think he needed our little group – he had no friends at school. Outside of school his only friends were apparently the men that frequented the gay clubs he described in graphic detail. I remember seriously wondering at times if this was just an elaborate tale he engineered. Most of what he shared was difficult to believe – sometimes far beyond what any of us had ever imagined. On certain days artistic endeavors took a back seat, because Tony honestly needed us more than we needed art – he bloomed.

Four in our small group were raised religiously conservative, one a football jock, another an average guy in tight jeans Tony admired, one a *stoner*, and me – none of the aforementioned. We were all an amazingly diverse group of high schoolers, but all drawn to Tony in the same uncanny way. He casually mentioned suicide once, but in the mid 1970's there was no protocol for reporting it – we just thought he was again seeking attention. In the hallways we didn't speak because we were already pushing social boundaries to the limit in art class by including him – an action I regret, allowing societal pressure to dictate our public reactions in other school settings, but Tony understood and never pressed those issues. The church people of our group reinforced in me something good about unconditional love and compassion – the others in our group did the same without church influence. Tony desired love and acceptance, he now had a group at school that made him feel good for once in his life – we didn't ask anything of him. I know he looked forward to art class – Tony created nicknames for each of us based on something he believed about us individually. I remember a few of the names, *Krystal Queen, Grapes, Jugs, Closet Queen,* and *Cliff Sunday* – Cliff, one of the church goers; his last name Mundy. Our nickname for Tony was simply, *Tony Girl,* and he liked it. One female member of our group, Lisa, actually shopped with him and said she had a blast. At times his language pushed our immature sensitivities to the limits. I think we intuitively knew how much he needed us but didn't realize at the time how much we actually needed what he was teaching us.

After graduation most of our group parted ways with Tony including myself. Reflecting on his influence, I know he indirectly taught everyone in our group valuable life lessons – slightly unalike for each person. The last time I saw Tony and spoke with him he was working in a pizza shop in old town Madison a few months after graduating – our conversation was regrettably brief – he appeared to be in good spirits. I didn't hear anything about him until several years later from another friend who sadly shared, he had passed away from HIV in New York City. The news of his untimely death truly saddened me. I recently discovered he's buried in Madison at Spring Hill Cemetery – I wish he could have lived to experience a total acceptance. Tony educated our group to show a greater tolerance for people's differences – my parents unknowingly modeled the same in their few associations – church friends in the art group led me to reestablish a faith I once cherished. Interesting how a disconnected trio assisted me to rediscover something I had temporarily shelved – quite the unexpected manifestation. Thank you, Tony!

Deoxyribonucleic Acid

He asked, *"Why do you need to know your paternity source?"* I didn't know how to answer the question. Another question to ponder on the drive home. My doctor said DNA results are reliable – mine arrived. My hope was to see a strong DNA connection to Raphael. The results revealed something I didn't expect, and again, not totally surprised. Obviously, my brother hasn't completed a DNA screening because results would have exposed our closeness of connection and shared matches. Being a half or full brother would give us a large shared DNA number. Instead, an entirely new group of matches appeared. This evidence points to something I sensed deep within – the father that raised me is not my biological father.

Several months earlier my wife and I visited my father's only brother in Madison. He and his wife live in the house my grandparents lived in, a house that holds many fond memories from childhood. I grew up staying with my aunt and uncle often as they raised young children. They moved into my grandparents' home after the death of my grandfather. We rarely see them now but decided it was important to reconnect. I immediately noticed the smallness where I found love and solace – the arched entrance to the cramped dining room without the chandelier I admired, and the tiny bathroom that didn't seem so small many years before. I asked my uncle if he would consider a DNA screening, and I offered to pay. I explained to him my interest in knowing for certain if my father, his only brother, is actually my father. He declined and said, *"Jim, what does it matter at this point?"* I thought the response was a bit odd but accepted his answer and didn't press the issue. At times this issue consumes me, at other times it really doesn't matter. My idealistic view of family drives a desire to know more. I want to know my family, all of my family, have deep relationships, visit often. I do not desire to just know DNA matches online, names and numbers indicating levels of DNA connection. I long to be connected to a real bloodline – faces I know and call by name, personally email, text. I desire to know more DNA connections.

What I currently have is a list of names with reliable DNA connections to my mother. These people are originally from Murfreesboro. Three brothers born within one to six years of my mother are possible connections to my paternity – it's likely one is my biological father. We have discovered the names of spouses, children, grandchildren and all of those people are listed in my DNA matches. Why couldn't my mother share truth? Why did she take secrets to her grave? My conclusion – generational – they didn't discuss those alleged failures. The overwhelming majority of her generation struggled with the same type of temptations we have, minus modern technology. As with every generation, sexual desire for the opposite sex engulfed them. My mother refused any admission to this because she couldn't imagine the thought of me knowing of her sexual union with other men. She communicated without words a strong impression of being bothered by sexual issues – she once jumped from our couch and turned off *The Graduate* before the seduction scene when I was a young teen – two generations clashing. I watched the whole movie many years later. My generation is open to sharing truth – my mother's generation never dismantled cover ups. I assured her nothing would change about our relationship regardless of what she shared – she instead remained true to her generational upbringing. The bond of silence and secrecy never betrayed by her because she was determined and steadfast scandalous truth would never be told – at least by her. Three potential DNA deceased men, two deceased spouses at this writing, one ninety-five-year-old living widow – so many DNA secrets buried in forgotten graves.

After learning of my brother and additional DNA information, I've pondered the many connections, personality traits, physical likenesses, and health issues of those names. I think of DNA as a multiplicity of tiny, powerful threads that weave a story together – those threads sometimes create a beautiful tapestry. The difficulty is pulling all those threads together from a sundry of unknown sources. It would be helpful to know health histories and reasons for death of those I discovered with the highest connection numbers. Where did excellent penmanship come from? My mother didn't have it. Where did artistic ability and flare for design come from? My mother didn't have that either, but someone did – likely my biological father – a man I do not know. I have a love for planting and cultivating flowers – something my mother loved – learned those skills indirectly. Raphael is a trained chef – I love cooking but lean more toward the presentation aspect. Where did our natural inclinations originate?

It's interesting how I obtained many likes and dislikes from those with whom I don't have DNA but close contact. I'm hurled to a contented past within seconds when I get the faint waft of Lucky Strikes and Old Spice that forever permeate a pair of bronzed baby shoes and two paint-by-number paintings from my grandfather Morris. The bronzed shoes sit on a shelf next to my bed and the two paintings hang within my screened porch. My grandfather Morris as well enjoyed amateur bird watching – loved using binoculars to spy on birds in his yard and inspired me to do the same. A grandfather and retired teacher in the trailer park, no connection to one another, educated me to know the various melodies of the mockingbird, how it can trap prey with the span of its wings, revealing white feathered stripes. The robin tilting its head to hear movement beneath the soil and how they construct mud nests lined with soft fine grasses, the forever angry and contentious blue jay squawking and stealing from less aggressive peers, and cardinals with their crowned crests and cone-shaped beaks, master builders of thinly weaved nests of bendable sticks lined with discarded weathered paper. My love for watching and studying birds is a legacy without DNA.

Grandmother Morris made a coconut cake to die for – absolutely the most delicious cake I ever indulged in of that type. Grandmother Tenpenny made a homemade yellow cake with candy caramel icing. The richness of the homemade icing bled into the yellow cake layers creating a thin, soft gooey layer just below the firm caramel candy coating – again, absolutely the most delicious cake I've ever indulged in of that type. Those are just two of the real deal truly happy food-oriented memories I cherish. I no longer drink sweet tea but if I do a remembrance takes me immediately to the grandparent's table where I enjoyed sweet tea on many occasions when it actually tasted like real tea. At the Tenpenny farm we never ate watermelon in the house – always in the back yard with an audience of jersey cows waiting for rinds. Somehow the cows knew when we were eating watermelon because they always made a path toward the fence along the backyard and waited patiently. After I gnawed the luscious ripened red down to the white rind, spitting out all the seeds, I walked to the fence and threw my leftovers to salivating cows – they unhurriedly chewed until it was completely devoured. A fond remembrance of my past. When I eat seedless watermelon today it's not the same but occasionally the taste will transport me to their back yard fence being watched by hungry patient bovine – sweet. Wouldn't it be delightful to somehow gather all those fondest remembrances and indulge just one more time – but I don't think it would be possible to fully grasp the unadulterated memory because so much has transpired since then and without the people that made those moments possible it wouldn't be the same. Perhaps that's one of the many reasons we have the ability to remember. How sad it would be if I couldn't remember the very things that enabled me to make life more whole and complete – fulfilled.

One of the best school moments occurred in sixth grade in conjunction with an extremely hellish period. The assignment from favorite teacher Rebecca Ramsay was to create a 3-D project instead of a written book report – exactly what I preferred. Checked out a beloved bird book and used playdough to form eggs of several birds and painted each one. I stood nervously before the class and shared the project – eggs mounted on a board, she praised me with cheerful, over-the-top exuberance I've never forgotten – she didn't realize how significant it was for me and how she boosted a diminished self-confidence. Years later I had opportunity to tell her face-to-face – a powerful moment for me and the identical emotion remains and resonates in the depths of my soul. Likewise, Grandfather Morris inspired me artistically because he worked as a professional painter and gold leaf artist. No shared DNA, but both people certainly influenced me by creating imaginative and artistic pathways I could embrace.

Perhaps my resistance to worldly vices come from the Tenpenny grandparents – my mother seemed to possess what I've termed the *black sheep* gene – perhaps I don't. During some of the craziest worse episodes of life I honestly felt like a spectator – not a participant. I know that sounds weird, but I think it was my way of emotionally disengaging – being an observer was safer, my psychological analysis. Escaping to my grandparent's home in Madison offered temporary intervals of peace. Growing up without the presence of paternity DNA explains much of the dysfunction and divide within my home, but love and acceptance from grandparents quelled the absence. What I now understand, the threading agent of DNA was the missing element I didn't know how to explain.

The DNA bond I share with two cousins in Melbourne, Florida has grown enormously more special. I do not know my new DNA connected family in and around Nashville and the surrounding counties and states, no emotional connections yet – just DNA. The history I share with cousins in Melbourne holds many of my fondest memories – hours upon hours of time together that mean the world to me. I long to be with them. We have visited Melbourne several times over the past few years. We reconnected our strong bond that once existed between the two families. My cousin Janice is single and plays a huge role in the life of her brother and his family. My cousin Bill is married and has two adult children – both children have recently moved out on their own – his daughter is mother to a teen son. Their lives are much busier than ours because they are still working full-time jobs. It's easier for us to visit Melbourne, plus the opportunity to visit the sunny beaches of Melbourne make each trip a fun-packed vacation. Our love for each other has grown stronger due to the recent visits. Janice is a faithful member of a church we enjoy visiting – we attempt to arrange our time in Melbourne so that it coincides with Sunday worship, another sweet family commonality. Visits are never long enough because they are the only DNA family members with whom I share a close common bond – a bond that is difficult to adequately describe. My wife believes the bond is rooted in the close connections my mother and their mother had as sisters.

In the extended Tenpenny family there are thirty-two first cousins. I spent the largest amount of time with my two most enduring cousins, Janice and Bill – the time together during our younger days built the lasting bond. Growing up we visited often, and our parents shared similar lifestyles in that they both loved cooking huge meals – usually two in a day when we stayed overnight at their country home in Spanntown. The Spann's rarely stayed overnight with us because the trailer space was too small, instead, only a full day. Breakfast at their home served around 10:00 – Bill and I fading from hunger by that time. My father usually had consumed a few morning cocktails and beginning to feel the liquor – slow blinking, stumbling steps. A typical breakfast on Saturday or Sunday mornings consisted of country ham, fired pork cutlets – never just bacon – my aunt's perfect scrambled eggs, hash brown potatoes, flaky biscuits, gravy, and homemade jellies – a lovely breakfast heaven.

Late in the afternoon preparations for the main course of meat began, which meant grilled steaks, barbequed ribs, chicken or goat – sometimes a combination. They never ate casseroles for a big weekend feast – still not a favorite of mine. Dinner was served late in the evening but as delicious as breakfast. At this point my father had consumed a lot of alcohol but typically tempered it with a couple of naps – then time for him to start the routine over. Meal preparation was a leisurely process, but always wrapped in a lot of loving care and devotion – everyone unhurried except hungry children.

These are some of my most distinct memories, and I'm certain the same for Janice and Bill. Sometimes those memories dominate our recent conversations when we share a meal – meals that don't quite measure up to the culinary expertise we adoringly remember. It's easy to allow fast-paced patterns of daily life to interfere with the sweet DNA bond we share – our mothers did share a close favorite sister relationship. I remember well the last conversation when my mother spoke with her beloved sister in Melbourne – used my mobile phone, she didn't understand how she was able to talk without a cord – she held my phone as if it might shock her. She heard the familiar sound of her sister Lora's voice – their conversation warmed both hearts, and both experienced the same deeply bonded feelings I've described for my cousins. It wouldn't take much to convince me to live the remainder of my life in Melbourne. Why? The DNA shared with cousins in Florida is a powerful example how it can intensify with time and how it entwines us emotionally – a bond first formed many years prior on a rural farm.

My daughter knows little of her Tenpenny family heritage – a large family – our family – one that I, unfortunately, do not know very well. Raphael knows even less but can claim a huge clan of DNA relatives in addition to his birth mother and me. A total of ten children birthed by Ossie and Vestel Tenpenny, originally from Auburntown, in Cannon County Tennessee – and that's not counting grandchildren, great-grandchildren and their families. It's sad to admit I know little about my Tenpenny heritage and cousins as a whole. What I know is an odd feeling of disconnectedness – with the exception of my relationship with cousins in Florida. Perhaps the closeness I yearn is just an idealistic long fading dream.

When I contemplate the disconnect with my DNA family, I often go to a dark cavernous place – a place where profound sadness and sometimes depression broods. My heart aches to know so little about my mother's family. Memories are limited for a vast swath of uncles, aunts and cousins. The disconnect seems similar to what one knows of an entertainer admired from a distance – usually very little. Not certain any of my cousins ever knew how much I longed to be like them as we grew – believing their circumstances were so much better than mine. What I know, and some of it is speculative at best, we were all navigating our own unique set of issues and as with all families, some flourished and succeeded better than others.

We gathered primarily for reunions and funerals, but emotional connections felt scarce or nonexistent. Niceties spoken, smiles and brief hugs exchanged, small talk, good food, not one word spoken of any past discretions or failures. Formality ruled the day. Seemed as if we had to be on our best behavior at all times. I'm certain beneath the *polished veneer* of all the proper acting people one would discover characteristic oddities of real humans, weirdness, dysfunction, sexual quirkiness, crude language, religious dogma and doubt to name a few. I didn't understand this as a child but clearly see it when I reflect. We appeared to be a perfectly handsome and attractive family. I longed to be who they were – possess what they possessed – live as they lived. I didn't recognize deceiving façades and multiple inadequacies.

Every Tenpenny family unit but mine owned material possessions I desired. At reunions I hated parking our older used vehicle next to shiny new vehicles – hated my clothes – hated my body and pimples. I wanted to be them – didn't perceive hidden truths beneath the polish. Why did I cry as a young child when family insisted on photos of the grandchildren? No explanation other than Jim was the child from the poor messed up family. Amusing looking at photos how I can see truth I couldn't see then. Can't explain the gulf – the lack of devoted connection, but it was real and remains real. My heart remains dismayed if I dwell on the absence of devoted family connections. Aside from the raw truth I know, my daughter and brother are linked, as I am, by DNA to a large family. I share limited specifics with a disclaimer of speculation for some details – family stories can become distorted as they are retold over time.

The first born to Ossie and Vestel was James Owen. He

married Mildred and they lived in Knoxville, Tennessee most of their adult lives. They birthed four children, cousins I've never really known, Martha Sadie, Joel, Edward, and Levi – all much older than me. Uncle James Owen was a big man, recall he loved eating desserts, as I do, and was generally quiet with an aloof type personality. Never got a feeling of warmth from him. My mother said they rarely visited his parents. I think her oldest brother was perplexed by his sister Velma and never understood her rebelliousness.

My mother's oldest sister Lee Oma was the second of ten. She married Lee Maxwell – he struggled with alcohol like my father – they birthed four daughters, Helen, Linda, Elena, and Judy. Lee Oma was the female version of my quiet, demure grandfather Tenpenny. She never spoke over anyone when we were together – her sister Velma did. The Maxwell daughters fondly labeled our grandparents, *"momma and daddy Penny"* – the only four of the Tenpenny grandchildren to use those endearing titles. Everyone else used the typical formal names, grandfather and grandmother. Lee Oma was diagnosed with Lupus in her late forties before a suitable treatment was available. I remember her skin looking red like she had a sun burn in the middle of winter. She agreed to an experimental treatment at Vanderbilt University Hospital, but it actually accelerated her disease. She passed away in her late-fifties. Raphael's birth mother, my mother was next – the third child of ten. My story frames the detailed history of her life apart from the fact she never had cancer, no heart disease, no major health complications until the very end – the official death certificate states her cause of death as sepsis. I overheard nurses say, *"...the smell of death."*

Thomas is the fourth child of ten. He was the quietest of all ten – rarely talked in a group unless he was spoken to first. He married Liddy Mae and they birthed one son named Benjamin. My aunt Liddy Mae was not intentionally funny, but it was her facial expressions and laughter that amused me and captured my attention. Even though she appeared restrained, a unique laugh defied her restraint. Her tongue pressed against the upper mouth and teeth as she stuttered quick shush sounds. She would often quickly contain the laugh with a gradual lowering of the sound, looked down to adjust her dress belt or straighten her skirt to shift focus off herself knowing she had garnered curious eyes. Benjamin is an exact copy of his father in personality but resembles his mother. Arms typically crossed, he never talked unless someone else initiated a conversation. Benjamin never married, and I've never met any of his close friends. He's extremely private about personal life, other than I know he was a university librarian. Uncle Thomas was killed by a drunk driver as he walked from his car to the mailbox in 1999. Liddy Mae was waiting in the car and just happened to look down to adjust a shoe, she didn't see the driver as he veered too close and hit Thomas so hard the impact knocked his shoes off. I attended the funeral with my mother – difficult to watch a grandmother grieve over the loss of a second child. Lora is the fifth child born and my mother's beloved sibling. Lora married William Miley Spann II and they birthed two children, Janice and Bill. Details of our life and times together are chronicled in detail throughout the memoir.

Nile is the sixth child of ten, the brother that drove his unwedded, thirty-four-year-old sister to Kentucky to give birth. Ironic how Uncle Nile is one of the brothers Raphael speaks with – the one holding the secret. The child born in Kentucky grew up to tell his birth mother's *driver* he uncovered a DNA family connection. Nile married Emma and they birthed four children – Jeanette, Freddy, Lucas, and Presley. The whole family has always lived in Murfreesboro. The house I remember most is their spacious two-story white brick with pillars across a large concrete front porch. I knew they had money as my mother would say because the house was furnished with big comfortable cozy furniture and each of the four children had a large framed portrait of themselves on the living room wall above a cream colored, tufted curved sofa. Downstairs they had a pool table, bar and Lucas's bedroom. I coveted the spaciousness of his bedroom and privacy; nor did I have a large framed portrait.

Aunt Emma easily intimidated people with a stern personality, but I liked her anyway. Even though the home was decorated with all the niceties I recognized and wanted, it was lived in – nothing was off limits. Aunt Emma often blurted commands to all the children with a serious tone but then displayed a half smile from one side of her mouth – cousin Freddy did the same. Her oldest, Jeanette was very much like her mother but didn't have a lot of luck keeping marriages together. I admired her and her husband for adopting three children from Russia. Freddy, in is mid-thirties, was shot in a fight outside a bar and later died of other complications. Freddy lived a rough and tumble life but always the fun-loving rebel – an adventure every moment. He possessed the tough exterior but displayed his softer, playful side in rare moments very much like his mother. The youngest is Presley and is by far my most interesting cousin of the entire bunch and of the four siblings. She is a *Mother Earth* loving, bongo playing, belly dancer. She loves to frolic through grassy knolls by gentle streams decked out in flowing white cotton dresses, wreath of fresh flowers on her head, a place of peace and serenity along with her organic garden. Presley is also fond of posting life on Facebook. Lucas is my age, but we never bonded as I did with cousin Bill – Lee looks exactly like his father.

Uncle Nile was fairly quiet and loved his beer and partying with my parents and the Spann's – blue jeans and flannel shirts his favorite attire. He liked to purchase business properties, build and sell homes. Aunt Emma died of cancer in her mid-fifties and Nile remarried twice more – both of those ladies died before him. He owned his own heat and air conditioning business now operated by son Lucas. Nile's first one-on-one conversation with me was at Shoney's in LaVergne when he was compelled to share a secret hidden for years. I attended his ninetieth birthday party and reconnected briefly with several cousins – exchanged mostly formal pleasantries which demonstrated nothing much has changed.

Uncle Nile may have known more truth than he spilled or perhaps he didn't remember. His sister-in-law Earlene, my mother's hairstylist, owned her own *beauty* shop. I was told by someone she and my mother were close friends. I'm confident Earlene knew everything because her days were spent gossiping with every customer. I also know my mother visited her hairstylist friend the morning of the exile to Kentucky. I find it hard to believe they didn't discuss the circumstances of her pending disappearance. A pressing question I've never been able to piece together is how did my mother manage to attach herself to a Catholic convent in Kentucky? Was her friend and hairstylist involved? My mother's family were staunch Southern Baptist folks with no connections to anything Catholic. Someone organized this exile away from the public eye for an unmarried pregnant thirty-four-year-old. I can't imagine the Tenpenny family having the knowhow or willingness to arrange such an undertaking. Someone Catholic was likely involved and arranged all the connections and perhaps the adoption. I know other people besides my mother must have known truth, but who – Uncle Nile, Aunt Emma, Earlene, parents, the father of the child?

I've wondered if the Catholic component was connected to my great grandmother Morris – that might explain the possible Nashville connection. Assumption Catholic Parish sat directly across the street from her red brick row house – I believe she was Catholic. Perhaps her grandson, the father who raised me, impregnated his girlfriend. My mother's Murfreesboro family likely absolved themselves from all responsibility, relinquishing the solution to another family to eliminate the messiness, shame and embarrassment. With complete assurance, I know my mother followed dictates laid out before her by the commander of the multi-layered predicament – likely orchestrated by a Catholic component. This is a mystery I may never uncover unless a lost diary of secrets is discovered.

Jay Thurman is the seventh child of ten and a career military person – he's the only sibling that attended my mother's graveside funeral. He married Linda who became a registered nurse. They birthed four children – Samuel, Martin, Clayton, and Jessica. I think his overly strict intentions as a father created a high level of dysfunction, opposite mine. He attempted the same around extended family. Once when several families were visiting Tenpenny grandparents, the older grandchildren watched American Bandstand together. Uncle Jay Thurman walked in and turned the television off without asking anyone – said the program wasn't appropriate to watch. He allowed strict religious dictates to rule his life along with military influence. I'm sure within his home it was likely worse, and I believe he probably meant well, but unfortunately running a family like bootcamp led to high levels of unnecessary strain and stress – especially for children.

Samuel seemed to manifest his hurt and pain as a bully when we were together – I feared him. Martin simply withdrew and displayed odd, loner type behaviors. He was considered weird by the cousins, and we wondered if anyone in his family recognized he might be on the spectrum. Clayton, on the other hand, seemed quiet, fairly normal; he's married with children and only slightly awkward in conversation.

Their youngest, Jessica, has beautiful dark piercing eyes that mask her apparent hurt. She became a nurse but sought refuge and escape with illegal drugs. I recall Aunt Linda stating several times with sadness, she didn't know where Martin or Jessica lived. She recently told me their children rarely ever visit – a troubling circumstance in their declining years. When Aunt Linda stood to say goodbye in my uncle's hospital room with her usual starched appearance, she came short of begging Pam and me to visit soon. I've only visited their perfectly decorated and spotless townhouse once – we haven't visited again.

Etta is the eighth of ten. She married Ned Foster and they birthed seven children. Her first two identical twins, Kurt and Burt, then Norah, Daniel, Wesley, Darla, and Deanna. I thought the twins were cool and looked up to them with admiration. Kurt has battled drug addiction and Burt became a well-known watercolor artist in Ohio. Norah is always reserved and very proper acting; Daniel likewise reserved and always perfectly quiet; Wesley reminds me of his father and seemed more of a quiet rebel; Darla is my age and the *perfect* child; Deanna is politically conservative and possesses her mother's spunk. I'm a little more familiar with this set of cousins because they visited Murfreesboro more often than the other out-of-state cousins. My mother and I spent two weeks in Ohio; I was about ten years old and loved our visit – a good escape from the paneled rectangle and I remember well their friendliness and hospitality. I recall a short visit to our home and all nine piling out of the station wagon – they were on their way back to Ohio – the only other cousins to ever visit our rectangle home.

Aunt Etta was outspoken and both Ned and Etta were strict disciplinarians, but not like uncle Jay Thurman. They really had no choice with seven children. Both always seemed good-hearted and hospitable – but Etta didn't mind telling my mother how she felt about things and would reprimand her if she thought my mother was misrepresenting a situation – which my mother did often. That was another clue as to where my mother ranked even though she was much older than her sister Etta. Ned died of colon cancer and Etta eventually remarried. She and her family remained in Ohio.

Randall is the ninth child of ten. He was Grandmother Tenpenny's pride and joy – a Southern Baptist pastor. Randall married Phyllis in Murfreesboro, and I recently discovered their wedding notice on Ancestry. My mother was in attendance but no one else is mentioned. It's odd she appears to be the only one – perhaps they married at the courthouse or perhaps there's a part of that story I do not know. Randall and Phyllis birthed three children – Silas, Amelia, and Tyler. Silas always seemed amused by my humor and stories as an adolescent. What I shared about adolescent follies in my setting was likely different from his more sheltered, pastor's son life. Amelia seemed rebellious pushing family limits but has remained connected and is politically conservative. Tyler is typically less social and recently lost a teenage son in a tragic car accident. The entire family resides in Texas where they have lived all their adult lives. I possessed a strong sense Randall was not particularly pleased with my mother and her choices. He possibly resented her moving back home with parents after the death of her first husband. I'm confident he didn't like the fact she birthed a child out of wedlock before me and was pregnant when she married the second time – some pastors are inflexible about morality issues but not necessarily their own.

Douglas is the tenth and last child born to Ossie and Vestel. Douglas married Dorine and they birthed two children, Donovan and Donita. Donovan has been married a few times and has children with each person. Donita has lived a fairly conventional life raising her family close to her parents.

Douglas and Dorine chose to live just a few miles away from the exact geographical center of the state of Tennessee where he lived most of his life as the youngest. Being regular fixtures at the Tenpenny house when we visited, they partook in the same delicious meal we were eating. My mother often protested privately about her youngest brother and his family making sure they became a fixture at the Tenpenny table. Aunt Dorine, like Liddy Mae, is known for her unusual laugh – she snorts. She loves to inquire about everything and is highly opinionated about faith matters but will always find a way to have a good laugh. When she phones for a family update, she starts the conversation as if we never ended the previous. Why did my mother's youngest sibling not pay final respects to his oldest sister? Aunt Dorine notifies us from time to time, *"We ought to get together and meet for dinner somewhere between Murfreesboro and Nashville."* I want to ask why they never did that when my mother was living? I was told they didn't attend her memorial because they had grandchildren to pick up from school. I may know the answer to my two questions.

The Tenpenny clan of ten siblings is a fairly unusual bunch of healthy folks – few have suffered any serious, life threatening conditions or diseases – all but two have lived long lives into their late eighties or early nineties. The majority of my mother's siblings never visited our home or visited when she lived alone for over twenty years – perhaps there were unresolved feelings of resentment or pain – perhaps she was being punished for poor choices – speculative on my part. I've struggled slightly with resentment toward a few of her siblings for abandoning their lonely sister – my mother never mentioned it.

A dichotomy clearly existed among the ten siblings that I never quite understood or comprehended. In times of celebration, family reunions, casual gatherings, even funerals, an obvious emotional divide permeated the atmosphere. Out of respect for the patriarch and matriarch I never observed any sort of verbal attacks or strong disagreements among the ten. On rare occasions my mother was the sibling to express dislike or repulsion – a retort typically born out of her own insecurities and suppressed wounds. Nine siblings I considered *the haves* stood beside the one sibling considered the *have not* – my mother. As a *have not* she would literally clutch her purse – a peculiar habit for the one with no monetary surplus to protect. I think she feared someone might see her cigarettes – of course they could smell it on her clothes. Among the clan of ten it was easy to observe the stark contrast in cars, clothes, and demeanor – also in the neatly ordered, spacious, and perfectly spotless dwellings as compared to mine.

As with most families, we stood patiently and respectfully at attention, smiling through multiple layered veils of secrecy and silence because we desired the illusive family photo for frame and album. Hidden dysfunction definitely existed, but unspoken, never acknowledged in this family. In my mother's simple manner of denial, I believe she put aside much of the deep hurt of rejection in her declining years and portrayed a greater acceptance of her circumstances. She and her sister remained close until Lora's passing. Lora, the one sibling who understood her sister better than the other eight, loved my mother unconditionally – love for her sister trumped all negatives. Lora wrote in her sister's senior yearbook, *"Remember me Sis,"* – my mother complied. I've made it clear, I'm the most comfortable with the cousins in Melbourne just as my parents and their parents found commonality. As I alluded, the same emotional divide among the other cousins remains. I wonder if someone in the family might be holding secrets from my past – few likelihoods remain. As of this *spilling* my brother and I have three DNA Tenpenny uncles among us from the Murfreesboro clan of ten – Jay Thurman, Randall, and Douglas.

Good Hearted

Within the haze of dysfunction my parents managed to cross societal boundaries that many others of their generation never considered crossing. For a few years in the trailer park two men lived together next door to us and I overheard my parents discussing their relationship in a way that made me suspect it was more than just two guys sharing a living space. What I never heard was insulting language about their supposed homosexuality or gay lifestyle in general. One man became very sick for a period of time, and my mother cooked a few meals for them. My parents talked often with both men between our trailers, always casually spoke and never seemed reluctant or embarrassed to do so. I didn't give their relationship much thought but was curious what my parents actually thought and why they chose to be so accepting. What I didn't know was if the two men knew of our family dysfunction.

When I attended the scam business college, an African-American instructor was searching for a babysitter for her two-year-old daughter. I shared my mother might be interested since we lived a few blocks from the school and how it would be convenient. My mother agreed and she ended up loving this child, and she loved my mother – there was no hesitation at all on my mother's behalf. My father was good with it as well – he certainly didn't mind the fact my mother earned extra spending money for herself. We were within walking distance to several retail stores – her extra money bought more junk.

I remember a time that my father was not a happy fan when his favorite college football team started a black quarterback – he listened to the games on a pink transistor radio and would become cussing angry if the quarterback messed up. My father eventually warmed up to the idea and especially once the new quarterback proved he was quite capable of leading the team to victory. He would occasionally voice a few strong feelings and held some misconceptions about Dr. Martin Luther King Jr. and the push for equality but never to the level of any racial hatred. It was interesting and educational to watch, listen, and learn indirectly from their openness and tolerance toward people of different races and lifestyle choices. Didn't fully appreciate or understand their openness traits then, but I remain grateful to this day for the unintended lessons these circumstances taught me. Through shadows of dysfunction my parents allowed a wide swath of grace outside of their limited white social circles.

My mother formed a few unique friendship bonds with numerous people in the trailer park. One such bond with Miss Goodpasture. I remember her looking frail and sickly – a person who hardly ever went outside her trailer. During a prolonged illness my mother cooked meals for her, and when she eventually died, collected money from trailer park residents and sent flowers to the funeral. I discovered many years later Miss Goodpasture was connected to a prominent Nashville family with the same last name. I don't remember anyone regularly checking on her except for my mother – she seemed lonely and somewhat sad, but graciously accepted the kindness my mother extended. This giving spirit continued throughout her declining years. As an educator and principal,

I received a myriad of small gifts at Christmas, gifts I simply couldn't keep or needed. I collected these and delivered a box full to my mother as a treat – instead of keeping everything, she decided to share the *wealth* by giving to everyone on the seventh floor. She never told the recipients where the gifts originated – everyone assumed she was being a generous giver full of holiday spirit – her flurry of giving ignited joy. Since the effort on my part brought her much joy as well, I continued the practice until she moved to a nursing home. I never insisted she broadcast to the seventh-floor residents the gifting source – we were coconspirators.

I didn't fully comprehend what my grandmother Morris attempted to convey – frustration perhaps as she talked to me a lot about my parents' extravagant spending on steaks and all the *get togethers* as she liked to say, for their friends – in reality it wasn't extravagant – perhaps excessive based on what they could actually afford. It was obvious she thought they spent too much money on other people. I politely listened, briefly pondered her comments then typically dismissed the concerns. What I didn't know was the possibility my father may have borrowed money from them – not certain that occurred but it's highly possible. My father kept a *running tab* at a local market directly across the main highway from the trailer park. He purchased beer, cigarettes and a few other items from the market. The market also cooked pulled barbeque I loved and piled sandwiches high – we brought the market's barbeque home on several occasions. I'm certain the tab ran too long, and he likely never paid it in full.

Another thing I know without doubt, my father and mother would give someone their last dime if they needed it. Their type of generosity was something they didn't speak about, never bragged – he and my mother just did it, and I observed those actions on several occasions. Something else I'm convinced about and witnessed – my father had difficulty paying off loans, paying rent and utility bills on time, but no problem giving money away. His manner of handling money most likely explains three bankruptcies. His credit rating was undoubtedly very poor. Expenditures on his addictions certainly contributed to his money mismanagement as well – liquor consumption erased concern for any money obligations.

An action I allowed to aggravate me greatly was their charity in allowing people to stay at our house. Some of the friends they visited had friends that ended up staying with us for extended periods of time – one such friend was Liz. Rough and crusty around the edges, she had a deep smoker's cough, and raspy voice. Of course, she consumed alcohol as my father did and most likely an alcoholic too. She would often stay at our house for a week and occasionally longer. I believe she may have been homeless before the term was fully recognized, but never heard my parents use the term in relation to her. Their benevolence annoyed me tremendously when I came home from school, work, or college and Liz was sitting on the front porch with my parents. Her visits meant three people smoking and drinking instead of two. This shouldn't have bothered me, but it did, and I don't truly know why their actions led to such annoyance. They were benevolent with limited resources toward others and perhaps I felt snubbed, or perhaps I lapsed into my pompous asshole attitude again. Their benevolent actions provided ample amounts of food and good times for anyone in need or anyone invited to stay under our roof.

During boyhood around age eight my mother agreed to keep a two-month-old baby while parents went out for the evening. They lived in a rented trailer across the gravel drive from us. The next morning, we still had a newborn. My father bought more baby formula, and my mother grew concerned because she had no way of contacting the parents – we didn't have a phone in our trailer for the entire nine years and I doubt the couple left a phone number or location. My mother used the landlord's phone when she called a relative or friend, but people never called us. For nine years schools didn't have a phone number to call in the event of an emergency. How were we much different than the young couple who left their baby? My mother eventually went to the landlord's house to see what information they had on the missing couple – they didn't have any contact information. The two finally returned later the second evening. I don't recall an explanation. I remember my mother taking care of the abandoned baby and wondering if she should contact the police department. I don't think we ever knew the true story behind the parents' two-day disappearance. Did this incident stir my mother to ponder the infant she named Jack?

Grandmother Morris knew the true story of her son's financial situation and how he over spent. As the oldest grandson I served as a sounding board for her frustration. Grandfather Morris on the other hand, remained silent on the issue. My father's parents made an annual trip with me to Sears because they made sure I owned a new winter coat each year knowing I walked to school every day, which included the coldest days of winter. We also formed a tradition of going downstairs to the Sears cafeteria for cheesecake – a cake my grandmother never baked at home. My grandparents never passed on dessert, nor did I when we were together. I looked forward to the annual trek for my warmth and creamy calories with drizzled fake strawberry sauce – unfortunately, desserts are a legacy of weakness for me.

When I was much younger, I occasionally shopped with my grandparents in old town Madison, and we made a traditional stop at the candy store. Grandmother Morris knew the chocolatier, and she would invite us to the kitchen and offer a freshly made piece of chocolate or chocolate covered cherry. Scrumptious moments away from family dysfunction with grandparents who loved me created a feeling of security and permanence I've never forgotten. Perhaps my grand-mother Morris was frustrated because she knew more truth than I ever realized. She enjoyed gossiping, gossiped a lot but held to certain boundaries she wouldn't breach which may have included my paternity. They didn't hesitate to spend money on themselves and enjoyed a few lavish purchases. I treasured their crystal chandelier over the dining room table – gave me a feeling of richness and fed my fantasy world as I created detailed renderings of amusement park rides or whatever creative spark was ignited. Their generosity, however, never included any truth of what I now seek to uncover. Whether they knew truth or not, when I was with them, I knew deep within my heart a closeness and unconditional love I often doubted in my home.

According to my mother's explanation she stood from the chair directly in front of the television and heard a pop – fell to the floor – couldn't move and was in severe pain from her right hip joint. She yelled for help several minutes until someone in the hallway finally heard and opened the door. They called 911 and she was rushed to the hospital. When I arrived, she was comfortable – pain medicine kicked in. The doctor informed me her hip was broken and would need replacement surgery in order to walk again. We agreed and surgery was scheduled the next morning. The surgery was successful and after two days in the hospital she was assigned to a local rehabilitation center for post-surgery physical therapy. I recall being concerned about finances but Medicare, along with her insurance, and Medicaid supplied all necessary funding. Amazed how the system worked so well on her behalf – didn't realize my mother wouldn't.

As it turned out, we had a big problem to address – my mother converted into a difficult patient. She wouldn't cooperate with any rehabilitation therapy – she simply refused to comply. She clutched an unfounded fear of falling again. Several therapists tried everything they knew, but she refused to cooperate. I was called into the facility manager's office to discuss my mother's non-compliance. With a somber posture the manager spoke in soft tones as she slowly charged my mother with an inability to respond to all physical therapy – I politely interrupted. I understood the circumstances and knew what needed to occur. The manager didn't hide her relief, she wasn't forced to fight denial. We discussed my mother's fate without conflict.

The next step was long-term care, a separate section of the nursing home facility where attempts to conceal urine and excrement scent fused with cleaning chemicals seemed a never-ending task. Everything looked clean, but I knew the dominant scent was a daily battle. I possessed no power to alter these circumstances but instead accepted her sentence. Failing eyesight was actually a blessing and another blessing in disguise was her gullibility and unawareness. I lied in hopes it would work – told her she was moving rooms to monitor her more closely as she continued healing. She would be sharing a room temporarily. Never voiced the words *nursing home* because I knew those words would not bode well. She lied to me for many years – figured no harm returning the *favor* to protect emotional well-being.

She thought she was in an upper-level room since she had lived for over twenty years on the seventh floor. The nursing home was a single level facility. We struggled to convince her to participate in communal dining or any programs – she hated sitting in the wheel chair – preferred staying in bed where she was safer. One evening during my visit the ninety-seven-year-old roommate took a slow fall in the bathroom and needed assistance from the staff. As they attended to the roommate my mother leaned over from her safe space and loudly whispered in disgust, *"That woman needs to be in a nursing home!"* I simply agreed with her skillful analysis since she did have prior work experience in a nursing facility. Shortly after that incident I knew it was time for her to know she was not returning to her seventh-floor apartment – she couldn't walk – there was no other choice. She didn't complain or resist my declaration. I was actually quite pleased with the care my mother received – attending nurses and staff conducted themselves in a highly professional manner at all times. The staff was kind and encouraged my mother to sit in the wheelchair – I did the same, wheeling her to a sitting area both inside and outside – she sought to quickly return to her room. I sought the spacious, well-decorated lobby or outside fresh air.

My mother seemed uncomfortable with her circumstances but totally satisfied to remain in bed. It was a waste of her money to maintain an apartment – my wife and I cleaned it out, giving away most of the worn and tattered furniture to other high-rise residents. We gathered numerous bags of accumulated junk and disposed of those. I kept personal objects like loose photos, photo albums, certain dishware items, and anything related to my father or the Tenpenny family. My wife visited the *facility* often to assist which relieved me since I was working full-time. My visits occurred primarily after work or weekends.

Our daughter was finishing college and decided to visit one afternoon – it was rare she had time because she lived thirty minutes away. I walked in after work one day to find the two chatting happily – Caroline sitting in my mother's unused wheelchair, legs propped on the bed. My mother seemed especially delighted to be in the company of the only grandchild she knew. Two days later my mother entered the hospital with an infection and never returned to the *facility* – providence? Perhaps a good-hearted nature pushed my mother through what she considered the worse days of her *facility* sojourn. To my knowledge my mother never knew she was in a nursing home; she never voiced those words – I never voiced those words. My deception appeared to work, but perhaps the joke was on me.

Spanntown

People with dysfunctional upbringings usually point to people or locations that offered comfort, peace, safe spaces, places that become some of the warmest, most cherished memories. One such place for me was a rural area a little over an hour away from our mobile home – a place where two boys convert a moss-covered cow pond into a fishing hole and hook a venomous water moccasin instead of a fish. My aunt Lora, called Pat by my family, Uncle Bill, and two cousins, Janice and *little* Bill lived in an area named Spanntown. I continually looked forward to visiting these two cousins. Janice was a few years older and Little Bill one year younger than me. Janice was always around, loved music, owned numerous music albums, and cherished the Beatles. She would regularly threaten her little brother and me if we interfered with her music listening, and especially if it involved The Beatles. I was at their house when The Beatles performed on the Ed Sullivan show – Janice went a little crazy – Bill and I stayed clear.

Throughout the years of our growth, we developed a closeness that has lasted to this day – separated now by an eleven-hour drive, flying my preference. For two boys the Spanntown farm served us a perfect landscape to romp and play until late evening. My cousin Bill knew every square yard of the massive spread dotted by cow patties. From one cow pond to the next, to the barn loft, then across several fields, we explored, pretended, created to our heart's content – his faithful bird dog on our heels. We circumnavigated acres and acres of rich soil far from watchful eyes. Parents had no concerns for our whereabouts. There was no better place for two boys to grow and discover life. At the house we did the same – endless hours of imaginary fun and discovery.

Margaret Magnolia Baskin Spann, known as Ma to my cousins Janice and Bill lived on the next hill past their house – only a quick walk through a cow field along a trampled path and through two wooden, weather-beaten gates. I recall the longstanding farm house smelling old but not in a foul way, surrounded by majestic oak and maple which created the allusion of persistent dusk. Ma Spann seemed thrilled when Bill visited, often more than once during a day because he knew where she kept the Nabisco Waffle Cream treats that she allowed without restraint. I stayed the night one time with my cousin at his ma's house. We slept in a large front bedroom where she slept in her big bed, we slept in a smaller bed next to a narrow staircase leading to another room or attic. I was scared of that location not knowing what lurked behind the door. Being highly suspicious, I thought it looked like a creepy place I didn't wish to see or know. As boys typically do, one of us forced a flatulent, started laughing hysterically, then both of us made the same noise with our mouths – boys being boys. Trying to restrain laughter made it worse and his ma finally grew tired of it and started tapping the wall. I think she attempted to frighten us, and it worked for me but not Bill. I also had knowledge of the overgrown family graveyard just beyond the house where William Miley Spann, called Pa, was buried – we never entered the graveyard, but I could see the tops of several neglected grave markers leaning to the left or right. By this time my mind was consumed with fear, and I lasted longer than Bill until my eyes could no longer keep vigil.

We rarely walked through or played in the living room and only played around the large front porch a few times. I was captivated by the secluded room where no one ever seemed to live. Bill didn't seem very interested – a part of his normal everyday life. The living room cloaked in faint natural light gripped my mind forcing attentiveness to what was once a vibrant plush space full of life. The room hadn't been occupied for years, prompting thoughts of an abandoned mansion frozen in time – like one would visualize in a good suspense novel or movie. I recognized the furniture as being old and dusty, a rounded sofa and matching chairs with plump tufted cushions in soft floral prints of muted yellows and greens. The plumpness flanked by side tables sat silently on thread-bear, washed-out Asian rugs. The floor creaked under our weight as we carefully stepped into the isolated chamber. The front door stood closed and never used as an official entrance. I stood in a room no one rarely, if ever stepped foot in, including Ma Spann – perhaps since the death of her husband. The abandoned room remained chilled during cooler seasons because the once vibrant space no longer warmed by crackling fires was now dormant and shut off from life. An emotional tug drew me to the lonely space for reasons I couldn't clearly articulate. Perhaps the plush stillness and imagined life that once occupied the room attracted me – perhaps a longing for material possessions I didn't own – perhaps a desire for what once thrived with normalcy.

Another interesting location we often found ourselves playing in was the large barn. Although the surrounding fields were still used for grazing cattle, the bygone days of a bustling farm now basically absent but cows still needed hay and it was in abundance within the loft. During spring and summer months barn swallows constantly darted in and out like miniature Kamikazes to firmly secured dwellings on the flanks of weathered grey beams. I could see feathers at the edge of each mud daubed nest – another fascination of mine. Climbing into the loft and rearranging bales of hay to stage make-believe scenarios was nothing but pure unadulterated entertainment – the most secluded yet perfect place for two youngsters to capture joy and contentment for hours upon hours. I know that feeling was the innocence of childhood freedom to explore beyond my wildest imagination which aided me in balancing the uncertainties of city life.

The water moccasin was fighting mad, and we dared not attempt to unhook an angry serpent. We dragged the stubby grey monster at a safe distance, eyeballing its diamond head and bulging cheeks of deadly venom. Our parents, especially my mother, acted appalled by the sight of it. Instead of ending life we returned to the pond – cut the long translucent barrier between us releasing our angry captive with hook and line connected. Spanntown experiences were life forming – creating unforgettable memories.

Peacocks, an outhouse and a former Tennessee governor's home remain unforgettable Spanntown memories too. Reflecting on cousin Bill's aunt Mary, she seemed very much the eccentric. I recall her being thin and sickly looking, typically clad in loose-fitting night gown type dresses sometimes with a housecoat. Greying hair unkempt and she constantly pushed scraggly strands off her wrinkled, weathered face – she was also an alcoholic. She lived in the dilapidated house of former Tennessee governor Newt Cannon. Cannon County is named after him. The vast property and her home were a couple of miles from the Spanntown farm. We would occasionally visit during our time at the Spann's, but I displayed little interest in the large stone monuments located a short distance from the house. The monuments were enclosed with a stacked limestone wall – the largest stone monument Newton Cannon's grave. He served as governor of Tennessee from 1835 to 1839, died at age sixty,

September 16, 1841. I knew none of the history when I was a boy or that we walked in a former governor's home. The house a simple two-story rectangle with a central hallway and four large rooms on the first floor – we never walked upstairs.

The house did not have a bathroom, so it was my first introduction to an outhouse. And of course, I had to go while I was there – not a favorite spot to tarry. The stench hit me first, then a decision as to which hole to use – one hole cut into the wood slab exposed unpleasant contents deep below and the other covered by a dingy, stained toilet seat. I likely used the exposed hole and made a quick exit. The outhouse was located to the right of the back door close to the sheep pen. I could see the large grave monuments from the outhouse but do not remember any discussions about the grave site by the adults. We played around the stacked limestone wall as curious peacocks strutted, sometimes showing off their ornamental feathers of iridescent colors. The peacocks fascinated and frightened me; didn't like the peafowl screams – a sound I wouldn't want to hear in the middle of the night. The peacocks appeared territorial – steering clear of their aggressive nature my safe choice – Bill never seem bothered.

His aunt also owned a lot of sheep – the kind with thick coats of wool for sheering – the sheep looked very fat in their dirty wool covering. I remember the sheep reacted to everything in a frightened manner and moved in confused bunches as Bill and I ran up to the fence or played close to the pen. We rarely stayed in the house because there was nothing much to do inside the sparsely furnished space. The inside looked old and in need of a lot of work and didn't seem very clean. The adults basically sat talking, drank beer, smoked cigarettes and sometimes got drunk. My mother believed Mary was a very rich person, but the only evidence was the expansive farm. Nothing about the house looked rich to me. I'm certain the history surrounding the location is intriguing but didn't mean much to me as a young boy. We romped where Newt Cannon's children played and walked the rotten, termite infested floors of a former governor's home. All is gone now but secluded graves and a historical marker posted at the entrance to the land Newton's father purchased in 1791.

My uncle and aunt's house stood as the primary location we typically found ourselves while visiting Spanntown along with my parents who likewise highly enjoyed their visits. Everything calmer, more orderly, not chaotic. Our visits included overnight stays unless it was just a Sunday visit, which left me feeling sad because our time together was too short. My uncle Bill and aunt Pat were basically quiet individuals – never saw them very upset or explosive about anything. It always appeared they loved visiting, talking, and partying with my parents. Aunt Pat was an excellent cook – flaky biscuits better than her sister's, perfect scrambled eggs, delicious homemade jellies served in a crystal bowl on a pedestal, and so much more. I watched her go about her work in the kitchen with confidence and loved the results. She was a meticulous housekeeper – hardwood floors like glass – sock feet only. Everything in the house had its place and always looked perfectly clean but lived in – it's what I liked and was drawn to and exactly what I longed for in my home. My mother told me her sister would sometimes actually sweep the front yard with a broom after mowing – cousin Jan confirmed it's true, so my mother obviously noticed the impeccably groomed yard as I did.

Uncle Bill was a master griller. I remember his large barrel grill and the many fine cuts of meat he barbecued – vivid memories of hearing the rotisserie slowly turn and watching meat drip juices onto the burning embers below as I anxiously awaited deliciousness. I love how our memories can be so sharply alert to remembering the most delightful manifestations of life. My uncle never seemed hurried, always enjoying his beer or whiskey along with my father. My father though, would often need a nap because he wasn't good at holding his liquor – never witnessed that trait in my uncle. Regardless of their surroundings, my parents seemed focused on their own needs and contentment. I never sensed that about my uncle and aunt from Spanntown.

One time at their house I fell off my cousin's bicycle and cut my knee; it was bleeding. I remember going to the back door and calling for my mother. She came to the door, quickly assessed my knee and insisted I was okay. I protested in tears, but she ignored my pleas and returned to the inside merrymaking. Aunt Pat came out with a wet cloth and lovingly attended to my tattered knee and applied a bandage. I didn't understand my mother's response, but her sister did. My memory is also sharply alert to remembering the most hurtful manifestations of life. Although life in Spanntown was never perfect, it was simpler, slower, less complicated than city life. For me it served as a needed respite for a trailer park city dweller.

Sojourners

Sojourners...*people who reside temporarily in a place* – slightly extreme but in the truest sense of the meaning it applies to nomadic patterns my parents adopted. One of my most favorite books to checkout in early elementary years, *The House of Four Seasons*, by Roger Duvoisin. I fantasied about living in that house. Loved how the family restored the old house then everyone selected their favorite color to match each season – not how twenty-five four seasons played out for me. Within that twenty-five-year span we lived in nine different dwellings, the longest nine years. My mother lived in eleven locations considering the last twenty-five years in a government subsidized high rise for seniors before her last few months in a nursing home – we dubbed the *facility*. To shroud their sojourns in a type of moral rectitude would be too lofty. All the sojourns were hastened for the most part due to financial sufferings brought on by poor choices, and those choices altered circumstances. But I dreamt of a beautiful house among tall trees just like the *Four Seasons* storybook house – little did I know what the future whispered.

Five months before my birth they married in *Podunk* northern Mississippi – I was full-term. They didn't have long to enjoy life without a child. The first place they lived together as a married couple was Ma Spann's – mother of my uncle Bill, married to my mother's sister Lora – suppose she was gracious enough to offer a hiding place for the shame they bore. I was birthed at the Murfreesboro hospital, but the homeless couple with a new baby couldn't move in with my mother's parents at the center of the state. Not an option because poor choices nine months earlier made that an impossibility in a strict religious household. Details of their time at Ma Spann's are relatively unknown, but I do know I was sick for several months. Perhaps my mother held me while sitting on the plump tufted cushions in the living room warmed by a crackling fire. My parents told me they listened to a country doctor who said I was suffering from colic – that I would eventually get over it – I didn't. Upon losing too much weight they realized I must be seen by a specialist. I've wondered who finally urged them to do this because my experiences with medical care were sparse at best throughout my young life. Around eleven months old I ended up in Vanderbilt Children's Hospital for surgery to remove a benign tumor from the opening of my stomach. As a young boy I was told my heart stopped during surgery and they revived me. Many years later I recall my parents in a serious discussion regarding Vanderbilt Hospital medical expenses – why so many years afterward? A collection agency garnished my father's meager wages. I do not know when they moved from Ma Spann's temporary lodging – what I know, *shame* wasn't eliminated as it was eighteen months earlier.

As a first official home my parents rented a small mono-pitched roofed house in Madison on Campbell Road – a few miles from my father's parents. I rode past that rental several times during childhood – the sloped roof appeared odd – nothing architecturally attractive, just odd for the time period. The next move was to Old Hickory Boulevard in Madison – one street removed from my father's parents. It was a small house directly across from Broadway's Market. A tiny general store with the classic screen door with a Colonial Bread sign and the blonde headed girl with blue eyes – as the squeaky door closed it would catch your foot if you didn't move quick enough. One of my earliest memories occurred at the Old Hickory Boulevard house. I ran into the street to retrieve a ball and got a spanking from my mother.

The next sojourn was a few blocks away on Maple Street, the same street as my father's parents – a short block away. This is the location where my parents began a long association with neighbors Ned and Blanch Derris and their children. The white shingled house with green wooden fence-like shutters is still there but totally remodeled. Three events stand out during my time on Maple Street. President Kennedy was shot and died in Texas – I was playing in the front yard when my mother heard the shocking news. On another day I fell at the back-door concrete porch attempting to pull my tricycle up the steps – the cut on my forehead required stitches, and the other event is indeed strange. One evening we heard a bizarre high-pitched noise, and no one could determine the source. Involving neighbors and grandparents, everyone finally discovered it was wind blowing through two slightly opened windows in the front and back of the house. Both windows were positioned perfectly to create a cross-flow air noise. We never heard it again, but I've never forgotten the disturbance. I turned five at this house and my mother threw a birthday party and invited several neighborhood kids – we played *pin the tail on the donkey*. I attempted to play alone with my new plastic car – my mother insisted I rejoin the party.

Next was our big move up in the world to Shepherd Hills Drive to a two-bedroom red brick house. The house had a fireplace in the den and a full-size basement. Life was good – my father worked for AVCO as an airplane mechanic – monthly house payments only $162. My parents bought my first puppy at this location but unfortunately, they neglected getting the puppy its vaccinations and it died a few months later. I didn't understand the importance of vaccines but recall my father trying a weird home remedy to keep the puppy alive – someone said the puppy likely died of canine distemper. It was buried at the edge of the woods in the big back yard. Close to one year later my father was laid off from his job at AVCO and never returned to the job. The new brick house went into foreclosure, and they sold it to my first-grade teacher – we moved to an eight-foot-wide rented tin rectangle on cement blocks. I didn't grasp the gravity of this unforeseen occurrence at six years old. Twelve years later I finally got a second dog.

The new dwelling on Monticello was only a few miles from our former brick home. The street name is spelled the same as Thomas Jefferson's home place but pronounced like cell with a long o – Jefferson's is like the musical instrument cello – more refined. Gateway School was close enough that I walked for six years. I never knew how much my parents paid each month for rent, but it wasn't much. I know they filed for bankruptcy after the foreclosure on the brick house and I believe twice more during nine years in the tin rectangle. The mobile home was first located on lot one, next to the road and a few yards from railroad tracks. We eventually moved to the prized spot on the lower backside of the complex – we had quiet instead of trains, more yard space, a stream to explore, and neighbors on the left side only. What else could I ask for? Longed for more space and privacy as I grew and family dysfunction increased.

Regrettably, life inside the trailer wasn't altered. In a peculiar way nine years in one mobile home might give the impression of stability – nothing close. I remember lying in bed countless nights imagining a different life. In fact, it was the most unstable nine years regarding my emotional growth and routine medical care. The first time I stepped foot in a dentist office was three weeks before I married at age twenty-five. I needed extensive dental care that had been neglected throughout childhood. I clearly remember writhing on the floor, in excruciating pain on numerous occasions due to the mess in my mouth. Thankfully I was fairly diligent in brushing because the damage due to neglect was secluded to molars, easy to hide unless I was in severe pain. My father's solution was not a dentist but Orajel – an over-the-counter remedy that numbed pain temporarily – and much cheaper.

Three weeks before I married an abscess developed below a rotten molar – the huge swollen knot needed immediate attention. A minister friend of mine knowing I had no insurance, contacted a dentist from our church and he agreed to see me. I was treated for an infection first – the huge knot subsided – got married – had extensive dental work over a three-month span. Pam and I paid cash for the majority of work until I was on her dental plan. Reflecting on childhood I remember getting vaccinations, unlike my puppy, but I never recall going to a doctor for well checkups. Somehow, I survived. It's easy to conclude it was simply a money issue. I know it goes much deeper than just money – it encompasses a chosen lifestyle, addictions and money mismanagement I had no ability to control – choices that altered circumstances. I'm not angry or resentful – all was forgiven because I had choices too. Since age twenty-five I regularly visit a dentist – she tells me after every checkup, *"Perfect, keep doing what you're doing!"* Started regular dental care for our daughter at age three – round one of braces in third grade – privilege I never knew.

After nine long years in a mobile home bankruptcy knocked again – time for another sojourn. After moving, a strange sadness enveloped me as I peered at our tiny home for the last time sitting half off the paved drive, leaning heavily to one side. The narrow rectangle, *the finest mobile home ever made,* appeared broken and dilapidated – ready for demolition

– my family in a similar predicament. I hoped no one else would ever endure the cramped space, or dysfunction caused by addictions and poverty.

We moved to Forest Park Apartments in Madison – a few blocks from my father's parents – funny how he gravitated back toward his roots. This time I had something new and exciting – a swimming pool. Our two-bedroom apartment was located just a few yards from the large pool – we could easily see the pool from our back patio and from my upstairs bedroom. My triple size bedroom was so much better than the past nine long years. We needed beds because the mobile home beds were built in. The Morris grandparents purchased a solid wood bed frame from a furniture thrift store. I'm surprised my grandmother didn't buy something new – perhaps she conveyed a message to her son. I discovered several tally marks etched into the wood where the top of the mattress met the headboard. I speculated the origin and purpose – why would someone etch tally marks on a headboard? Didn't immediately occur to me but after further speculation I drew a conclusion – a tenth-grade understanding answered.

During three years of apartment living, we met several interesting folks. Outside of the bus route for high school I was forced to walk most days. Walking to high school embarrassed me because I thought about what others might be thinking of me. Buddy lived in the complex, and we were the same age. Somehow, he had his own car – I rode with him some days, but his personal lifestyle didn't align with my more reserved choices. He liked driving fast, smoked, cursed a lot, and one day followed a school bus because a girl in our class flashed a portion of her upper body from the bus window. I didn't know where the exposure would lead but prepared myself to wait patiently in the car until the encounter ended – nothing actually happened, just a tease – unfortunate for Buddy I suppose.

Monica lived on the opposite side of the pool from our apartment – she was a little younger and developed a crush on me. I wasn't interested, but her mother invited me to Opryland, so I went because she paid for it. Ironically, I ended up attending the same big church as Monica and her mother a few years later. By that time, we moved twice more and Monica had a boyfriend she eventually married. Monica's mother gave us two handcrafted Christmas tree ornaments as a wedding gift, and we place those on our tree every year. Tammy was another girl I met, also younger than me but quite unlike Monica – not sheltered – more worldly. She was thirteen but acted and looked more like sixteen – a big flirt. Her father played steel guitar in the Opry. She lived with her mother and was often home alone. As our friendship developed, I could have easily taken advantage of our alone time, but I knew it was up to me to practice self-control – didn't wish to shame two families as my parents did. Tammy then met my cousin Bill and fell head over hills for him – she loved what she described as his *dreamy eyes* and dark long eyelashes. Suddenly she was no longer overly concerned about our attachment – she desired him. Bill and his family lived in an apartment on the south side of Nashville at the time. Tammy's mother allowed her to stay overnight at Bill's once – totally surprised by that decision, but Tammy and I remained close friends.

The most interesting situation in the apartment complex was an association with famous radio disc jockey Coyote McCloud and his girlfriend. I met the girlfriend at the pool one day with her three young children. We talked several minutes, and she asked if I would be interested in watching her children that evening for a few hours. I agreed. I was probably fifteen at the time. She went to the radio station to be with her famous boyfriend and didn't return until 3:00 am – a little longer than three hours. She paid me, and I became her regular babysitter until they moved. At fifteen I liked being around young children, very responsible, and possessed a natural ability to manage kid behavior – enjoyed being in charge and earning extra spending money too.

For reasons I don't recall we moved toward the end of my senior year, and I missed the pool. They rented a small two-bedroom house on Harris Street directly across from the back entrance to the apartment complex. I stood in the front door and resented seeing expensive vehicles with unknown drivers using our street as a cut through – what I really wanted was a nicer vehicle. From this dwelling on Harris Street, I started attending the scam business college – walked each day and resented that too. The best part about this move was a second dog – my new dog already had its shots because he lived – named him Samson – a shepherd, collie mix. I loved Samson, but my parents refused to allow him in the house. Samson stayed within the fenced yard until one day he escaped – he was lost and there was no sign of him for several weeks. I was riding with my best friend in his junk car. We were a few miles from my home and across a major highway when I noticed a dog that looked like Samson. I had him stop quickly and jumped out and yelled Samson – the dog stopped and looked – I yelled for him several times, and he hobbled toward the car. It was him – I was overjoyed. He was thin, beat up a little and weak but managed to timidly wag his tail – I put him in the back seat and immediately returned to my house. I fed Samson lots of food for several days, and he quickly gained weight. My parents decided it was time for another sojourn – I was out of the house more often and couldn't give the same level of care to Samson as before. Thankfully, Samson was adopted by a family and sojourned to a big farm – never saw my furry friend again but thrilled he had a spacious place to run, bark, and be the happy dog he was meant to be.

Life on Harris Street seemed disjointed and unfocused for

me – nothing settled, lots of uncertainties. The most intelligent friend I knew from high school and grew very close to during my time on Harris was Lisa. Her intelligence and self-deprecating nature never interfered with us having what I would term a rip-roaring, hysterical time. We managed to laugh so incredibly intense at times ribs hurt and eyes burned with tears. Lisa always cracked me up with clever quips and risqué jokes. Both of us enjoyed doing impersonations of people, primarily a few parents of friends and famous people. Mae West one of her favorites and when I broke into a chorus of *Everything's Coming Up Roses*, in my spot-on Ethel Merman cadence, Lisa often had to pull her light blue Volkswagen Beetle off the road to calm her convulsive laughter. Other episodes of crazy laughter were prompted by *cussing sentences* – the rule was every word must be a cuss word – again, uncontrollable hysterics over something so stupid. Other episodes involved my over exaggerated movement when she shifted gears in the Beetle. I would thrust my body toward the dash then throw myself back against the seat – my antics sent Lisa into a fit of laughter leaving her gasping for breath. I purposely voiced crude remarks to provoke laughter – we shared a lot of vulgar jokes which often left us both splitting our sides open – innocent young adult immaturity. We entertained the thought of intimacy once but quickly drew the conclusion that our uninhibited laughter must never be tarnished – a vow we never breached.

When I was somewhat disconnected without a succinct, clear focus for my future, a few friends offered a sense of permanence and stability, the humor was my outlet for emotional release. Healthy endorphins flooded my bloodstream during those episodes of wild laughter – but I yearned for more. Lisa's friendship served as the conduit through which I found temporary contentment. The common bond we shared was humor, and we fed off each other with skilled comedic timing – although most often crude in nature. In retrospect, the laughter and sometimes brackish banter was therapeutic but immaturity didn't recognize that at the time. I cherished my friendship with Lisa and the many hours of camaraderie and uproarious hysterics. Reflecting upon the unique bond we shared many years ago, I can now chuckle with a fondness and contentment I didn't know or fully understand then.

I didn't know this next house would be my father's culminating sojourn before a final passage to Veterans Cemetery in Madison. A blue shingled house trimmed in white with black shutters, located on Idlewild Avenue just a few yards from our previous dwelling on Harris Street – Idlewild like Monticello struck a fanciful, *bourgeois class* tone and I liked the enunciation and color – both important aspects of the charm. *Anne of Green Gables* described her *Idlewild* as, *"(her) most romantic spot"* and *"poetical...?"* Perhaps a bit of a stretch for our Idlewild dwelling but overall, it was a warmer, cozier type country allure unlike the other surrounding homes of my recent past. Or perhaps I was more tolerable as their dysfunction mellowed a bit. Exaggerated perceptions of *Idlewild* are reminiscent of a pattern garnered from my mother, making something more favorable in her mind made it more tolerable – my mother desired the finer things in life but was forced to settle for much less due to lifestyle choices.

Our home on Idlewild with a covered front porch and white railing, rose trellis on each side of the porch, two dogwoods in the small front yard, hedge bordering the street – a quaint dwelling. My mother cultivated giant zinnias and placed hanging flower baskets of petunias along the porch. A brick paver sidewalk led to the front steps – porch converted to a regular retreat for my parents. And yes, everything did seem a bit calmer and serene but deep-rooted habits prevailed. One evening when a group of my friends gathered in the small front yard before departing, we were talking and laughing loudly when my mother suddenly made an appearance at the door and yelled, *"It sounds like a damn circus out here!"* Needless to say, she was feeling her liquor, and I was embarrassed by the abruptness. Lisa couldn't stop laughing and the *damn* phrase was immediately adopted as a favorite go-to within our group. My friends were very amused by my mother – best friend Cliff nicknamed my mother *Velma darling* – it stuck.

The Idlewild house was slightly bigger than the previous house on Harris, both only two bedrooms – the locals called it an *Old Hickory* house because it was relocated from an area of the city named after President Andrew Jackson's nickname. Life was busier on Idlewild because I worked several part-time jobs and attended college on top of church activities which kept me away from home. The separation from home was good for me, but once I started dating my future wife, I robbed focused time from college studies. Found myself struggling to balance a plate full of interests. Knowing college work couldn't take a back seat, I forced myself to remain unyielding in reaching my goal of becoming a teacher. I couldn't allow my life to take a destructive turn at this juncture – my yearning for a different life was alive.

Grandfather Morris visited often at the new location when he didn't forget where we lived. He lived only a short distance away on Maple Street – enjoyed popping in most mornings for a cup of coffee with my mother and a biscuit with lots of butter and jelly. We knew he was declining mentally when he told I was in the military overseas and we discovered him sitting in the dark because he forgot to pay the electric bill. He passed away shortly after that discovery. My last remaining grand-parent was grandmother Tenpenny in Murfreesboro – she occasionally visited Idlewild to stay with her favored daughter.

The owner of the blue house decided to sell instead of rent which meant another move – my parents liked it well enough that they made an offer to buy – somehow a deal was brokered, and my parents became homeowners again – perhaps they would be able to finally keep this house. This is where I lived when I got married at age twenty-five. My wife moved into our newly purchased brick home one week before we married. Knowing my parents would not be comfortable nor could they afford to rent or cater a rehearsal dinner, I suggested they cook the rehearsal meal at our new home and serve the wedding party there. They agreed to the plan. Bill and Velma triumphed. Everyone experienced a delightful time and delicious meal – a well-matched event for simple, good-hearted people.

After the rehearsal dinner I stayed my first night in our new home; Pam went home with her parents to finalize last minute preparations for the next day's wedding festivities. My groomsmen stayed around for a surprise bachelor party, and I confessed those *sins* in the car after the wedding – nothing too sinister. After our celestial honeymoon I returned to the blue house to retrieve personal belongings. Pam assumed I would make a few trips back and forth. Upon returning she stood at our back door as I removed two boxes and a bundle of clothes from the back seat. She appeared confused why I didn't load more things on the first round, told her that was all – *"That's it!"* – she blurted with a tone of unbelief. We've laughed many times reflecting – she simply perceived I possessed more things – she had so much to learn.

My dad's younger brother called a few months later to inform me the meat packing company where my father worked called him – my uncle worked for them several years before. They told him my dad was drinking on the job and probably needed some help to stop. Being a *mom-and-pop* business, they didn't have an official HR department that would normally handle issues of this type. I decided to spy on my dad first to see what he was doing during his breaks – sure enough he went to his car, and I saw him drinking what I assumed was liquor because I recognized his typical movements when taking a *swig*. This was not wise for someone working with sharp knives all day. I first mentioned this to my mother and her typical denial kicked in. She said he wasn't an alcoholic – complete denial – I knew truth – she did too.

Shortly after this disclosure, Father's Day 1985, less than two years after marrying, that's when my father returned from the grocery store, stepped into the house, took his last breath falling onto the sofa. My mother called his brother instead of 911 – his brother called 911 then called me and we all met at the hospital emergency room – his final sojourn. My mother lived alone, now in the not-so charming blue house on Idlewild for less than a year after his death. I finally had no choice but to complete a quick sell, take over her minuscule finances because she didn't know how to handle any part of it. Her next sojourn lasted nearly twenty-five years on the seventh floor of a government subsidized apartment high rise – her final sojourn occurred in a nursing home after breaking a hip – she chose never to walk again. I chose a private graveside service. No visitation – no more sojourns. She is buried next to her second husband William Bates Morris, a military veteran – the two grave sites, provided by the federal government are located on the back row to the right of a concrete and stone gazebo on sixty-four acres in the Nashville National Veteran's Cemetery located in Madison, Tennessee. When I drive past their final resting place I think and wonder about many things but mostly how fleeting life seems to be.

Bourgeois

Dysfunction provoked my mother's desire to be bourgeois, although she never knew the word or meaning – that's how she lived. She viewed certain material possessions as bourgeois, and never hesitated presenting the false impression we were middle class – a characteristic of her routine denial. I adopted similar notions which pointed me in the same direction and could have caused financial hurt and pain – an inherited fondness for an epicurean way of life. Classical music is an example that captivated me, loved school field trips to the Nashville Symphony – have loved classical music to this day. How does that occur in a low-income environment? Exposed at an early age to forms of bourgeois led me to admire with great respect those whom I perceived to live lives of luxury. An immature perspective did not allow me understanding beyond the disguise and dysfunction lived out in those situations too. The origin of my attachment stood firmly rooted in a mother's way of perceiving her limited resources. She was quite masterful at making something cheap appear expensive – making choices to buy one or two accessories to upgrade another item. The same was true for clothing within her sparse wardrobe. I watched.

I vividly remember a black skirt and matching fitted jacket that flared below the waist. The three-quarter length sleeves were finished with white polka-dot ruffled cuffs, the same at the collar – the outfit made her guise bougie. She later purchased a pair of short white gloves and a solid black sheer, bowler type hat – the style that looked like a small lamp shade inside another larger lamp shade. She carefully handled and stored the prized hat in a box – I knew how much the hat meant to her. She wore the ensemble to my school chorus performance. I beamed with pride and knew everyone must notice how *rich* she looked. Jackie O. and Audrey Hepburn rolled into one. I didn't voice those names or any words like elegant or classic, wasn't part of my vocabulary yet. She purchased the black dress at Three Sisters in Madison where the wigs on the mannequins looked like wires, not hair. The store may not have been considered *high-end* but that didn't matter – my mother was *rich* in the black dress – she knew it and I knew it. I didn't know what my father thought – I never heard him compliment her.

My mother did something similar with house accessories. The smallest trinket or new set of curtains prudently placed and admired for *fineness* – she often talked about the *finer qualities* of her material possessions in glowing terms. Strange, yes – another form of her ever-present denial – distracting her from truth. She was well aware of her financial limitations but when allowed to buy something she deemed important, that thing was the most important thing in the house, or in her closet for weeks to come; she cherished it. I never felt cherished, at least not in the same way she looked at and admired her material possessions. I held to an innate desire to be cherished by parents as all children do.

It was easy to adopt her attitude toward material possessions – obviously a distraction for me too. The positive side to our lust, we didn't allow material things to ruin us by making unwise purchases – a trait we both shared. I'm thankful my mother never held a credit card. I possess and use a credit card, but I make a conscious choice not to over-extend or use it on unnecessary expenditures because those choices could alter circumstances. My mother, on the other hand, was strictly limited by financial circumstances. Both of us operated within the parameters of our personal means. I know in the past it was more about how we misperceived bourgeois *things* because I recognize the trait in myself. Mind-games and fantasies I playout in my head seem rather ridiculous but typically harmless. My brother, on the other hand, actually possessed the real finer things in life as he grew and developed. I only fantasized about finer things. I never truly separate the past from the present – as brothers though, I regret our past remains separate from our present. I find it fascinating how we are similar in that we found and have maintained monetary successes in our own unique ways – obviously, both of us enjoy the *finer things* of life.

We arrived at a stately, white antebellum home nestled in the woods – my curiosity was immediately peeked by its grandeur – four large pillars across the entrance, tall stately windows, all surrounded by beautiful trees – my cousin Bill, not so impressed. I had no idea why we traveled to this home. I did not know where we were – my uncle Bill, my father, my cousin little Bill, and I walked in. I remember one other gentleman being there, most likely the home owner. The adult men walked into the oversized kitchen and helped themselves to an adult beverage of some type. The men went into a big sitting room and we, the boys, started a self-tour. I was curious about the house, high ceilings, plush furnishings, hardwood flooring and beautiful thick rugs throughout, and a spectacular staircase. I wanted to see the entire house and we did. I don't recall the adult men giving us permission, but we walked into every room.

A vivid memory flooded my mind as my cousin and I made our way through the house – opening tall, white, raised paneled doors, thick decorative moldings – Christmas at Cheekwood. As a third grader I visited Cheekwood mansion in Nashville, Tennessee during a school field trip. I stood profoundly gripped and impressed by the beauty and opulence of the grand home. Nestled in every room all around the house were decorated trees of Christmas representing many countries. I didn't want to leave the splendor of the perfect day. Didn't realize I was within a few miles of a brother I didn't yet know – a brother already familiar with beauty and opulence. Of course, I went home and grabbed my drawing pad to recreate a tiny bit of the splendor I witnessed at Cheekwood. I don't believe I did the same for the stately, white antebellum home. Staying with my cousin at the time, I didn't have artistic supplies, but I stored the memories away for safe keeping. Memories like these influenced my life on many levels and continue to hold a special place of attachment and desire.

My great grandmother's home in a portion of downtown Nashville known as Germantown served as another similar experience and fond memory of finer things. Her dwelling, a red brick, corner lot, row home, black wrought-iron fencing around the small front yard – red brick sidewalks bordered all the homes – a picturesque and charming old neighborhood. I was impressed by the high ceilings, red velvet tufted, uncomfortable, Victorian furniture. Above the arched backed sofa, a large painting framed in gold leaf of a beautiful lady in an elegant red satin dress reposed on a piano bench – an Afghan hound sitting at her feet. On the oval marble top coffee table sat a collection of delicate Dresden lace figurines I was not allowed to touch. The only occasion I remember visiting my great grandmother was Christmas. The Morris family gathered there, four generations, connected by DNA except my mother and me. We enjoyed gift giving, delicious holiday food, spiced aromas, and a giant flocked Christmas tree adorned with blown glass indent ornaments – lights reflecting a legion of silver ice cycles – bourgeois at its best.

Great aunt Fannie Mae often walked in late to the annual gathering draped in a mink coat, whispers and wide-eyes prevailed – my mother took notice because I recall her gossiping about the *"show off"* – hand over mouth whispering. My uncle nicknamed Fannie Mae, *"asshole."* I viewed it all not fully grasping their sensitivities toward her domineering presence. This and other experiences fed my desire to feel bougie, feeling bougie at various times my experience – becoming bougie my desire. Not understanding until mid-adulthood, a truer meaning – learning life is not related to the material grandeur I once coveted.

Two boy cousins, one twelve, the other eleven playing outside in a wooded area behind the white antebellum house after the self-tour ended – seemed like an eternity – bored pre-teen boys usually find a way to deal in a little mischief. I never understood why we were there, but I suspect to borrow money, pay a debt, something a little shady – just a hunch. Perhaps all four of us dealt in a little mischief that day. We headed back to my cousin's home – a home I also cherished. Nothing opulent, a white three-bedroom modest country home nestled on a family farm. Gleaming, slick hardwood floors, no dust, everything had its place – everything I desired. Didn't comprehend I possessed one of the *finest things* in life – family.

Designer

Fuller's Business College was a financial rip off – a money scheme that preyed on the poor and those wishing to satisfy a desire to attend college. I had no money to attend, but the college quickly approved a loan for the full amount with a hefty interest rate – of course I didn't care about those details – just teach me how to become a famous fashion designer – money wouldn't matter in the end. I fell *hook, line, and sinker* for the scam but realized later, all of it wasn't corrupt. Several positives were derived from my experiences, which proved to be consequential for my future. My goal at the time was to pursue a career in fashion design, although the emphasis focused on fashion merchandising. I considered myself talented and creative in the area of design – at least I was told so by several people outside my family. My style and preference at the time, high fashion with a flair toward female entertainment clothing – Cher, Diana Ross type clothing. Instructors and peers quickly learned of my pursuits as I shared original designs. I wanted everyone within my sphere to know beyond any doubt my goals and desires for success.

Shortly after classes began a local Nashville fashion designer called the school looking for a sketch artist to assist on a part-time basis. I thought the opportunity signaled a good chance to get my foot into the business a little deeper. She lived in Belle Meade close to where my yet to be known brother lived. He was at Duke University, a real college – a business college scam for me. Jean Smith, a well-known, high-society elite, started her own fashion design business in her home. She specialized in vintage type dresses, imported laces, silk ribbons, silk satin materials, and lots of tucks – all handmade and expensive. Many of the local, high-society, private school debutants purchased one-of-a-kind presentation gowns from Jean Smith. Young ladies in my circles didn't purchase presentation gowns. Suddenly thrown into a world I didn't know – I secretly wondered, what are tucks? My brother probably dated high-society debutants.

The first official assignment was to sketch numerous gowns to be cataloged into a booklet for retail stores buying from her – Saks Fifth Avenue, Neiman Marcus, Bergdorf Goodman, Bloomingdale's, Lord & Taylor and so on. At first, she was a bit picky about the sketches – she wanted detail but not too much. Once we found a happy medium and understood each other I gained her trust and knew exactly what she desired. As her trust grew in my ability, she allowed me to make suggestions and even submit my own designs, always under her name and in her unique style. My first public display was four watercolor renderings of gowns selected for the Memphis Maid of Cotton Queen. The four watercolor sketches ended up on the front page of the fashion section in The Tennessean newspaper – my signature in clear view. The article focused on formal cotton gowns and Jean Smith's business; four watercolor sketches published for thousands of people to see – a proud moment for me to say the least – don't recall my parent's response. The world I suddenly found myself immersed in created a level of intimidation for parents like mine.

Later, Smith allowed me to work with different clientele and sketch ideas as they described what they envisioned or desired. As I sketched for a high school debutant in her private school plaid skirt and white Peter Pan Collar Blouse, she suddenly jumped from the chair and hugged another girl entering the room. As she hugged, she silently mouthed "*bitch*" behind her back to another friend standing across the room; a new world I didn't fully understand. I once sketched for Jimmy Carter's sister-in-law, and opera singer Beverly Seals. Another article featuring Jean Smith and my watercolor sketches ended up on the front page of The Tennessean's fashion section – another enormous moment for a budding designer.

Jean Smith was known for her local fashion shows – sometimes private home showings. I assisted her during some of those, but my name was never mentioned unless she occasionally referred to me as her *assistant* – that was fine with me. It seemed I was now fully immersed in the Nashville fashion business. She hosted a major fashion show at Opry Land Hotel – I assisted. I remember feeling excitedly attentive as the music started and models started walking the runway – spying on Jean Smith's face lighting up as her creations were elegantly displayed – she overflowed with pride – so was I – a fun time for a novice designer. Once Jean learned of my talent with flowers, she asked me to arrange flowers for her parties – flowers in every room where quests sipped wine and downed cocktails or whatever they do at high-society gatherings. My background in flowers started at Seller's Florist – my first official, full-time job after high school graduation. I knew nothing about the floral business, but a natural artistic talent for creating allowed me to learn the floral business without a lot of sweat and toil. The florist owner taught me several basic techniques and then unleashed me to create on my own with little guidance. After several months he told me I had become one of the best floral designers he knew – a nice confirmation for something I knew was not a life-long career. I continued part-time with Jean Smith but realized it was a dead-end.

After getting engaged I suggested my future wife use Jean Smith – I would design the wedding dress without seeing the finished creation until she walked down the aisle. I finalized the sketch and Pam approved without any apprehension. The day of the wedding I used my floral talent to create her bridal bouquet – it was good to stay busy – I was a bit nervous. Her wedding dress and bouquet inspired by Lady Diana's – I desired both to appear *high-society*. Part-time fashion design work and how I perceived things allowed me to do something similar to what my mother taught me unintentionally many years before – but this time it was truly the finer things in life. The door of the church lobby opened – classical *Here Comes the Bride* processional resonated throughout the candlelit sanctuary announcing my bride's entrance; the wedding director fluffed her designer dress before she walked. I fixated my eyes on beauty walking toward me – a stunning dress, but she more radiant than ever. I momentarily lost my breath, finally regaining composure and avoided fainting – I kept replaying, how can this be happening to me?

Two DNA connected brothers – entrepreneurs – one in New Orleans preparing fine-dining cuisine and one in Nashville – *James Morris Originals* – my own business alongside a teaching career. With Pam by my side as the trusted brain handling paper work and finances, I would be the chief designer. The focus of the business was high-end wedding gowns and evening wear. We planned a trip to New York City to buy exquisite fabrics and laces – we were serious. A fabric store owner we met in Hillsboro Village agreed to guide us through the buying process and share the best locations to buy what we needed.

This was our first time to be in New York City together. I had been before with the group from the business college and

Pam returned to the Big Apple after our initial trip together with Peterbilt Motors for a training seminar; we thought we knew the big city well. Upon returning to Music City, designed and ordered business cards and secured all the necessary permits finalizing the new business adventure launch. At the same time, I created a booklet of original designs for clients to view but I would also create designs to match any specific taste. An expert seamstress in our church agreed to make a few dresses so that we could show the quality of materials, design, and workmanship. She was an outstanding seamstress, and was able to work from sketches and create exactly what I envisioned.

One of our first clients was planning a big wedding and the family asked if I would direct the wedding as well – I agreed. Everything worked out perfectly with the exception of a few minor issues at the actual wedding. A busybody aged uncle asked me to have the air adjusted prior to the start – his wife thought it was too cool. I addressed the issue immediately in a simple, respectful manner – *"Yes sir, I'll take care of that, thank you for letting me know"* – he walked away happy, and I said nothing to anyone about the air. The family had specifically requested the building be cooler due to the large crowd. The wedding was beautiful – went off without a hitch and the designer gown admired by all. We created wedding gowns and veils for a few other clients as we struggled to manage life, work, and the start-up business.

Maintaining separate full-time professions brought us to a realization of how difficult it is to pursue a new business with a strong resolve to be totally dedicated. It's a stressful business anyway because we were dealing with people spending a lot of money and emotions are forever fever pitched. It's rare if everything works out perfectly, and of course I wanted perfection. The expert seamstress had another bout with cancer and was unable to continue working with us. Another factor was the location in our home in Madison and a lack of desire to devote every moment away from our other busy professions to making the business flourish. I was highly interested in design, but our overall focus slowly shifted. Once we moved to our new home and baby Caroline was on her way the business took a back seat and eventually faded. I have never viewed it as a business failure. Instead, a business adventure that taught us valuable lessons about life focus – something about the high-end emphasis became less important to us. A flair for high-end design and observing finer things runs thick within my blood – always near and dear to my heart. Raphael told me his culinary work as a high-end chef was all consuming – hard work he did for over twenty-years, perhaps fond memories of his former work run thick in his blood.

New York City

New York City and Atlanta – both known as centers of high fashion – I was scheduled to visit both cities within a year's time. Both trips part of the business college money scam – the cost of each trip included in the overall tuition rip-off – didn't concern myself with that issue because it would be my first time to visit both cities. The first trip was New York City – also, my first time to fly, and the best part, we didn't have to plan anything. My brother was likely an experienced flyer – probably family vacations and such, but I was a novice – flying never a consideration in my life to this point for any reason. I boarded the airplane as an inexperienced eighteen-year-old – had no idea what I was doing – just followed the lead of my peers thinking they knew what they were doing. The first thing I remember about the flight was bumping my head on the overhead baggage holder – I'm certain someone laughed – I was embarrassed. I don't recall any serious feelings of anxiety or fears about flying – my mother probably had fears, but I don't recall her voicing those – my parents did have a few days free from disapproving eyes.

My mind was totally focused on absorbing the trip, everything I could possibly take in. I knew flying to one of the fashion centers of the world might be my big break – *hey New York City, it's me!* We arrived at our hotel – couldn't stop looking up – enormously tall structures everywhere. I don't remember what floor, but it was high – the cars below looked tiny from our room. In the early morning hours before daylight, I heard vehicle horns – mostly yellow cabs everywhere at all hours – all of it seemingly surreal. My roommate Roy was a very odd man – veteran of Vietnam and probably a person looking to better himself with a business college diploma or whatever the scam college swindled him into. He concerned me a bit with his constant talking and naked yoga. I returned to our room shortly after arriving to find him seated on the floor naked – he asked if I was bothered by him doing this and I said no. Roy seemed basically harmless, but he did walk around our room naked and even stood in the window – of course no one could see him. In the evening he shared a lot of stories about Vietnam – his experience noticeably messed with his mind, and he obviously tried too many illegal drugs. He didn't smoke – which I liked, and he didn't bring any illegal drugs to my knowledge. Roy always tagged along with our group but never really fit in – we tolerated him. He did seem a bit sensitive about certain issues and not highly interested in fashion merchandising. Most of us in the travel group were close to the same age with the exception of Roy who was in his late twenties, and we never looked to him for any wise advice. I felt compelled to treat him respectfully to avoid rifts between us since we were roomies.

During the day we had prescheduled events to attend and some free time. During the first longer period of free time, I wanted to see the big city close up, so I walked and walked until my feet ached – did my sightseeing all alone. As I strolled the crowded sidewalks, I stepped into every famous New York City store I was able to locate during the self-guided tour. The famous window displays of each store were designed and crafted to perfection – much more stunning in person than photos I had seen. I also noticed several people that looked like professional models – female and male – many of them carrying large portfolios. I wondered about their lifestyles. What was it like to walk a New York City runway in designer clothing? One of our scheduled events was a designer's showroom to see an authentic New York City fashion show, the first time anyone in our little ragtag group from Tennessee was exposed to something of this high quality. The music was loud, the models professional, it was incredible. I was totally sold – this was exactly what I desired. I fantasized this could be my fashion show – my designs – my showroom – I loved the thought of the possibility and didn't want the experience to end.

In the evenings after our scheduled dinners, we were free to head out – time to party in New York City. Our first evening out we went to Tavern on the Green, and the place was packed with revelers. I suppose we were officially *"disco hopping"* as we made our way to several other night spots full of partygoers. The music at each location extremely loud – lots of flashing, spinning lights – booze for everyone. Some in our group didn't hold to any limitations regarding alcohol intake – Roy didn't – I did. Each night spot had a large dance floor – we danced on every floor – it was electrifying! Dancing in New York City – how could there be anything better than this? Back in our room, drunk Roy suggested we pool our money and invite a *"lady"* from the street for a visit – *"Absolutely not,"* I insisted. As I pondered the day and attempted to avoid Roy's horny antics, a stream of dialogue developed inside me – not literal words – but an uneasy sense about something different – something I was unable to articulate or clarify – something I didn't fully understand. But I knew it was a yearning for something that wasn't in New York City.

After an exhilarating few days of excitement, I faced the reality of it all ending, the plane separated from the runway and banked toward the big city, I stared at the tiny skyscrapers below – Statue of Liberty – Brooklyn Bridge – lasting memories. The dialogue became a truth deep within my heart – returning to Tennessee I somehow knew I would not be returning to New York City for a fashion design career – it simply wasn't a sensible option. I experienced a brief hint of a lifestyle that had the potential to go in many wrong directions very quickly – something didn't feel exactly right. Perplexed by this nagging truth, I struggled to hang on tightly to a long-held dream – didn't share my truth with anyone. Atlanta was next on the agenda. Perhaps that trip would reveal a clearer path for the future. Time did eventually show me a new direction. I eventually found a new focus – a new career – a new family I never dreamed possible. Reflecting over the years, what I couldn't explain then is now perfectly clear.

Atlanta

Chicago of the South – *The Big Peach* – Atlanta. This time we boarded a charter bus to drive four hours south of Nashville. Our trip basically had the same focus as New York City – minus the concentrated high-end stores and old-time fashion district – this trip primarily focused on the Atlanta Fashion Mart and Atlanta Underground. I knew nothing about these two locations – just heard all the buildup. In Atlanta we were scheduled to participate in a fashion show – nothing like I had previously experienced in the Big Apple. Actually, I don't remember much about this particular trip with respect to the fashion business, but a few other events do stand out. Once again, Roy was my roommate – he shared more war-time stories, some very difficult to believe and some centered around a group of men who must have been very bored at times, perhaps the reason he used drugs so often. Told me about a time someone offered LSD and what his drug induced trip was like – not totally certain he was recalling exact events or what he experienced in his mind. This was the first time for me to be in close proximity with someone who had actually experienced LSD – something I never desired to experience.

One evening in our room alone after dinner another person in our group knocked on the door – everyone was gathering in a particular room to play cards or something like that. I'm not fond of card games, so I waited to join the group. When I decided to check out the gathering, I realized it was actually far more than card games – a marijuana smoking party ensued. I immediately smelled it upon entering the room. Not wanting to appear prudish I chose to stay on the outside of the *Woodstock* circle gathered on the floor – a joint was being passed around. First of all, I had no desire to place my mouth on something several others placed their mouth on. Second, I didn't like the smoke-filled room or smelling it – had grown up smelling cigarette smoke all my life. The joint was offered a few times – I politely declined – to this point in life I had not smoked anything – why start now? I stayed for a short amount of time, made an excuse and returned to my room. Roy stayed and participated. He returned buzzed this time – wasn't surprised – he acted horny again, stripped down and hopped on his bed – he talked about his sex life. I listened, looked at the ceiling not knowing what was true or fabricated. Roy prompted me to share but I shared nothing – he then got off his bed and approached mine, asked if he could join me. I expressed a categorical no without freaking out. The next morning nothing was spoken about the evening before.

The next day we traveled to a large department store and were fitted for two outfits for the fashion show. I clearly remember the guys had a very small dressing room – entirely too crowded and basically on top of each other. I recall changing quickly into a second set of clothing and basically bumping into everyone around me – at least it wasn't a stinky, damp, concrete floor like the boy's locker room in junior high. Also, no bullying issues this time – we were too concerned about getting changed quickly for our return to the runway. For the record, none of us from Tennessee signed a modeling contract and I seriously doubt if any agents were in the small audience.

I don't recall very much about the Fashion Mart other than

its size and lots of venders and opportunities to buy the latest trends and the hottest market items. I do, however, remember Atlanta Underground – a dark, literally underground cave type environment. Restaurants, bars, lots of *dives* – places we probably should not have entered. We visited a few night spots with dance floors and drank alcoholic beverages, danced – but nothing to the same level we experienced in New York City. All in all, Atlanta was fun – not what I had anticipated – somewhat disappointing. I left the city on the charter bus looking forward to being home – not necessarily my home though. A longing for something different continually nagged – something more meaningful – fulfilling – more rewarding. The business college sat next to an elementary school. From a second-floor room I enjoyed sitting at a table by the window watching teachers lead students in and out of the building – why was I so intrigued?

School Teacher

Dreams do come true. My brother told me he attended Catholic schools as a boy and teenager – St. John's Lower and Father Deegan High School. He then attended and graduated from Duke University with an engineering degree, a degree he wasn't thrilled with – he truly wanted to be a trained chef. He convinced his father MSU's culinary school was the right place for him – and he fulfilled his dream. I had to convince myself to fight and scratch for every penny in order to fund my education, no family college fund for me until I married in 1983. My wife worked full-time at Peterbilt Motors and was happy to fund my last year at Lipscomb and pay-off the scam debt so I could achieve my newly-held dream of becoming a teacher. I graduated with a 3.0 primarily due to the fact I wasn't very interested in the required classes one must take as a freshman and sophomore. To buffer those dreadfully boring classes and useless information I made sure to include additional education courses. High interest and nerdy attention to teaching endeavors saved me from failure. I often found myself alone in the library between classes reading educational theory books and classroom management techniques – another nerdy exertion.

The first two years of college I spent at Volunteer State in Gallatin, north of my hometown Madison, tuition much cheaper. During this time, I substituted at a local private elementary school – also an endeavor that saved me from failure. Many teachers possess natural instincts, referred to by some as *withitness* – something universities cannot teach. A principal I worked for used the word often and it describes good pedagogy, but in laymen's terms – you know what's going on all around you. My desire to succeed as an educator guided those practical experiences, also allowing me to gain a level of respect among several professional teachers and administrators. An enthusiastic yearning to have my own classroom and students kept me laser focused and determined nothing would sidetrack my labor.

I arrived at the school location where my student teaching experience would begin – third grade, Mrs. Larson. I clearly recall her welcoming me into her space without any hesitation and much to my surprise, almost handed over the reins from day one – she trusted me greatly, or perhaps she needed a long-awaited break. Whatever the reasoning, I was eager and thankful all at the same time to have this distinct opportunity. It was an outstanding experience because Mrs. Larson allowed me to learn, fail, and work through a lot of the behavioral issues on my own, but I also watched her interactions – how she loved the unlovable. She basically let the classroom become my own. Mrs. Larson's classroom was located in a portion of the original building. Dark thick hardwood encased bulletin boards and chalkboards. A coat room separated from the main room constructed with the same scarred and scratched thick hardwood whispering memories of the past served as storage for books and supplies. The only visible updates were the two window air-conditioning units and solid sections of white durable plastic panels that replaced the old metal framed windows that once occupied the entire outside wall. It was now an excellent place to display student art work and other student accomplishments. I didn't want student teaching to end.

After completing student teaching, I finished the summer quarter at Lipscomb, classes I missed due to seeking additional education classes early on. It was an easy quarter though, and I finally concluded all undergraduate work. Upon graduating, the first in the Morris family to achieve a college degree, I finished all the necessary employment applications for both public and private schools. Mr. Jordan, principal at the elementary school where I completed student teaching told me of an opening that would occur October 1st. His one sixth grade teacher was retiring September 30th. I could hardly believe it, an opportunity to have my own classroom and so soon – could this possibility become reality? At that time Nashville Public Schools hiring was extremely limited and especially for new hires – my chances slim to none. However, I didn't realize a force was pulling political strings – one might call it Divine intervention or perhaps unmitigated persuasion. Whatever it was, I got the job and certainly not due to my sparse resume or credentials. Truth is, principal Jordan worried the *stew* out of the director of elementary education until he finally gave in. Mr. Jordan fought hard for me and won – I was grateful to have my first official teaching job – dreams do come true.

With the job secured – the retiring teacher walked out of her classroom on the last Friday of September with only a purse hanging from her half-left arm – a disability she managed to overcome while achieving a full-career teaching. She left everything for her replacement – all mine now. My wife and I went on Saturday to convert the classroom and worked all day – the room had to reflect my style. The portable classroom was in need of a much-needed update and we somehow managed to overcome the dullness with updated bulletin boards, a new seating arrangement, and two ferns. Thirty-four curious and expectant sixth graders trudged in – my official teaching career underway. I was thrilled and contented – no desire to change course. Graduate school was my next college experience twelve years later – an administrative leadership degree. A new dream birthed – a new path I never expected or thought possible. But I first needed several years of practice before I was persuaded to climb the education ladder.

Year three, I paused, looked at the old, worn concrete steps leading down to a door below the school cafeteria. Why had I never given any attention to those steps? My mind immediately recalled the steps discovered by Howard Carter in 1922 that led to the tomb of an ancient king. A colossal idea popped into my head, but I needed to see behind the door – just as Carter. The custodian reluctantly opened it and my idea grew bigger than what I originally envisioned. Was it possible? Could I actually pull this off? Would the principal approve it? My mind raced with lots of crazy ideas of how to make this idea become reality. I went to the principal with a plan. One of the first units in social studies in sixth grade is ancient civilizations – ancient Egypt always a favorite because the students enjoyed it most and loved learning about the mummification process. I presented a plan to the principal to teach an integrated unit of study centered around ancient Egypt – create an Egyptian tomb and encompass all the subject areas – she loved the idea too and said go for it. When I presented the plan to the students and what it would require, they were enthusiastically all in and when asked for a commitment by show of hands, thirty-four students shot a hand up. An old boiler basement, now just a storage room, would become a pharaoh's tomb, the inspiration, King Tut. The first semester we primarily used for planning the project and collecting lots of materials and large cardboard boxes. The students' enthusiasm overflowed most days.

In the words of a Tennessean staff writer, *"We didn't have a dead pharaoh anywhere around the school and all students were accounted for and there were no missing teachers – they had to make a mummy.*" Everybody in the class had a hand in building the mummy – the cheese cloth wrapping was dipped in a secret sixth-grade solution of white glue and water. We ended up with something that came awfully close to a genuine mummy. We used an empty room next to a first-grade class just inside the building close to our portable classroom – a perfect set-up for making tomb props. The mummy needed a cardboard sarcophagus with two inner coffins, and a crook and flail to represent Egyptian royalty. Each of those items needed elaborate Egyptian paintings and lots of ancient hieroglyphics – lost count of how many cans of gold spray paint we used. We created our own papyrus from brown paper grocery bags by soaking it in water and gently crumpling the paper, repeating the process and drying gave it an ancient, crinkled papyrus appearance. Then the students added colorful Egyptian art and hieroglyphics.

Another major task was learning how to present this information and the elaborate creations to our visitors. The task of teaching public speaking skills – how to project and speak slow enough to be heard and understood. Every student was assigned a specific job for the upcoming tours. Invitations were sent to all of Nashville's government office holders and to local public and private schools – of course every class at our school would visit first to give us ample practice time. There were certainly moments when I thought we had taken on too much. Then the acceptance calls started coming in – we were thrilled that so many accepted our invitation as the May calendar quickly filled.

Assigned student greeters met our guests as they arrived and directed them to the start point – students were positioned at several locations throughout the tour providing detailed information, explaining displays, and answering questions. One group was in charge of music and slowly removing the lid of the sarcophagus to reveal the mummy in the grand finale of the tour. I remember the students being overly excited each time a new tour was about to begin. I was amazed how the students embraced their specific roles – the special education students especially seemed overjoyed with their roles and fully participated. For all their work, there was a fun culminating event – we traveled to the Ramesses Exhibit in Memphis, Tennessee. I loved the closing words of the Tennessean article referring to our trip, *"It will give them* (the sixth graders) *a chance to see if ancient Egyptians really live up to Neely's Bend standards."* My original work highlighted again in the newspaper but this time a school project instead of fashion designs.

During our tour of the exhibit, I overheard an official docent say how well informed our students were – a heartwarming moment of teacher pride. One of the greatest rewards was to hear from students many years later say they have never forgotten this experience and how it enriched their overall knowledge. I was enriched as well by their enthusiasm and total dedication to excellence – many hours of hard work and stress paid off with a high level of hands-on accomplishment. Maria Montessori provides a fitting quote, *"The greatest sign of success for a teacher is to be able to say, 'The children are now working as if I did not exist.'"* In this particular instance it's precisely what occurred.

The pseudo-Egyptian tomb project closed forever; suddenly I felt consumed with an overwhelming sense to move beyond my three-year stint. Was it possible to top what just transpired? I was restless for something new. Neely's Bend Elementary where my career began as a sixth-grade teacher – wonderful memories but I was ready for change – desired a new challenge. I applied for a transfer and was granted a move to Delamere Elementary in the eastern part of our district – the school had grown to be the largest elementary in the county. I started in third grade until an additional sixth grade was needed – I quickly volunteered realizing my preferred grade level was sixth. The Delamere building was undergoing renovations and additions, only fourth-grade classes remained at the original location. Everyone else was temporarily moved to an old vacated high school building. The large structure provided a massive amount of space for elementary students to navigate, but there was something else that loomed larger – Carlton Reynolds, the executive principal – two meek and mild assistant principals served under his subjugation.

He was a domineering figure both in personality and strongly held beliefs, his authoritarian dictates ruled the day. He only supported teachers that fully supported him or pretended to do so. The two assistants carried out onerous, menial tasks he didn't wish to handle – both knew who was clearly in charge by marching to his commands. Otherwise, there would be no chance of advancement for any future role. To my knowledge neither person ever challenged him regarding his demands. I discovered his distaste for teachers who smoked, he didn't particularly like black teachers, and was not fond of male teachers if they had domineering personalities that might compete with his – there were two of us. In contrast, he was very fond of attractive white female teachers who were viewed by some as *brownnosers*.

"Yes Sir." The answer Mr. Reynolds preferred. A large physical presence and intensity afforded him instant command of a room – dress coat typically hanging slightly off one shoulder. He often popped into classrooms unannounced with some type of pronouncement – didn't matter what the teacher was doing or how engaged the students might be – he shifted the focus of attention to him. Technology was his number one priority – although, not certain he actually knew very much about it. He wanted computers throughout the

building so that he could tout Delamere's cutting-edge approach. One day in his typical mad rush style he stopped me in the hallway to ask if I wanted six computers from the other building – he insisted these had to be moved immediately – I said *no sir* instead of the answer he wanted because my classroom was not equipped for six additional computers – our relationship began to sour after the exchange. A domineering male personality and reason challenged a reckless and cavalier dictate.

It was December, year two of my tenure under the rule of a *dictator*. I realized staying at Delamere would not be best for me after attending the Christmas breakfast where he used unauthorized funds, according to a reliable source, for the festive meal. He never invited custodial or cafeteria staff. Those jobs were beneath him, and I finally discovered this injustice as I walked out of the library for a quick break. Releasing a waft of southern cuisine into the hallway I nearly stepped on the dust mop gliding past the door – my stomach full of country ham and scrambled eggs – we both did a quick, uneasy downward gaze of embarrassment. Two years in the old high school building was enough time to realize I didn't wish to be in a renovated building with Mr. Reynolds. That same year the district opened a new elementary school in the area which reduced our large staff by almost half. We were asked by Human Resources who was willing to take a voluntary transfer – my name was first on the list. Not my desire to be under an autocratic, unprofessional, *dictator regime* – but I did value learning something I never wanted to become.

Throughout our vacation in the Ozark Mountains with Pam's parents I knew time was drawing near for transfers to end. I called central office to discover they had misplaced my contact information. I was given the choice of three inner-city schools and chose Jere Baxter, sixth grade, a lesser drive from our new home among tall trees. I quickly realized my choice was a mistake. Jere Baxter was a school in desperate need of strong leadership but instead had a mild-mannered weak leader who understood everyone from a counseling point of reference. He told the entire staff in our initial faculty meeting how wonderful it was that I chose to be at Jere Baxter – true, but not in the way he led my new colleagues to believe. The poverty level was nearly 100% which aggravated any attempts to teach in traditional ways – I simply wasn't prepared for the bombardment of social and emotional turmoil and mayhem that existed.

On several occasions I needed heart-to-heart discussions with the principal – he was a good listener – a good man. I truly believe he empathized with my plight – he just didn't have suitable solutions. One thing he did was plant a seed – he said to me one day, *"Mr. Morris, you think like an adminis-trator – you should pursue that avenue."* I truly appreciated his trust in my ability to lead but was not in a position to think beyond the extremely difficult and challenging circumstances. What I did know beyond any doubt, another transfer was necessary or my career in public education would be jeopardized by me. On most days I forced myself to direct the car into the parking lot – then I prayed – one day I almost drove away.

The director of elementary staffing reached out and took my hand to assure me she would do what she could to make a transfer occur. I told her in the politest terms leaving the district was the only option if a transfer didn't occur. I interviewed at Dan Mills for a fifth-grade position and was granted the transfer. This principal was all business and highly professional at all times. She allowed teachers to do their jobs without a lot of interference but was stringent on district mandates. One example was leaving a class unattended – I totally agreed with her but reality must be dealt with using a little common sense. At times a teacher needs a personal break – it's typically understood among colleagues that another teacher is capable and willing to watch two classes while the other teacher takes a quick restroom break. We managed this minor adjustment without incident. During faculty meetings, standing with perfect posture, she would rattle off district mandates without allowing any discussion or debate. I raised my hand once and asked if we were going to wash their clothes next – my colleagues laughed in agreement, fully understanding my satire and point of concern – the principal didn't find the comment amusing. My veiled prophesy became a reality – within a few years schools in high poverty areas installed washing machines and dryers. A lack of empathy and obliviousness toward my past plight blinded current reason.

The principal surprised me by asking if I would serve as designee in her absence – I was honored, but I didn't have a master's degree in administration. She said it was her choice, trusted my leadership abilities and didn't realize she cultivated the seed planted at Jere Baxter I had all but dismissed. Walking in her shoes changed my perspective. I left Dan Mills after five years, pursued a master's degree while teaching in a private school – remained in private education sixteen years. Returning to public education I was acutely aware of the privileged but longed to serve and be immersed with the underprivileged once again. I was better equipped with a healthier empathy and understanding for the devastating plight and hopelessness poverty brings to so many lives. Returning to the heritage which had originally grounded me in life allowed me an opportunity to employ a level of maturity I did not initially possess.

While at Dan Mills Elementary I met Janis Pickney – we were hallway neighbors. Shortly after meeting we discovered some interesting connections. Janis grew up in the Madison community as I did and lived in a neighborhood where we shared several close acquaintances. Janis's father owned a bar a few blocks from the big church I attended – I'm certain my father visited several times. Janis attended elementary school six years at Amqui where I landed as a public-school principal after sixteen years in private. She also graduated from Madison High School just as I did. Her classroom being next to mine allowed us to divide the fifth-grade subjects and switch students at mid-day – we taught our favorite subjects and reduced planning time significantly. Janis smoked, drank heavily (after work), partied late, and dressed everyday as if she was going to a cocktail party. In spite of our purported differences, we melded quickly because I seemed to have a clearer understanding of her lifestyle than others. I stood determined to forge a close bond since we shared students, and as a result, we grew to become best friends.

My wife and I met Janis and her third husband Ray after work for dinner on several occasions – our relationship outside of school worked well because I respected her differences and she respected mine. My wife worked with her first husband at Peterbilt Motors. Janis assumed I had grown up a child of privilege – I must have displayed my pompous attitude on occasions. When I shared truth of my childhood Janis appeared shocked. Little did we know how my story would change in a few short years – that my brother grew up just as she suspected I did. After five years at Dan Mills, restlessness rose again – ready for another change but dreaded sharing my decision with Janis. When I gently broke the news of my departure, she said without hesitation she would retire if I left – and she did.

I moved from public education to a private Christian school, but we purposely maintained a close relationship until she died. Janis asked me to preach her husband's funeral, and I was honored to do so. She told me that same day I would preach her funeral too. I had the privilege and honor to fulfill her request. With a heavy heart I shared my fondness, memories sprinkled with her extravagance. Our professional relationship and friendship operated perfectly. I absolutely cherished the uniqueness of our bond because it was at all times deeply rooted in heartfelt mutual respect – I think of Janis often.

A dear friend told me in confidence a long-time teacher was leaving her sixth-grade position – thought I might be interested – my interest was immediately piqued. I officially applied at the private Christian school knowing if hired I would take an eight thousand dollar cut and perhaps more considering the loss of benefits and retirement. I had grown increasingly weary with the day-to-day struggles of public education and was close to total burnout. My wife was ready for me to make a change but wasn't truly sold on the idea of private education, although our daughter had been immersed in private since age three, now in kindergarten. After a few serious financial discussions and some tense, but respectful back and forth debates she was willing but still cautious. I was hired as the new sixth grade math and science teacher. Stepping into the private world of Christian education required a major paradigm shift.

The first official day was an amazing, eye-opening realization of profound differences. As I wrote class rules on the board I paused, slowly turned to look at my homeroom students, everyone, sharpened pencil in hand, obediently writing what I had just written because I told them to write. They only paused because I did. I finished writing rules – everyone completed what I wrote without a word, without touching someone else, without making any odd noises to distract others, without telling me they didn't have the correct supplies, or no supplies – they wrote without incident – I was stunned. During my first break I immediately walked to the principal's office and shared my first teaching experience. She listened intently, smiled and affirmed what I experienced is the norm. Emotion welled – I needed a tissue from her desk to clear my eyes. She repeated my story numerous times. I was totally ensnared and hooked by my first experience. As always, reality sets in and some of the usual challenges of teaching become obvious even in a pristine setting – nothing, however, close to what I left behind in public education. I was now actually teaching and having fun doing so – I looked forward to each day and the eagerness to learn by the majority of students. Sixth graders are a delightful bunch to teach anyway because they have just enough childlike qualities remaining but are also moving quickly into the wonderment of budding adolescence – an interesting contrast to witness.

Experiencing less job-related stress led me to pursue a graduate degree in administrative leadership. I was able to balance work while earning credentials to become a principal. Trevecca Nazarene University in Nashville accepted my application, and I passed the Miller's Analogy Test – barely. I was in and loved the process, treasuring every moment of higher learning. Devoured all the theory books, writing all the research and opinion papers, sharing insights and experiences – it was a nerdy endeavor for certain, and I was passionate about every dot and tittle – ready to conquer the world of graduate education. I graduated with a perfect 4.0. How does a poor little trifling, fearful trailer park kid manage such a feat?

During my last set of classes I was told about a principal position at another private school on the far southeast side of the county, several miles from my home, but nonetheless, I was interested in at least gaining the experience of applying. I previously attended church with the current president of the school but didn't know him well. He taught a young adult class I attended for a few months – we easily reconnected by phone, and he invited me to interview. The interview lasted over two hours and included a tour of the school. The actual position was principal of the elementary, grades PreK to fourth. Before the interview ended, I was offered the job and my mind suddenly filled with so many questions I couldn't answer. Am I actually ready to do this? Why would I take a job so far from my home? Do I really want to uproot my daughter from a school she's been in since PreK? How will I convince my wife to agree to this change? She had just agreed to a major shift two years prior. Would we need to move closer to the school? What about my future at the current private Christian school? Did I have a future at the current school? How would I tell them I'm leaving for another private school? A plethora of unanswered questions raced through my mind over and over on the long drive home – I told my wife.

Principal

Desire roared deep within my soul – a yearning, a throbbing, a sense of calling I couldn't shake. The seed Mr. Northern planted grew, no longer dormant. An opportunity to actually be a school principal. I wanted this more than anything else in the world. So many ideas and practices to put into action – theory and opinion could now become reality. My idealistic mentality already racing to the start line – just a few hurdles to overcome. Her reluctant stare coupled with an awkward silence made the moment seem like forever as I waited for a response – *"It's so far from where we live!"* I agreed but believed we could make it work. The salary increase made the opportunity more appealing, but the distance and increased responsibilities for both of us remained hurdles. One additional hurdle – our daughter. After a day or two of reflection, we agreed to accept this new challenge, we shared the decision with our second grader – not happy. All her friends left behind – that's what kids think about. The only school she had ever known was being taken away. The only consolation at the moment was the fact I would be her principal for third and fourth grade and work at the same school she attended. My wife, daughter and myself visited the school and were given the full tour of facilities. A new calling was now becoming our new reality.

Shortly after finalizing the hiring process, we boarded a plane with my wife's parents and her sister's family for a Colorado vacation in Pagosa Springs. My mind still racing with all sorts of thoughts and plans for the future. I noticed on my second tour of the school the large meeting area directly in front of the elementary offices. The president said it was known as the *"commons"* – I thought a dull, uninviting name for children's chapel and other elementary events. The open space was big enough to accommodate everyone in the elementary school. *Commons* just didn't sound like an appropriate name for elementary students – name change a must. As we walked around the beautiful resort in Pagosa Springs each area had a designated name – one caught my eye – *The Eagle's Nest*. That's it! An appropriate name for a gathering place for elementary students in a private Christian school – the eagle already its beloved mascot. The name spoke to me as a warm, nurturing place for little people – like a real eagle's nest would be for little eaglets. The first major change – rename the Commons – one of many changes that to my surprise challenged a well-established status quo. I faced a mammoth learning curve and shackling force I wasn't prepared to tackle or fully grasp – at least not in the beginning. Battle strategies needed to be sharpened and improved as I contemplated my new opponent.

She swiftly pulled me into an empty office across the hallway from the business office, and I was promptly reprimanded by an office staff person. Allegedly, I'd embarrassed her daughter at dismissal the day before – I didn't know her daughter. It was immediately clear to me this impromptu scolding had a well-defined purpose, *put me in my place*, plainly communicate change is seldom tolerated, and who possessed the real power. I suppose asking someone to move a car to a different place was offensive, and she tattled to her mother whom she knew carried more power than had officially been granted. My second battle was a disorganized and chaotic dismissal procedure – lots of elementary children standing everywhere, teachers randomly stopping cars to load someone – a process that lasted too long, a change for the sake of safety was imperative. I remained polite but not apologetic because I did nothing wrong – the new motto for anyone receiving pushback about updates in dismissal policy procedures – it's all for the safety of children. This was not the last or most serious confrontation over change.

Within a few weeks of school starting, I noticed the usual things new principals begin to notice. With an enthusiastic spirit I began to appropriately address issues for the good of everyone involved. That's what new principals should do – right? My close observations slowly brought me to a realization the elementary school had operated with a lackadaisical type atmosphere since its beginning in 1973. Pushing for real change would not be easy but obviously necessary. I decided to move slowly, gain support from a few influential, long-term staff members, and take down one by one *sacred cows* that existed – unfortunately this *barn* was full. Several of the so-called sacred cows existed within school policies but others were considered untouchable employees – reality check for faculty and staff – no one is untouchable.

One such person was a long-term teacher. On the surface all seemed well, beloved by many, and often received several requests from parents. This teacher, a classic self-promoter, used the school for personal advantage and gain. Once I started receiving direct complaints from a group of parents, I decided it was only fair to make the teacher aware so that concerns could be appropriately addressed. Nothing in the personnel file indicated anything negative. Teacher files were shockingly sparse – another challenge that needed a fix. The teacher consistently denied all complaints – never once accepted responsibility for any concerns. After finishing the first year as principal my daughter had also successfully adjusted and completed her first year at our new school. I purposely placed her in this teacher's classroom with all the complaints – it was to show support and allow me a direct look into the issues if indeed there were issues to be addressed. Surely there would be no major issues since my daughter was in the class.

My daughter is easy-going, laid-back, a type of child that didn't stress about very much. I wasn't sacrificing my daughter's future on the altar – she would be fine – and she did survive. The school year for this particular teacher went fairly well with only a few minor issues – nothing that was overly serious. The usual quirkiness, an overabundance of busy work, general disorganization, lots of food and pandering to the boss was the norm. I began to realize there was a desire to draw me into this world like so many others in the past – I resisted the tugs. Regrettably, the next few years proved much worse, numerous complaints steadily increased to the point that serious conversations occurred, many tears were shed. Everything continually denied – the file grew. I meticulously documented issues and consistently shared these with the school president. We faced a barrage of issues and complaints surrounding this teacher.

Coming to terms with truth highlighted what I quickly learned about the school shortly after arriving, many issues were ignored – this teacher one of many. But the board hired someone in leadership refusing to ignore glaring issues any longer – enough, I told myself. I delivered a bold edict to the president that something must be done and if not, I would not place another child in the teacher's classroom – it would be his responsibility – risky move? Probably so. Complaints non-stop at this point. He was slow to act but finally responded to the next major incident in early April – gone – a long career finished at the school. For seven long years I attempted to encourage, offer advice, issue directives, observed closely to determine if changes were implemented, offered a different position – all to no avail. The teacher was compensated for their entire contract – the school happily did that hoping to move beyond.

A well-suited substitute finished the school year. We received a full-on bombardment of concerns and complaints regarding the decision to terminate. How could we do something like this to such a beloved, long-term teacher? Others spoke off the record thanking us for finally taking a stand for the school. The teacher with guidance from church elders sued the Board of Directors, president, and me – a regretful and sad time in the school's history. We eventually settled the suit to avoid dragging the teacher's name and reputation into public record. As part of the settlement the teacher requested the school president provide a letter of recommendation – he composed a one sentence letter stating the dates of employment and his signature. The teacher retired from public schools after a short second career.

"Some Christian school you are; it's not very Christ like to treat us this way!" I sought wise counsel from my former principal at the Christian school where I taught sixth grade for two years. She told me I must not only be an advocate for the child struggling with behavioral issues but for everyone paying tuition. In other words, it was my responsibility to advocate for all students – not just the one. After many weeks of attempts to reconcile this dilemma, it was my decision to expel a first grader for defecating on the bathroom floor seven times. Of course, many other issues existed, simply more than we were equipped to handle. His grandparents paid tuition and obviously didn't agree with my decision – I merely advocated for all the students being affected by him and his teacher. Unfortunately, life for him didn't improve.

After eleven years as elementary principal I had opportunity to apply for the top position – I sensed a readiness and preparedness I had not before – Pam would be an impeccable *first lady*. The new role now afforded me full access to opposition from all three schools and to everyone in-between. Everyone with any type of stake in the process, including parents, would have access to me and likely take full advantage of the opportunity when they felt so compelled. On one occasion I was told in no uncertain terms I was taking the school straight to hell – the reason was over prayer – prayer led by a spiritually mature, beyond her years, high school student. Her father happened to be a local minister and very supportive of our school. Our school held to some strict conservative views regarding women and their public involvement in prayer and teaching. Females were not allowed to teach in chapel unless it was designated all-female nor could they pray publicly if males were present. These polices were ludicrous. No, our school was not a cult or located in Iran or Saudi Arabia – it was located in a southeastern suburb of Nashville. The office staff person meant every word spoken, and those words were meant to hurt – but I knew the accuser well and maintained professional composure – chose not to address the student or any future situations of that type. With a similar disposition, a high school teacher expressed concern for one of our parents renting a venue for a dance after our senior banquet. I told the teacher it was not our event, so no concerns – not the answer she desired – perhaps she thought we were on a fast road to hell too.

On another occasion, after a two-hour lecture by the board chairman I voiced one simple question, *"Are you asking me to override the high school principal's decision?"* His answer was no, but I knew otherwise. His grandson had been suspended two days for pulling sports pants down on a female peer in the hallway. She was wearing gym shorts underneath, but he didn't know it – that didn't matter. His grandfather was concerned this discipline infraction might jeopardize a potential baseball scholarship – the grandson did not land in the major leagues as grandpa envisioned – not certain if a scholarship was offered. The same board chairman called furious because I had moved forward on offering an employment contract to a new football coach he didn't agree to hire. As president it was my final decision on new hires, not the board or board chairman. I held my ground, and the new coach accepted his contract. After my eventual departure from the school the coach this particular board member wanted was hired – he lasted one school year – the football program and school overall suffered tremendously under his leadership.

During a quarterly board meeting I suggested the school chorus sing at several local churches to promote the school with the potential of increasing enrollment. A new board chairman objected to my suggestion. His son was a member of the chorus. His exact words, *"My son will not sing under a denominational roof!"* I was dumbfounded with only one thought – how utterly idiotic and stupid can one be? I basically fought the board on so many issues during my fourteen years in leadership – the status quo had to be challenged. A divorce policy not allowing anyone divorced or married to someone divorced could work at the school – again, I promise we were not a cult. A policy stating what type of church every employee must attend – it was all about the name – and it didn't seem to matter if the person occasionally attended – only the name, *"Church of Christ"* on paper mattered the most. I knew several staff with sparse connections to a church.

October 2010, my third year to serve as president, a general meeting with three board members occurred in order to clarify a few routine issues – nothing serious. The meeting was cordial, and I shook hands with each board member as they stepped out of the office. Lynn, the last board member to exit, shook my hand and paused; his eyes captured my eyes.

"Jim, you're doing a good job. Don't worry about anything, okay." I believed the supportive gesture but not necessarily the other gate keepers. Something was different about his tone, even though I knew he personally backed my efforts. As I turned and looked across the plush setting with a view, I somehow knew it was time – time to give up the battle. I chose to submit a resignation letter to the board in January 2011 – fulfill my contract and turn over the reins to the next enthusiastic president. I accomplished all that I could, it was now up to someone else to fight the well-established power structures – leadership in private Christian education concluded. Fourteen years of life dedicated to seeking necessary, constructive change – considered *evil endeavors* at this school – but I harbored no bitterness or regrets. The uniqueness of my transition into the president's role was an out-and-out major life changing shift. It's a story all its own of emotionally charged experiences. Suddenly, there I was in uncharted territory I had never navigated, an executive leadership role demanding every morsel of my life and more, but I was willing to climb the mountain – didn't fully grasp the steepness.

Mountain Top

Stepping into an executive leadership role is a mountain top experience that required me to also step into a deep sea of uncertainty. The juxtaposition was profound, eye-opening, and jaw-dropping, all of which I experienced first-hand on more than one occasion within three short years. A lifetime of insecurities screamed this can't be done – I'm not good enough – don't measure up – not equipped to handle the complexities. Doubt-filled questions uncontrollably erupted. Why did they want someone like me to lead the school forward? How could a former indigent trailer park kid do a job with so much at stake? How would someone without church pedigree be suitable to oversee a long-standing, strictly conservative, white-washed machine? I didn't have answers to those doubt-filled questions, but another voice deep within at the same moment articulated acceptance and courage in a calm quiet tone urging me to say yes to this monumental challenge. I listened and the little insecure boy retreated momentarily.

The new title afforded me power that I knew must be used wisely but in strategic and astute ways. My mind raced with ideas, but I knew what must come first, and I needed full support from the board of directors to make an audacious move but a necessary one – and especially within a few days following my job acceptance. The machine I now commandeered was running desperately low on oil – in much need of a major overhaul – not a simple tune-up. The more I pushed forward with the plan I sensed God's will being revealed. A clear message was planted upon my heart and mind. Was this the moment I had been prepared to accomplish? A part of me still screaming impossible. At this juncture in the history of the school no one entrenched in the school's past was listening or responding to God's call for change. An overwhelming majority of staff and patrons didn't recognize the norm of mundane efforts and weak spirituality – most seemingly satisfied with lackluster efforts.

New leadership was necessary in order to pry loose corroded long-held positions of rigidness that for too long choked the very life blood from its existence. I couldn't speak those exact words publicly, only veiled references to a few individuals and to one fully trusted confidant within the walls of the institution. One thing I learned quickly by way of several direct hits and resulting bruises, one cannot stay on the mountain top. Honeymoons end. Machines must be serviced often to work well. Layers of old paint need to be scraped away before adding a new coat. It's lonely on the mountain top because the weight of so many people, complex situations, considerations, major decisions, and day-to-day perplexities ultimately rest upon the one at the top. Any expectation to please everyone will never be achieved. I knew as executive leader I'd be miserable if my goal was to please all the barking voices. At this institution the barks were all within walking distance – sometimes too close for comfort.

I first spoke to the vice-president of financial affairs. We had formed a good working relationship early, and he was pleased I accepted the new role. Sam was a pure numbers nerd in every way and preferred to work behind the scenes. He knew where every penny the school possessed was located. He also knew the detailed history of our financial situation and what was necessary to move forward. I trusted him completely and he trusted me. He was the first to hear my plan because it required his approval on a sticky salary situation that had the potential to cause a major upheaval. He agreed to the plan. Spoke directly to the board chairman next. He seemed delighted that I desired a new administrative staff to lead each individual school. The high school principalship would be a fairly easy shift because the current principal decided to retire. The elementary school principalship was an easier choice because I already targeted my replacement if and when I moved to the president's role. The messy decision involved the middle school. I was about to step where no man had stepped before and survived – a lot of undeserved power rested within the middle school office.

This was territory within a few steps of my domain perceived by many as untouchable. Entrenched might be the best way to label it. He was deeply-rooted in a position he had no desire of exiting until retirement. The president who hired me attempted to pry him loose, and it ultimately led to the loss of his job. This principal's entrenchment was primarily based in his success as the girls' softball coach, and he was a good Christian man. I was impressed by and honored his coaching success because he brought unprecedented acclaim and attention to our institution. After eleven years, I knew he was incapable of doing what I would insist he do as an administrator – he didn't possess the skill sets I needed to achieve my vision for the administrative staff. Enough administrative philosophy differences were between us to warrant this significant change – a skillful maneuver on my part to protect his integrity was required. I moved quickly.

We met on his turf, and I told him there would be a significant change in the administrative staff. He stared with a look of what I interpreted as fear then nervousness. He interrupted once to ask if he was being fired – a recognition of my new level of power – I said no. What I carefully explained was his skills could be better utilized by overseeing our high school sports programs with the title of high school athletic director. He would also likely teach physical education again – his background. And he could be utilized in several other capacities that he previously felt very comfortable doing. He asked if his salary was being reduced and I assured him it would stay the same – preapproved by the VP of financial affairs or until he officially started drawing social security. I also shared there was no reason to force him into all the changes I had in mind. Why deal with all the stress of change at this late juncture? By the end of the conversation, he seemed somewhat reassured by the plan but slightly shaken due to the abrupt change he didn't see coming. We shook hands, and I shared how much I appreciated his long service, coaching expertise, and overall dedication to the school and how I looked forward to working with him in a new capacity. I walked out of his soon to be vacated office and took a deep breath of relief. The most difficult phase of my whirlwind plan complete. I penetrated *hallowed* ground, *slayed* a giant, and survived to tell it. Spiritual author Eugene Peterson reflects on an ancient biblical story, *"Only a prayer-saturated imagination accounts for what made holy history that day in the Valley of Elah..."* [*] My *holy* day occurred in a middle school – no smooth stones necessary. Power taken down. I was enormously pleased and thankful.

She listened well – pondered and also patiently tolerated my musings, sometimes tirades on a range of subjects, most often related to our work or spiritual matters. She didn't allow her personal convictions to collide with mine. Instead, she broadened her own sphere of thinking and understanding without compromise. When I pondered my potential long-

---

[*] Eugene Peterson, *Leap Over a Wall: Earthly Spirituality for Everyday Christians* (New York: HarperCollins Publishers, 1997), p. 45.

term future at Southeastern Christian, I began to take notice, to target her as a replacement for the elementary principal's role. Skilled leaders should develop other skilled leaders to step in when needed. That's exactly what I set out to accomplish. My choice for elementary school principal was easy because I considered this choice long before it was necessary. She was a highly professional teacher I observed for eleven years. Without any hesitation I approached her to ask if she would take the position. I handed an envelope to her which I had placed a new salary to contemplate. Salary was not her major focus. She taught Transition One at that time – a class for students needing additional time to grow and mature before taking on the rigors of first grade. I had no doubts regarding her ability to shift to an administrative role – she had a few.

Throughout the past eleven years I witnessed up close her skilled pedagogy in the classroom, how she treated peers, and how she consistently functioned on a day-to-day basis. My brain, full of all the data I needed, made my decision an easy one. Early in our careers at SCA, we began to have numerous conversations about leadership topics in general and around specific issues pertaining to our school and especially during the two years when she completed a Master's Degree in school leadership. She's a thinker – liked to gather facts before making decisions. She is excellent at knowing just the right questions to ask – sometimes the hard questions most are not willing to ask. I would often allow her to think with me over certain situations when I needed serious advice before moving forward. I could do that because we had developed a deep mutual trust, and I knew she would never divulge any sensitive information. Simply stated, my comments were safe – no fears of retribution or slander. She is excellent at looking between the lines and seeing things others do not. She once advised me privately of a situation occurring all around me, but I was totally unaware. I soon learned she was completely accurate. She never exploited our friendship for professional gain. Both inside and outside of her classroom she never raised her voice at students but maintained excellent behavioral management. Students in her classroom were always well-behaved, even the most challenging. I finally decided it must be consistency. Students knew exactly what to expect regarding her behavior, and they were clear on their own behavior and learning expectations. Bundling all her expertise into one, I knew she was the right person for the job.

I'm glad she said yes because I wanted our professional relationship to continue growing just as our personal friendship had grown during the past eleven years. I was tremendously excited to now have a highly competent leader committed to stepping into my former position. She would be the first person to say she is humbled and somewhat embarrassed by my description of her natural abilities and professional skills. I'm thankful as a leader I was alert to her skills and recognized her abilities to move to the next level of leadership. While her overall leadership style looks different than mine, we were in full agreement as to the focus and future of the school. Always extremely measured in her responses, leads with a quiet tone and soft touch, tough questions one-on-one, and holds high expectations for everyone under her observant watch. We attained three years in our new roles before departing. Another insightful quote by Peterson on the biblical friendship of Jonathan and David may be the most appropriate way to describe our association, *"And then someone enters our life who isn't looking for someone to use, is leisurely enough to find out what's really going on in us, is secure enough not to exploit our weaknesses or attack our strengths, recognizes our inner life and understands the difficulty of living out our inner convictions, confirms what's deepest within us. A friend."* [†]

The current football coach had expressed interest in pursuing the high school principal's position. He was next on my list, and we talked briefly. I was satisfied with his leadership abilities and all I had observed would meet the challenges in the high school. I offered the position and without hesitation he accepted. He asked to remain in his head football coaching position – I agreed. In retrospect, it may have been better to seek a new coach, but with so many major changes occurring it seemed best to move forward without an additional search for a high-profile position. Prior to my conversation with him, an unexpected clash of *powers* occurred in the out-going president's office. I walked in with a few transition type questions and noticed a large stack of folders on his partially empty desktop. He mentioned he was searching through applications for high school principal candidates. He was planning to schedule an interview with someone from Florida. I paused, mentally collected my thoughts, then told him I would like to take care of that process. He took a deep breath, placed both hands on the stack of folders and shoved the stack across the desk toward me – clearly a testy moment of irritability – his facial expression spoke volumes. In an instant, his grip on power was relinquished with a symbolic shove. In that brief space of time, he momentarily forgot how I had recently sat for hours in quiet reverence honoring him and his family during the darkest trial of grief for the loss of an adult beloved son – but that's okay. I knew he needed space to grieve his lesser loss of nine years on the mountain top. I knew this wasn't easy for him. In a respectful tone I said thank you and quietly slipped out. He was still my superior and I didn't need to tread on his last days, hours, and minutes – no additional conversations

---

[†] Eugene Peterson, *Leap Over a Wall: Earthly Spirituality for Everyday Christians* (New York: HarperCollins Publishers, 1997), p. 54.

occurred between us. I set up a temporary office in the library after vacating mine in the elementary building.

The first professional conversation with the new high school principal after accepting involved some long-held concerns for the school that I now had direct influence over. I didn't wish to dictate verbatim, but I wanted to be clear on the issues most concerning. One such issue was the overall resistance for what I perceived as a systemic lack of academic support for struggling students. Too many high school students dropped out because the academic rigor was too challenging for many coming from public or home schooling. Several teachers in the high school claimed to offer academic support, but I didn't believe it was consistently accessible. The data simply didn't support their claims. Several teachers in the high school could easily be labelled academic elitists. He agreed with my concerns, we discussed potential plans to encourage higher levels of academic support – gaining that support from stubborn high school teachers might be another steep mountain to climb.

We also discussed a delicate situation involving a teacher. After receiving an anonymous letter stating we should check on a relationship involving a roommate, I decided it was best for me to conduct a quick check of the teacher's social media. Nothing particularly worrisome, but we did see a few photos posted of a recent cruise with the roommate. I spoke with the teacher privately and any involvement beyond being just roommates was denied. We ended our investigation, although I did make the principal aware of a situation involving the same teacher that occurred five years prior. Again, nothing serious, but the teacher was seen by me in a park where I occasionally rode bicycles with my wife and daughter. The teacher immediately left the location once we were spotted. This particular area of the park was known as a safe spot for nefarious networking – to my satisfaction all concerns were resolved.

Being an employee in a private Christian school requires adherence to whole set of different standards related to personal behavior than that of public schools – at times forcing difficult conversations. One quick change was made that didn't earn me any points with high school staff. I eliminated the copier position – a person who copied mounds of worksheets for teachers – it simply wasn't necessary, the new principal agreed. Professional leadership takes one into messy endeavors – often more so in Christian based institutions. Anyone unwilling to confront difficult situations should not be in the leadership arena. Private Christian schools are certainly not immune to the pitfalls of life circumstances. He remained in his dual role of principal and coach two years then transitioned out of the coaching responsibilities. We sustained a healthy, supportive professional relationship for three years until we parted ways with the school and both of us returned to the public arena.

My last hiring task was slightly more challenging, I would enter again *hallowed ground* – middle school, this time without a fully articulated strategy laid out in my mind. Resistance might thwart the loose plan from materializing from this branch of the school. Everything related to the middle school seemed more complicated, and most of the staff was highly suspicious of intruding eyes. An air of being untouchable permeated the atmosphere. To this point I had not discussed future plans and thoughts with anyone in the middle school, but I did have someone within the staff I would consider for the open position. I sought a new generation – a different type of thinker – someone open to being mentored, and someone not locked into rigid formality of faith and spirituality.

She was teaching eighth grade English; served as middle school cheerleading coach and a graduate of the school. Her two children were students in the elementary school, and her mother was a well-established, highly respected eighth grade math teacher. She was fully engrained in the school's culture, but of a younger generation not entrenched in the regressive conservatism I loathed. I asked if she would come to my office for a brief discussion. She knew I accepted the president's position but was not yet aware of the major shifts to follow. As I spoke of my vision for the school, she appeared a little surprised – I'd never discussed these issues with her. Then I asked if she would consider being a part of the administrative *revolution* for the middle school. She was speechless for a moment and laughed nervously. The expression on her face left me wondering how she might eventually respond. I didn't know how to read the initial reaction. I knew time was necessary to think and reflect on what I just proposed – something she was not prepared to hear but hopefully intrigued. I asked that she let me know as soon as she was able. A new team almost mobilized, but one open spot remained – my hope was to hear a yes.

The next day she returned to my office with an answer – yes. She spoke with a tone of gratitude for my trust in her ability to do the job and simultaneously questioned her decision. Assured her I would be present with full assistance and guidance as she maneuvered the new leadership role. Those supportive words seemed to bring comfort, but I still sensed apprehension, and that's to be expected. The plan overall was to mentor the new administrative team offering my full support. In the past it was *sink or swim* but not anymore. Mentoring administrators is something that never occurred on the campus. I was navigating uncharted waters but ready to take the plunge. Enormously grateful to have three new principals positioned beside me ready and willing to move the school forward along new paths. I was taking a calculated risk knowing we must abandon a few archaic practices – little did I know.

Eleven years in the elementary school allowed me to gain a clear perspective of not only the elementary but also of the middle and high school. I knew the strengths and weaknesses of all three schools. I moved quickly because I wanted to communicate a sense of urgency. Needed the staff to understand I didn't accept the position to possess a plush office with a view. Additionally, it was my desire to communicate newness – three new principals to lead each school division, and expect to see new things happening. I pursued the three individuals within our staff for the purpose of communicating continuity and stability. I thought the people under their leadership would feel connectedness because the leader is someone they already knew – someone they could easily talk with and share dreams and concerns.

Urgency was necessary because we didn't have time to waste. Too much time had already been wasted on useless issues in the past that stifled progress. A major paradigm shift needed to be ushered in – *old* power structures were gone, new leadership at the top, new leadership in each school division – a new start, a new horizon. We immediately began to meet as a team to map out plans for the approaching school year. It was an exciting time to be on campus, dreaming big dreams and generating big growth. I loved every moment of every administrative planning meeting. It was my goal to challenge faculty and staff with a unique spiritual focus – starting this time with the nucleus – the new administrative team.

We worked tirelessly as a cohesive team for three years to enact change, shift hearts, move the school out of a conservative rut. Unfortunately, the new spiritual focus each year didn't do it. Speaking from the depths of my heart on spiritual issues and challenging everyone to look deep within their own hearts didn't do it. Urging the board of directors to reconsider draconian dictates and policies didn't do it. Speaking often to the board to loosen their overall grip of power and control, not to view themselves as church elders, instead fully support the strategic plan for the school's long-term future, they didn't do it. They were offended when I told them we are not a church – we weren't. Instituting a school-wide plan for academically struggling students didn't do it – nor was it supported. Creating high-quality advertising campaigns featuring our diverse student body titled, *"Affordable Excellence"* didn't do it. Recouping a huge amount of past due tuition, more than any president before me didn't do it. Organizing first-class fundraising campaigns and dinners for our patrons didn't do it. Revamping the school's news publication, *"The Soaring Eagle"* into a glossy updated look didn't do it. Responding quickly to alleviate situations that had the potential to bring negative public relations upon the school didn't do it. A willingness to reduce faculty and staff to save money didn't do it. Speaking truth when faced with strict conservative push back didn't do it. Why didn't these achievements change the course of the institution? I stood baffled by a general lack of interest.

Reflecting, I sincerely believed those efforts would improve our chances to remain relevant in a changing community – we had good bones. Nothing seemed to penetrate the dominate culture – it was too engrained – infused into every fiber and sinew of its existence – impenetrable. Old power structures still had breath. But during all the skirmishes I fully appreciated the support and camaraderie among the administrative team. We worked together well, respectfully disagreed at times, debated issues, finalized plans each spring to improve our previous year's work, and continually anticipated a brighter future. Then a moment of complete and utter clarity flooded my every thought. Fourteen years of doing good things is not always adequately rewarded or appreciated, I no longer desired to fight the veiled cloak of overly strict, conservative *church* orthodoxy. I dreaded sharing the news with the administrative team – didn't wish to let them down after lifting them up, but it was time for me to find another home for my heart.

The elementary and high school principals made the same decision to leave after completing three years in administration. The middle school principal was more invested regarding family and her long presence, decided to stick it out a little longer. I honestly desired the school to succeed in spite of its narrowness and overall lack of vision for the future. Here's good news, all four of us eventually landed and thrived in public school administrative positions. Here's a sad footnote – a once vibrant, highly competitive sports program is now in shambles. Enrollment dropped to its lowest numbers since early beginnings. The academic program can no longer boast, as we did, of *"affordable excellence"* – several highly competent teachers have moved on or retired. What was once a significant part of the private school community is no longer significant. Why? At a time when change was desperately needed, they dug collective heels in deeper and refused to budge. A *no change here* mantra prevailed – results have been devastating. The little boy that retreated momentarily put forth a valiant effort and would soon face another steep climb.

As we drove through north Atlanta returning from Tybee Island, Georgia my cell rang. The Director of Elementary Education for Metro Nashville Public Schools offered me a principal's position at Amqui Elementary in Madison; she was a former Amqui principal – *"Amqui is my baby, and you better take of care of my people"* her immediate dictate for my new role – she wasn't joking. Returning to my boyhood stomping grounds I accepted another mountain top position without any hesitation. What a quick turn of events – one moment I'm without a job and the next moment I'm employed again with a parallel salary – providence? Amqui, a school nestled in the northern part of Madison – a school I knew all my life – a school where a close friend now worked – a school where several well-known, distinguished teachers completed long, respectable careers. I personally knew so many of those people – so many connections. The school had changed drastically over the years due to dramatic changes in the community. Amqui was now a school where 96% of the families were at or below poverty level – educational and economic challenges for those families and children are enormous.

Truly an amazing twist, returning to my community roots – a way of life I knew well. I was immediately inundated with numerous issues to address and overcome. A reliable source said my first challenge was to make a positive impression upon a forty-year veteran kindergarten teacher – her entire career at Amqui and she hated the former principal. A meeting of the Leadership Team was scheduled at the district site to make specific plans for the upcoming school year. This was my first time to meet with a group of Amqui teachers. We politely introduced ourselves and started our work, the day was tightly scheduled, but we met our goals. As we gathered materials to leave, the forty-year veteran whispered in my ear, *"This was a good day, I can tell I'm going to like working with you."* She offered an affirming nod as she walked away in her confident aged stride. I passed the first test – *taking care of people.*

In four years at Amqui I was continually amazed and thankful teachers returned the next day to again face monumental challenges. I often described our efforts as clawing and scratching our way up a steep mountain with loose, ever-shifting rocks – we made strides to only slip back then start the climb again. It was a constant test of our will and fortitude. We never faced a day without huge obstacles to overcome. At times our test scores showed slight gains – a green bar – we celebrated. The next year we would fall back – a red bar – no celebration – more meetings and plans to bring scores up – a process that became a never-ending cycle coinciding with the never-ending cycle of poverty.

Walking the long hallways became a daily ritual due to major discipline issues erupting all over the building – some burning out-of-control, others simmering. Many times, I didn't know which issue needed priority – words under my breath deteriorated into trailer park verbiage – burgeoning stress spurting forth releasing pressure. *"This is a fucking insane asylum!"* No one heard my invective. Unfortunately, harsh words didn't remedy chaos or relieve me of any responsibilities. Inhaled and exhaled deeply – stood straight – battled the biggest out-of-control fire first with firm calming words hoping for immediate de-escalation. Although trained well, poverty is always a tricky opponent to contend with.

In our district every school employs a bookkeeper. The bookkeeper is the only other twelve-month employee along with the executive principal in each school. The bookkeeper is vital because they hold the purse strings even though my signature was required and most importantly, they handle payroll. The former principal had just hired a new bookkeeper, and it was her first time to be in the position. Thankfully her mother held the same position at another district school and was just a phone call away. Rachel possessed a spitfire, high-energy, get after it attitude toward her responsibilities – I liked her immediately. Rachel also possessed a characteristic reminiscent of my local grandmother – she peppered language with a lot of choice words and was hilarious. After gaining a better understanding of her general character, I granted permission to step into my office anytime she needed to vent – close the door and let it rip – no judgment on my part, and she did so on several occasions. A school like Amqui required a cohesive working relationship with the bookkeeper, and we were able to form a close professional bond. Rachel was also excellent at protecting me from unnecessary intrusions and conversations and never put junk mail on my desk, and I loved that too. After three years she moved to a school closer to her home and with less chaos and stress – she was a mother of two young children and needed to be closer to their daycare and school. I advised her new principal to give her a safe space to vent and all would be well.

My next bookkeeper was Barb, and she was as efficient as Rachel but in a different way – we were the same age. As I alluded, the bookkeeping role is critical – it must work well or life in a school will be doubly chaotic. When Barb arrived for the interview, I was intimidated by her apparent corporate demeanor and style. I visualized her walking across a large plush corner office to a glass top desk. I liked her but thought she would be miserable in a school like Amqui. I selected another candidate, but she didn't pass the initial background check – I called Barb and she accepted the job. I know it was providence because Barb immediately seemed at home, and we quickly formed the necessary professional bond required of a principal and bookkeeper. Once our relationship was well established, I shared my reason for not selecting her initially – she laughed uncontrollably for several minutes, and we have joked about it ever since. I share these two bookkeeper stories because I would not have survived the daily pounding Amqui brought to bear without them. Both bookkeepers were loyal employees and made my job more tolerable. I will always be grateful for their intentional patience and kindness toward me – blessed and fortunate twice.

Likewise, I was fortunate to be surrounded by smart professionals. One of those smart professionals was the building literacy coach – she understood the serious nature of our task and searched diligently for interventions that would make a positive difference for students. She applied for a

$10,000 literacy grant to improve sagging achievement levels and we got it – an amazing opportunity we desperately needed. The literacy coach discovered an intervention program named, "Measures of Academic Progress" – otherwise known as MAP. The program provides teachers with accurate, and actionable evidence to help target instruction for each student or groups of students regardless of how far above or below they are from their grade level. Numerous reports for data-informed decisions are available. The program appeared to be exactly what we desired. She presented MAP to our building literacy team and I presented the same to district leadership and it was shot down because the program didn't align with district curriculum and standards – also told the cost was too high. My literacy coach insisted MAP was the right way to go and I trusted her judgement – grant money we were allowed to spend at our discretion.

Final approval for MAP in spite of negative voices from leadership declaring we were wasting our grant money came directly from me – unconventional rebellion? Perhaps. We moved forward and once teachers were trained and the first phases of the program were implemented, we started to gather mounds of critical data on every student tested; we could see clearly areas of deficit and areas of strength. During a district-wide meeting of administrators and literacy support staff I discussed MAP with a few colleagues. A district literacy director overheard my conversation and inquired with a tone of high interest. She looked stunned and seemed amazed we were implementing MAP – she had obviously done a study of the program and its highly touted benefits. I recommended she speak to our local literacy coach about details. MNPS now fully implements and embraces MAP district-wide. Amqui never received any recognition for piloting MAP. Likely due to the fact we did it without direct approval from the ivory tower.

MAP is now all the rage thanks to a few smart professionals at Amqui searching for a better way to serve and understand the needs of struggling students – that's what caring professional educators do. Everyone involved from the grassroots level at Amqui should be proud of this legacy.

The never-ending cycle of poverty required time and attention toward our neediest families. My goal was to discover new ways to connect with families – especially poverty-stricken families already struggling with simple trust. These families had to be convinced we had their best interest at heart. A starched dress shirt and silk tie created barriers – required dress by the district superintendent. Forced to work doubly hard to overcome the visual barrier, I had to convince people stuck in the mire of poverty I understood their plight. Convincing them their children needed to work doubly hard was a huge task, but the most difficult task was convincing teachers to work doubly hard to overcome these obstacles. Several long-term teachers were beaten down emotionally – barley hanging on. The ruling class safely lodged in their ivory towers insisted we couldn't use poverty as a talking point – not even acknowledge it. How were we to overcome something without acknowledging the root cause? I recognized denial – this edict made no sense to me. The executive director started a meeting once with principals from failing schools stating, *"I do not want to hear one word about poverty or the difficulty of dealing with your specific populations."* Another stunning declaration of denial. From my perspective, the first step in solving our difficult problem was to acknowledge it and work from that point of reference. I'm certain resistance and contempt for the absurd approach radiated on my face as the proposal I shared before the failing group of school peers betrayed the truth of my convictions. The executive director gazed with disdain and an air of superiority.

Returning to the real world where people need to be treated with dignity and respect, I put aside the declarations from on high and went about my work of caring deeply about those in the trenches. One simple task I found to be quite effective was being out in the community. This effort along with a few community partners, one being my big church, started hosting a monthly food give-away on Saturday mornings until noon. I made a point to be there, greet people, assist in the actual process. No talk of test scores, discipline issues or failing schools – just natural one-to-one conversations in jeans and casual shirts, breaking down barriers. At dismissal one day a young grandparent raising three grandchildren told me how much she appreciated the extra food and how much it helped at the end of the month when funds were sparse – barriers removed and long-lasting positive connections – *taking care of people.*

I often rode one of the school buses in the afternoon, usually due to discipline issues but parents at the stops noticed and appreciated the efforts to get their children home safely. It was also necessary at times to search for parents because none of the phone numbers listed were operational. Driving to the address was not always safe, but it was the only way to connect with some families. I remember well the time I stood in the narrow hallway of the Section Eight apartment building knocking several times. Directly across from me, behind another door, I overheard a discussion about the TV dropped as it was being stolen the night before and cocaine they needed to sell. Was my life at risk? Probably. Someone finally opened the door I knocked on, a male, he was half dressed and just a boyfriend but agreed to come to the school and talk to his girlfriend's second grade son who was out-of-control – we were desperate for assistance. I waited at my car several minutes when he finally appeared. I drove him back to school making him aware of the circumstances. I had no choice but to suspend the student two days due to his violent behavior choices – sent home to most likely a worse situation. Watching news a few evenings later a convicted offender's photo was displayed on the screen – he was in my car three days ago – we had a decent discussion; he was polite and thanked me for the ride. I called the police department the next day and shared my story – it was now in their hands. I could share so many other similar stories, the stories and unique challenges were never ending.

"Prescription for Success" was an all-out assault on the ravages of poverty upon faltering literacy at Amqui. My second trusted assistant principal, Angela, and two highly competent and wise literacy coaches devised detailed strategies to battle a myriad of overwhelming odds. In an effort to inspire the *troops* we dressed during pre-service training in full medical scrubs. As *head of surgery,* I wore a white doctors coat and a stethoscope around my neck – Angela did the same – we viewed the effort as serious business. As a team we presented a united front to rally our beleaguered *brigade* with a detailed battle plan and began to sense an immergence of renewal and inspiration – a *we can do this* attitude. Green bars the ultimate goal. We employed a good team – a good focus – hearts dedicated to students' success. The all-out assault was fully implemented with the usual bumps and delays along the way. I knew success or failure of this effort rested solely on my shoulders even though more than fifty professional educators, from the assistant principal down to the classroom teacher were all working toward the same goal. As self-titled *head of surgery* I faced a brutal *malignancy* – POVERTY – *do or die* the name of the game.

Taking care of people necessitated positive working relationships with every staff member – even the most difficult. I needed their best efforts in spite of enormous difficulties they faced every day. Pam cooked homemade birthday treats, I wrote positive notes and cards, listened carefully, acting joyful to be at work even though every cell in my body screamed opposite, conducted difficult conferences by giving each person the benefit of the doubt – looked for a positive spin every day – not an easy task at Amqui. I'll say it again, I was lucky dedicated teachers showed up each day. In four years, we made enormous gains in spite of enormous challenges – social/emotional gains were critical. Unfortunately, those couldn't be quantified and computed by the State's testing formula. Testing formulas mattered most to district leadership. I wisely retired after officially being told they wanted to move in a different direction – a new direction that didn't quite go the way they envisioned. A former principal colleague informed me Amqui was honored at the first official principal's meeting before the start of the next school year. Amqui students once again made gains – green bars – *"Prescription for Success,"* successful. This time the percentage of achievement growth was enough to merit a graphic on the big screen and shout out of distinction among peers – Amqui landed on the green growth list – well deserved due to many hours of detailed, steadfast service to children in poverty by a dedicated and bewildered staff. I commandeered Amqui's literacy focus, and it led students on an upward trajectory – but I missed the public recognition among my former peers because I was at home – retired.

Reflecting on my return to public education I remain amazed how some relationships turn on a dime and can't be explained with any type of human logic, circumstances that defy common norms and typical outcomes – my first assistant principal assigned to Amqui fit that category. I was in Gatlinburg, Tennessee for a short vacation before my official work began – my mind occupied with anticipation for a return to public education and to a community I knew well. Pam and I had just started our drive through a steep narrow snaking road for an afternoon of sightseeing when my phone rang – it was a second call from the elementary school's director. Betsy Potts had been assigned the new assistant principal role at Amqui. Stunned and basically speechless, do not recall what was said after her statement; the conversation was short. I navigated the car off the road at the next available spot to breathe – stunned. Told my wife in amazement and unbelief – *"How can this be? How will I navigate my new role with Betsy by my side?"* A sense of intimidation and foreboding consumed me – breathe! How can this be?

Before resuming our quiet and relaxing afternoon drive in the mountains, I phoned a close friend who happened to be a teacher at Amqui. She was as surprised as me – her son knew Ms. Potts well – she had been his principal at the private school where I substituted many years ago and applied for the principal's job – a job Betsy acquired instead of me. Betsy Potts and her husband were also part of the big church but had recently departed for a more conservative environment – issues her family didn't accept as scriptural. Betsy and I did not see eye-to-eye on much of anything and we were now forced to work side by side – how can this be? My thoughts quickly shifted from planning to dreading – again, how can this be?

We managed to complete our afternoon jaunt through the mountains, but I barely engaged trees, sharp curves, and beautiful vistas – my mind absorbed with making this new adventure effective. Did the powers that be somehow know we had known each other for thirty years – that Betsy and her husband married the evening after us in the same big church, that we were once seeking the same administrative position, but she won out? For two years we served on the same faculty at the private school where she taught first grade and I taught sixth – we hardly spoke and rarely crossed paths. Betsy did eventually leave the private school after serving as elementary principal. She then had a successful stint as a first-grade teacher at a local public school and was selected teacher of the year. She was now returning to administration, and I was her direct supervisor. We scheduled our first official meeting. How can this be?

Our new forced relationship must succeed or we will both be sunk – I was determined. We met in my office and after a few moments of small talk I told her how we would conduct our work as principal and assistant. *"In our respective roles we may not always agree on every issue, but when we walk out of our offices no one will know – we will present a united front on whatever decision we decide and move forward in that manner."* She smiled and agreed that was the best way to move forward. We cleared our first hurdle – not so bad, but what did our future hold? Our past experiences unmentioned.

What I didn't fully realize in the first few days of our new administrative roles, this was going to play out like soldiers in a fox hole – we had no other choice but to have each other's back – I mean that in the truest literal sense – differences no longer mattered – we intuitively knew – but never uttered those words. Immediately I realized her training in public education had changed her whole style and way of seeing people in a public-school setting. She was born and raised in a protective bubble and the bubble reinforced by two private Christian Universities, then a long career of teaching in the very school where she walked the halls as a student for twelve years with her father at the helm – CEO. I observed a person I didn't really know – someone I needed to know and utilize her newfound capabilities to help us reshape a failing school stuck in the throes of poverty – the task before us monumental.

On numerous occasions Betsy stepped up and took care of situations I never believed possible. The first open house we took turns working as *bouncer* at the front door as parents streamed in from around the community. We were told former students might slip in to sabotage classrooms or help themselves to whatever they could carry out. These folks were my folks – I was taken back to my childhood. While I listened to teachers talk about expectations in the gym I was summoned to the front entrance. Two parents were sparring in the parking lot ready to fight. I rushed to the door, but Betsy had already handled the situation. She stood between the two arguing women and told them in no uncertain terms stop or she would call police – also gave them the option to take it off our campus. I was impressed. On numerous occasions we covered different sides of the building to avoid students eloping – an almost daily occurrence. As I turned the corner into the long back hallway, she was sitting on the floor holding a student after his tantrum – her arms were loosely clasped as she spoke softly in order to maintain his de-escalation. I motioned if she needed my assistance, she shook her head no. On another occasion after being kicked by the same student several times she promptly let him know in her high-pitched tone, *"These are my new boots, and I don't appreciate you kicking them!"* I had to disguise my laugh because her response was just plain funny, and the student appeared a bit surprised by her concern for boots. She later assisted this student in writing a letter to his father who was in prison – the student specifically asked Ms. Potts – not me. She was *taking care of people* too.

Betsy was much smarter than me in a lot of ways – a detail person – a meticulous note taker. I always depended upon her to remember minutiae. Toward the end of our first school year, I was so pleased with how everything had played out – we actually balanced a stressful workload very well with no personal conflicts. Betsy applied for an open principal's position at another elementary school within our cluster and got the job. She was leaving Amqui to be an executive principal again – hated to see her go but happy for her promotion – well deserved. During district-wide administrative meetings she always chose to sit at my table – thought it might be her silent gesture indicating we had formed a strong professional relationship. Once again, we all depended on her expert note taking skills – we basically sat back at our table to occasionally listen as Betsy recorded significant information. For every assigned cluster project, we looked to her smartness and exhaustive notes to give us the edge – she never failed us.

Roughly two years into our successful cluster group Betsy got very sick and underwent a series of tests to determine the source of her health issues. It was determined she had a rare blood disease – her health unfortunately declined quickly. The time frame was summer break, but executive principals worked twelve months. The student Betsy had wrangled to the floor and de-escalated with a calming voice, the one who kicked her several times on her new boots, the one she assisted in writing a letter to his father in prison was at our front door – he was now a middle school student. I knew he was going to ask for Ms. Potts – he did. I explained she was now a principal at another school then gently broke the news of her serious illness. He appeared crushed by the news and saddened – Betsy had unknowingly made a lasting connection with someone far outside her sphere of privilege – that's who she had become – I was sad they could not reconnect. She would have been delighted to know he had attempted to visit her.

We were sadly informed she lost her battle with the dreadful disease – it ravaged her body. I stood in line two hours in order to offer my condolences to her husband, two children, her parents, and extended family. I told each of them what a privilege it was for me to have her as assistant principal for one short year and how blessed we were to have had her in our district cluster. I arrived early at the district-wide training site the next day and placed a bouquet of white flowers at our table to honor Betsy and turned her chair down

– several colleagues commented in agreement and were touched by the impromptu tribute. Her funeral coincided with our administrative training at a local university that day. All principals were expected to be present, so I Informed our direct supervisor we would attend Betsy's memorial service but return to the meeting – that was her plan as well. Our decision didn't sit well with the executive director, but we went anyway. I sat in the packed auditorium watching throngs of people pay final respects and pondered our time together. Amazed by the intricacies of our long and sometimes divided relationship. Amazed how our relationship was solidified through adversity and struggle. Amazed how two people with diverse backgrounds worked cohesively managing the ravages of dysfunction and poverty. Amazed how opposing viewpoints finally found common ground, not allowing those to ever divide again. And I asked myself one last time, how can this be?

Retired

Retired was not a word I had even contemplated at age fifty-seven – my career was uninterrupted. Shortly after signing the official retirement papers, I was uneasy – literally fearful. Too young to retire I said to myself, I'm quite capable of continuing work, so I pursued several potential openings in MNPS. Since word had spread among administrator colleagues about leaving Amqui – it was probably assumed by several that I had not measured up to the standards of the current ruling class – we all knew the high-stakes of the game. Principals in our district at the time suffered under tremendous pressure to raise achievement levels regardless of *unspoken* poverty or other difficulties. These issues were not viewed as potential barriers but as circumstances that must be overcome but remain in the shadows. The building executive principal was the sole proprietor held responsible for huge achievement gains each year among the general population and for closing achievement gaps between disadvantaged groups.

Fighting against the ravages of poverty is never an easy task, especially when the root causes can't be discussed. The district had implemented several initiatives to assist the achievement process – one such initiative was hiring a director of literacy. She focused primarily on struggling schools like Amqui and visited often. This person was already familiar with Amqui because her job before becoming the literacy guru was Director of Reading Labs sponsored by a local university. We housed a Reading Lab in a classroom within the main building – students with the greatest literacy needs would go to the lab to work on reading skills with trained volunteers and university graduate students. Following the first year of the lab our student numbers grew, and I needed the classroom for a regular teacher. I informed the director she had to move her lab to a portable room just outside the current location – she was not pleased but complied. Being the executive principal, it was my decision to assign teachers to grade levels and classrooms. It made more sense for the lab to move outside instead of an entire classroom of students. The Reading Lab continued with a robust additional group of volunteers I helped recruit, including my wife – all seemed to be working well, but the director remained unhappy with the outside room. The reading lab director was then hired by the district to oversee all elementary literacy initiatives. Additional pressures landed on executive principals as she pushed a bloated agenda. Amqui was on the list to receive regular focused literacy visits – monitored closely to assure we were implementing all literacy initiatives.

During my fourth year at Amqui pressure ramped up to a ridiculously high fever pitch. *Prescription for Success* in full-swing. An upcoming literacy visit was scheduled – we met often as a faculty, and I laid out specific directives for our literacy plan. Teachers were instructed by coaches and me on exactly what they must do, and I assumed it was perfectly clear. All guided reading tables must be prepared and ready for use and appropriate literacy strategies implemented every day. The director arrived for her visit along with my direct supervisor. The three of us visited random rooms during literacy time and recorded strategies being implemented. In the majority of classrooms decent strategies were being implemented and students were engaged. In some classrooms it was not clearly evident the strategies being implemented, and I could sense concern by the director's body posture and scowl expression. In one particular fourth grade classroom the teacher was completing a math lesson using what is known as *drill and kill*– not on the director's list of appropriate strategies – I didn't like it either and was furious with the teacher. His literacy table for guided reading was not prepared for students. I walked out in disgust during the observation and waited in the hallway. When the other two observers walked out, I expressed my dismay, and the literacy director just shook her head in disgust. We conducted a few remaining observations then the required debriefing session.

The literacy director bashed several teachers and strategies she witnessed, and I attempted to explain how teachers were given specific directives. I clearly expressed disappointment in a few teachers, and she continued her negative feedback with increasing force. My emotions toward her tirade built to an overflow – she began making her rant very personal – I finally interrupted. *"I suppose I'm not being the bad ass principal you want me to be?"* She recoiled with a look of astonishment – not certain she expected such a response. She concluded with a few more useless remarks and hurriedly ended the debrief. My direct supervisor later told me she wanted to kick me under the table – the literacy director privately shared with my supervisor she didn't feel welcome at Amqui. I was seriously stunned by her take away because it must have been obvious; I was as upset as she was and for the very same reasons – we were both enraged by the same issues. In retrospect, I believe she was determined to make this circumstance all my fault – allow me to take the fall for the lack of appropriate literacy strategies because it was not to her personal liking. During her literacy reign, the university reading lab remained outside in a portable classroom.

Unknown to me until it became apparent, the Executive Director of Elementary Education turned against me at some point due to low achievement test scores – she basically didn't like me – sensed hostile feelings on several occasions – perhaps she read my facial cues. Here's another truth, she never stepped foot on the Amqui school campus one time during my entire four years. I'm certain her mind was made up based on sagging achievement scores from the previous year and from information being fed to her by the literacy guru – the two were inseparable. The two people didn't really know me – didn't know my compassion for people in poverty – putting my life at risk seeking parents with no contact information – how many times I was forced to ride a school bus to make sure students got home safely – didn't know how well I knew the community where I grew up as a boy and lived most of my life – didn't care about anything but the damn achievement test scores and their reputations.

When my direct supervisor told me the plan to place a new principal at Amqui I was surprised but not totally. Prior to being informed of the plan, my assistant principal had accepted a position at a new school in the district, so it was my responsibility to search for a replacement. Amqui could not operate with only one principal – we unquestionably needed two principals to manage the daily onslaught of chaos. I was told to wait – not interview anyone yet. I started to get suspicious after several weeks. I asked my direct supervisor to tell me the truth – didn't wish to hear it from an executive director who didn't care enough to ever visit Amqui once. She told me the plan even though it was not her responsibility to do so. I appreciated truth from someone who actually visited on several occasions – she insisted, *"Jim, you haven't done anything wrong."* I also knew she most likely wouldn't challenge her superior on this issue.

During one of the last official group meetings with principal colleagues, I walked toward a table where the literacy director was sitting. She conveniently looked down at her laptop – instead of ignoring her I intentionally spoke and smiled – forced to look up she returned a stressed half-hearted grin. Based on less than desired test scores accompanied by her misperceptions of my labor, she and the executive director desired a change for Amqui, and I was their target. I believe the two conspired on a plan to install a new young principal whom they thought would perfectly institute the mandates they desired. Unfortunately, test scores the next year dropped to the lowest number yet, low morale rampant – a calculated plot completely crumbled after two years and was brought to an embarrassing, very public, abrupt end. I held my head high and remained gracious – a learned reaction I witnessed from a mentor many years prior.

I had opportunity to apply for open assistant principal positions – the district leadership would not place me since they conveniently instituted new hiring policies. After pursuing several administrative roles, it seemed likely executive principals had been urged by the person who never stepped foot on my campus to seek specific candidates – which did not include me. I visited a former Amqui principal now serving as executive principal of a middle school – she experienced a similar fate after one year at Amqui and ended up teaching high school biology for two years before returning to administration. She needed two eighth grade teachers – science and English. We talked briefly, very informally, a friendly conversation and she asked which position I wanted – I chose science. She could easily relate to my circumstances and trusted my ability to teach eighth grade. I was thrilled to have an opportunity to work full time.

I officially rescinded a short-lived retirement. With a rejuvenated attitude I transformed a skimpy classroom into an eighth-grade science lab. As new colleagues visited the room they commented on my penmanship, visuals displayed throughout the room, and the overall organization I brought to their middle school – an elementary background is to blame. But I appreciated the compliments and was ready and excited to begin a whole new chapter in my career. Then the eighth graders walked in – an overwhelming number of eighth graders in this school were not interested in the science I was teaching. Yes, science, but only their version of science. Suddenly I was totally immersed again in the junior high boy's locker room of a distant past – one major difference – this time the space included females. Students could not keep hands off one another or control vulgar, hateful remarks toward each other – middle school.

The daily schedule of hour-long classes of different eighth graders each period made Amqui seem like nursery school. It was a chore to just get through a day – a grueling 9:00 to 4:00 every day. At 3:00 the elementary school next door dismissed – from my well-organized, chaotic science laboratory I could see buses leaving. I longed for my past elementary school 3:00 dismissal. Glancing at the clock only reminded me another hour of excruciating stress awaited my fragile endurance – could I actually do this? On a rare day there were a few manageable moments – most days were full of highly disordered situations and behavioral issues that made no sense at all – the students were so cruel to each other. Every day turned into pathetic situations that were extremely difficult to manage.

The worse part of every day was knowing I had three years before I could officially retire again after rescinding my initial retirement. While confiding in a close friend, now assistant principal at another school, she empathized with my misery but also urged me to at least check with human resources to have the retirement issue clarified. She is smart like that. I phoned during planning time as I stood at the window peering at freedom and asked the dreaded question – fearing the answer which would seal my fate three more years, she answered without hesitation. *"You can retire anytime, it's up to you."* I was stunned with pure overwhelming joy and relief. I looked up and said, *"THANK YOU!"* A dark chapter of my life will officially end. It was mid-September, and I walked into the principal's office and carefully laid out my decision to retire again and apologized for taking a job she had so kindly offered. She looked straight at me and spoke without any expression, *"I would walk out right behind you if I could – no reason to apologize."* She understood completely – I was grateful for her kindness and trust in my ability.

There's a little providential evidence to take note of. I was allowed to officially retire due to my first teaching stint of eleven years then four as executive principal, but the higher percentage of retirement compensation required fifteen full years and I had a gap of employment due to my initial hire date of October 1st, 1984. My short teaching stint of craziness in middle school perfectly filled that gap and I was able to draw the higher retirement rate. My second retirement started November 1st – monthly retirement compensation and pandemonium free. After a sixty-day required waiting period I started substituting in the same district, this time it was my choice where to work and when. A retired educator can work 120 days – a total of 900 hours within a school year – retirement can be profitable for a public-school educator if one prudently plans or providence is a guiding factor. Substituting was short lived; next interim positions, then instructional specialist positions, and now back to what I originally searched for but didn't find, administrative positions – assistant principal. I'm pleased and satisfied to be officially retired and working again as an administrator – Divine providence may account for perfect timing.

Transformation

Raised Catholic, Raphael told me he and his family are now Episcopalian and said Episcopalians are very similar to Catholics. Not certain what that means for him on a personal spiritual level or how he processed his earliest spiritual influences. We've not yet had opportunity to share the details of our spiritual lives, but it's my hope the conversation will one day occur. As I've noted, my earliest spiritual influences were primarily through grandparents – my mother's parents. Neither my mother or father were ever officially connected to a particular religious body of people – my mother most often identified with Southern Baptist because she was raised in that structure of strict, conservative values. My mother's parents remained faithful Southern Baptist folks throughout their lifetime.

My mother pretended when asked by anyone who knocked on our door with a religious tract – she was quick to tell them she was a Baptist – I knew the truth. Nothing about our lifestyle seemed particularly religious, spiritual or Baptist in any way, but my parents did faithfully watch *The Old Time Gospel Hour* – a Sunday morning program featuring gospel singers. My father's parents were not spiritual people but were law-abiding citizens. My grandfather Morris, likely raised Catholic, his mother, my great grandmother, and her extended family were also Catholic. A few Catholic symbols within my great grandmother's Victorian row home was the extent of my understanding and Assumption Catholic church across the street. I walked inside the sanctuary once and statues of Mary and Jesus captured my attention.

I assumed the Morris grandparents attended church at Madison First Baptist occasionally because they received the church bulletin in the mail – but I have no memory of them actually going. My aunt Wanda, married to my dad's younger brother, a faithful member at Madison First Assembly of God – next door to the First Baptist and Krystal. I visited with her frequently but was never totally comfortable with the charismatic type of worship. Nashville has churches on almost every corner – known as the *buckle of the Bible belt.* I've been surrounded by pretenders and believers all my life.

A few of my closest high school buddies were members of Madison church of Christ – most of those in the art class group were from the big church – never once visited their church even though it held a very prominent presence in our community. The churches of Christ both directly and indirectly did play a major role in my spiritual development both as a child and throughout adult life. The trailer park owner and landlord who knocked on our door a lot seeking late rent was a member of Gallatin Road Church of Christ. He and his wife invited my mother and me to attend their church – my father wasn't interested. We visited a few times and my mother pretended to be religious – I knew the truth. I attended their Vacation Bible School and really liked the daily snack time of Hawaiian Punch, butter cookies and especially the hotdog and chips lunch on Friday. Discovered an aged vacation Bible school certificate in a pile of saved junk when we emptied out years of collected memories in my mother's seventh floor apartment.

During my high school senior year, two buddies started

inviting me to several youth events at the prominent church – I never accepted an offer while we were still in school. I have vivid memories of hearing my grandmother Morris disparage her neighbors who were members of Madison Church of Christ, called them nosy hypocrites, but most often *Campbellites* – a reference to church restoration founder Alexander Campbell. She often used graphic language I didn't repeat as a child. She never said any of it to their faces to my knowledge. She believed the minister was trying to control the whole community – and he was extremely influential throughout the religious and non-religious community. My father claimed a local bar closed down because of his influence – a favorite spot for my dad – he often mimicked his mother's sentiments.

On Sunday mornings I sometimes rode with my father to what he called a *bootlegger* – only two blocks north of the big church. How did the influential minister not know about this *depravity* so close to his church? I think he probably knew. As I rode past the big church, throngs of nicely dressed people were streaming in to hear Dr. Ira North proclaim the gospel in his unique style – likely in his signature red jacket. I innocently recognized we were riding by a large church building and I wasn't going. I watched as my father drove to the back of a small building – walk to a solid wood door barely ajar – an arm and hand reached for money in exchange for a brown paper bag wrapped tightly around my dad's Sunday whiskey. The nicely dressed church people were still streaming in and out on our way back home – an unknowing glimpse into a destined future – had no idea my future held a thirty-five-year stint.

A few months after graduating, I finally accepted an invitation and visited the big church. My first Sunday in the three-thousand seat auditorium I sat with Cliff and John in the oval half balcony – a highly enthusiastic song leader led several songs I enjoyed – later learned he was a back-up singer for Elvis. This particular faith group didn't use musical instruments – it was considered an addition that was sinful, only voices. I didn't admit to my friends I liked the singing – wanted to keep my initial impressions private. Eventually I attended home Bible studies my friends organized. A curiosity was piqued, I followed the study closely, which led to my own reading and study of scripture. I had not established a Sunday morning routine of attending regularly since the days of the bus ministry – Easter a few weeks away.

More people than usual do attempt to attend a church on Easter – I felt compelled to do the same. Following Easter Sunday, there was a new yearning deep within my heart – it was time to make an official commitment – be baptized in the Church of Christ. This would be a second baptism – did the first baptism not count, I wondered? According to friends my first conversion occurred in the wrong church – so I made it right. On the following Sunday evening I responded to the gospel invitation and was baptized by the youth director. When I walked out of the dressing room the homecoming queen of my high school senior class hugged me. Wow! Didn't realize baptism had those benefits. I barely knew her – we never talked at school – briefly on a few occasions pertaining to artwork for cheerleaders. A few years later she sent a basket of goodies to my honeymoon suite at the Sheraton where she worked – another surprise benefit.

Being baptized in a prominent church like Madison suddenly propelled me into a new group of well-connected people. I immediately got involved by teaching a junior high boy's class with Cliff, the best friend who originally invited me. Confident in my teaching abilities because I was beginning freshman classes in education at Vol State in the fall. I was not as confident in my overall Bible knowledge but worked hard at thoroughly planning lessons. I was extremely serious about the new responsibility – even though I really didn't know what I was doing. My dream of teaching was now becoming reality in a non-professional way. My own class of rowdy eighth grade boys every Sunday – a gigantic challenge.

I discovered people in churches have a way of messing things up too – self-righteousness is not much different from the usual forms of dysfunction within a home. But I was totally committed to my newfound faith, which led me to meet my future wife. Pam was born and raised in Portland, Tennessee – into a family who were lifetime members of Clearview Church of Christ. Every time church doors opened, they were expected to be present and counted. Pam brought those same expectations to our relationship and marriage. We married in the oval three-thousand seat auditorium August 12, 1983. After the honeymoon, we returned to our newly purchased home in Madison a few blocks from the big church.

Four years later we purchased two and a half acres covered in tall trees in a rural part of northern Davidson County and built a home; my wife created floor plans and I selected all the decor. A few months after moving Pam discovered she was pregnant – the odor of the new kitchen cabinets made her nauseated, so we ate on a card table in the empty dining room. After the birth of Caroline our life changed dramatically but church attendance remained top priority – Sunday morning worship and Sunday school, Sunday evening services, and mid-week services, never an option to miss unless someone was sick or dying – felt like guilt driven, pious attendance to me. Being present and accounted for seemed most important in my opinion – more important than focusing on what God does – instead, more about what I do. For many years the big church perfectly met our needs. Although we had questions, we didn't see a need to question anything publicly. We were comfortable. Is church designed for coziness and comfort?

As we matured and studied on our own, we perceived something slowly changing – the change was an emerging desire to seek something more profound than perfect attendance, comfort and self-righteousness. We remained intrigued in a deeper spiritual relationship as many others expressed the same. This yearning was occurring within several young families at our big church – also within the broader church community outside of churches of Christ. We had excellent Bible teachers who were attempting to lead people toward something we didn't yet know – personal spiritual transformation.

A passionate new song leader ushered in a new way to worship in song – introduction of a Praise Team, male and female singers in a group on the front row with microphones. This did not set well with the most conservative church orthodoxy – they rejected this innovation because it didn't fit into what they referred to as *scriptural* – women were not allowed a public voice, so the addition of a microphone gave them something they had never used. So, the most distressed folks didn't believe the new innovation was authorized by God-inspired scripture. I had a few questions. If we could hear women singing what difference did a microphone make? I can still hear them – just slightly louder than before. No one could ever answer with a logical response. The whole issue instigated a major uprising among the ranks. So-called dedicated Christians on both sides of the matter did lots of arguing and bickering over something that didn't seem worthy of that much attention, toil, or worry. We believed Christians were called to love one another above all else – it didn't seem to apply in this circumstance – at least it wasn't evident to us.

My wife participated on the Praise Team for about seventeen years. We were determined to stay at our big church in Madison through thick and thin – we were not quitters.

Powerful preaching, lots of good fellowship, deeply meaning-ful Bible studies, super Sunday school programs, extravagant spending on Summer Spectacular events – all of those led several thousand through our doors. Unfortunately, resulting in little spiritual growth overall or additional people that remained with us. We were seeking personal spiritual growth and believed that was a key ingredient to a healthy church. Spiritual growth for us occurred through individual endeavor – something we must pursue on our own – only then were we able to grasp it as a supernatural occurrence. There remained a disconnect in our relationship to the church at Madison – transformation in its infancy, and we were unquestionably moving in a new direction.

I rose to the pinnacle of church leadership in my late forties – the title in our sect, *elder* – probably wasn't the wisest thing but in the end my role facilitated a specific purpose. I was first a deacon. It seemed being a deacon was required before one could be an elder – even though scripture does not state that stipulation. I gave up the *sacred* role of deacon a few years prior to becoming an elder. In my thinking, I could effectively function as a deacon without the title. I also detested deacon's meetings – lots of old men sitting around looking very bored and basically doing nothing. Most of them probably didn't read their Bibles. I officially stepped aside from the official role and title of deacon but continued serving and being involved. The choice made sense to me – I felt liberated – didn't need the official title to serve.

A few years later someone asked if I would be interested in serving as an elder. An elder within our church structure served as an overseer of the flock and that's actually biblical – within scripture. Another name for elder is shepherd and I liked the term shepherd – conjured tones of kindness and gentleness in my mind – though nothing like a real shepherd. But just like many other church roles, people made a mess of this leadership role too. The role had become something it was not. A lot of *sheep* must not read their Bibles because several didn't understand the true biblical role of elder or shepherd. A host of people in our big church, mostly older members, had come to believe an elder must be wealthy, or an executive in his secular work, and possess all the usual material things those people typically possess. The mindset was not fully engrained, but holdovers from the past held to strict traditions. Nothing about that mindset is biblical. I did eventually agree to accept the role and was installed – didn't like the word *installed* – sounds too churchy and uppity, a *high church* word – another one of those holdovers that needed to be banned.

Elders met weekly when I joined the crew. It's a smaller group of men because we were considered the most *spiritual* among the flock – we were overseers of the *lowly sheep*. What I quickly learned and admired: they were regular men, seriously concerned about the spiritual well-being of the flock, concerned about the preacher doing his job well, but hyper concerned about the weekly budget – a concern I didn't admire and the least of my concerns. We started every meeting with prayer for those with specific requests. But like all regularly scheduled meetings, we frequently got bogged down in the minutiae of church business. I didn't like that aspect of our lengthy meetings. One evening as we debated a particular situation involving one of our *sheep*, I noticed one of my fellow elders nodding off. As we arrived at an impasse in the debate the sleeping elder popped his head up and affirmed emphatically, *"She's a nut, and she'll always be a nut!"* He settled the debate immediately. I liked his candid, straight forward approach. It was rare something like that occurred though – usually we were too nice because we didn't wish to hurt anyone's feelings or state the truth people really needed to hear.

A *sheep* walked up to me following a service and asked if I could do something about the large podium the preacher stands behind – thought it was too big and dominated the pulpit area. I smiled and lied; told her I would look into the issue. Sometimes *sheep* are dumb and say stupid things. Comments like that confirm to me they are not reading the Bible. That's why the Bible refers to followers as sheep – sheep are dumb – that's why they need a shepherd. At the conclusion of each service two elders stood close to the pulpit to receive anyone coming forward for prayer or repentance. Every time it was my turn, I stood looking out across the crowd of *sheep* thinking the same thing – I don't know these people; how can I shepherd people I don't know? I was greatly bothered by that question and could never formulate a reasonable justification until I was able to be honest and finally concluded – resign. It was the only way to relieve myself of the nagging guilt and tension I couldn't shake. To shepherd sheep one must know the sheep – the flock – it simply wasn't possible in a big church like Madison. I blamed my resignation on the demands of my daughter's sports schedule and my executive role at the same school – another lie.

Reflecting on two years of serving as elder, the greatest purpose I served was most definitely for one of my dearest friends and her two children – I actually performed as a true shepherd on their behalf. For several years her husband, a good friend of mine, cheated on her, and when she finally had enough and gathered all the damning evidence she needed, it was time to end their marriage. He left her and the children with a house literally falling down all around them from all the remodeling he never completed. I had opportunity to talk with the children and urged them not to hate their father, hating his choices was okay, and perhaps one day they could forgive him – my first real shepherding moment. I recommended to the elders we offer her a home the church owned and allow her to pay a small amount of monthly rent, something she would insist on doing. They whole heartedly agreed, and a crew of church friends moved her. The week before the move another church friend in the financial loan business called me to say they must foreclose on the house. I begged her to wait until after the move then take possession – she agreed to wait – a second real shepherding moment.

A few months before I resigned a discussion among the elders ensued about selling unnecessary church property which included my friend's new dwelling. One elder wanted to make the announcement before the church but without specifics. I spoke up, *"We can't do that because she and her children will be sitting there – it would be terribly upsetting for her to know she had to make another move."* They agreed that I could share it with her privately before the public announcement. She didn't take it very well and was upset by the news as I suspected. I then proposed we only sell several acres on the back half of the property first, sell road access to the property between two houses, leaving three houses for situations like my friend. They again agreed and she remained in the house with her two children. A third real shepherding moment. My short service as an elder was not completely in vain – my service had a specific purpose and I believe the purpose was fulfilled according to a larger plan.

The conclusion of our time at the big church was perfectly clear as we listened intently to the seventh minister in our thirty-two-year stint of emerging spiritual growth tell us he was leaving – he was done – we knew we were done too. Not because we would follow a minister – we didn't have a clue where or what Jason was planning to do with his life. We simply left to seek another spiritual family. We didn't leave angry with anyone – this chapter of our faith journey closed forever.

My father-in-law was enormously unhappy about our

decision – his golden child was born and raised in the church of Christ and was leaving it behind. He feared we were jeopardizing our salvation because he firmly believes the name of the church matters and being non-instrumental is crucial to being in a right relationship with God – not exactly sure he can thoroughly justify that stance, but that's his belief. My mother-in-law on the other hand, didn't take a hard line on those issues. We remained steadfast in our determination to move forward. Thirty-five years earlier a rekindled faith journey began in the churches of Christ and that choice altered circumstances in many positive ways – numerous significant events and people, including my beloved in-laws, all played vital roles in redirecting my adult character. I remain eternally grateful for each of those events and to every single person that influenced my spiritual path.

We are presently both partners of an independent church that meets in a rented sanctuary – we don't own a church building – sing with instruments – part-time staff – simply a small group of imperfect people serving a perfect God. We no longer desire an institutional church but have learned all churches, regardless of size and focus, have matters of dispute and never-ending struggles because it's comprised of people, and people will forever be flawed. We've learned it's not possible to have our spiritual journey all figured out. The one thing we know for certain – it's an individual's journey – the choice to seek spiritual transformation. Our spiritual journey is just that, a journey of discovery – we are always open, allowing a Divine presence to direct and open new levels of connection and deeper understandings.

Darkness

The darkest moments in my life regrettably coincide with the darkest years of my emotional growth and physical development – adolescence. Guilt driven rage accentuated by alcohol led to spousal abuse. Confusion and fear colliding created helplessness with each turbulent year. This is by far the most difficult portion of my life to expose. Pam struggled to understand why I didn't seem to like much of anything to do with Christmas – she loved every moment. I played along but often felt down-cast – a gloomy type sadness drifted over me resulting in a stagnant fog that wouldn't lift during most holiday seasons. I finally divulged the culprit, but she was unable to fully grasp or understand – it wasn't her experience, she had absolutely no point of reference to comprehend the gloominess. Christmas in an eight-foot-wide rectangle offered decent moments – but when alcohol in copious amounts is consumed the result leads to a not so happy, joyous place to be and especially for an only child. I had no place to retreat – hide – there was no room to go where I could shut it off – not hear the dysfunction when the *monster* raised its ugly head. I know there are more tragic situations than mine regarding alcoholism – situations far beyond anything I experienced. But my circumstances are mine and shaped who I am – both for good and bad.

Fog of addiction creeped in, shrouding holidays and obscuring life because my father used days off to doubly enjoy intoxicants, often becoming sleepy – long naps the best-case scenario. Other times, usually late in the evening, guilty rage triggered him, and he turned toward my mother. The worse time span for his alcoholic rage was during my most awkward stages of adolescent life – sixth grade to ninth – junior high. Perfect timing. My sixth grade was part of the elementary school I attended – junior high school was seventh through ninth. As with every adolescent, life is already filled with abnormal to extreme mood swings, compounded by physical changes and sexual maturation. Adding addictions to normal growth and maturation ballooned my chances for catastrophic outcomes – *"he didn't have a rat's chance in hell."*

It was late evening on Christmas Eve – my parents had given in to my begging and allowed me to open one gift. I picked a big box – the board game Green Ghost. I worked a long time taking out all the tiny parts from the packages and putting pieces together creating the maze and traps – I was totally immersed.

Deep-seated emotions are stirred when I think of this particular evening and during a favorite scene from Santa Claus II when Tim Allen, alias Santa Claus, decides to spice up the boring teacher holiday party by giving vintage toy gifts to everyone. Joy abounds once everyone is suddenly immersed, as I was, in playing their favorite childhood games – Green Ghost is one of those. When I see it, stored memories are jogged loose in my brain then tears every time. I know exactly what generates the deeply-rooted emotion – a penetrating, dreadful memory – as fresh today as the moment mayhem ensued.

My parents finally went to bed, but I needed to finish my game construction project and study rules – within the hour I overheard my parents arguing from the back bedroom just a few feet from my spot on the living room floor. I ignored their quarreling voices because I had experienced similar conflict many times before. My mother suddenly bounded through the narrow passage, stomping her feet in disgust and anger through the tiny bathroom and my bedroom – my father followed her with a staggering irritated gaze. I was immediately told to go to bed. I slowly rose and walked toward my tiny space and pulled the pocket door shut. My parents were now in the living room on the green couch – the arguing worsened. I could hear every word, but my mother tried her best to keep things quiet with her typical denial – didn't work this time. A muffled, *"Tell me the truth,"* from my father and hushed denials from my mother.

Their arguing escalated again then heard my mother scream stop – heard a slap – she screamed again, and I heard thumps against the floor – perhaps their feet. Got out of bed and walked slowly into the kitchen, stopped at my desk – heart thumping out of my chest – he gripped my mother's arm – jerking her arm toward him – asking if she was cheating on him – she said no numerous times – he raised his hand to strike her again – she yelled, *"No Bill!"* I intervened with a loud *STOP.* Both glanced toward my direction and told me to go back to bed – I refused. He hit her again – she dropped her head – I knew the hit shamed her; he looked enraged – lips pursed tightly. She attempted to escape – told me again to go to bed. As she lifted herself from the couch, he wrapped his hand tightly onto her arm and pulled her back to a seated position – she complied and shielded her face. I cried, begging them to stop fighting. I don't recall exactly how the horrible confrontation deescalated.

The next thing I recall is sitting on the floor next to the new board game – Green Ghost. I reached slowly for pieces I hadn't placed – arm and hand still trembling – looking through foggy eyes, smearing nose droplets on my pajama sleeve – the room quiet now – heart pounding. My father went to bed – probably passed out from his inebriated rampage. He successfully ruined another Christmas – another drunken holiday season to remember. What was she thinking? Did she cheat on him? If she did, she didn't deserve what just occurred. Thoughts crashing around in my mind – continued working on the new board game. The game must be perfectly assembled as I wanted my life perfectly assembled. I had full control now. Played the game in quiet, peaceful solitude – easy to lose track of time – glanced at the worn green couch, flattened cushions where abuse occurred – heard my father snoring – didn't really matter at this point. Hurtful memories buried again to reemerge at unexpected times – life must go on.

A family denial routine in daylight – quiet movements – few words – breakfast – remaining gifts opened. We typically traveled to Murfreesboro Christmas Day. I don't remember if we did – gifts were not exchanged at the Tenpenny grandparents – too many grandchildren. My father, my mother, and I knew the drill. We pretended with precision – *Oscar worthy.* An invisible veil of secrecy covered our true faces, usual hugs, smiles, delicious food tainted on Christmas Day by abuse. Found comfort in the decadent holiday jam cake in the round aluminum holder on top of the Tenpenny refrigerator – eyes focused immediately on that location upon entering the back-porch through the screen door. My brain still a collision of exploding emotions – must remain hidden – not approved for sharing. Secrets never to be told – wounded joy over temporary pleasures of a grandmother's holiday feast. Nothing ever voiced about these incidents and my mother never confided in anyone to my knowledge – denial her preferred mode of operation.

I nearly revealed our dark secret on one occasion. Don't remember the time of the year but it wasn't cold. The same recipe of holiday ingredients made for another night of mayhem. Noritake china ordered from Seoul, Korea sent from Japan became an additional ingredient for a fit of rage and frustration. I now possess the partial set – originally ninety-three pieces according to a 1952 letter from my father to his parents, William and Lucy Morris. My father purchased the set of fine china for $40, paid $20 for postage and insurance. I have the original Japan Central Exchange customer's copy. Lucy passed the set to her daughter-in-law. My mother didn't understand the value or quality – I witnessed fine china thrashed to the floor not knowing why. My father got involved, he thrashed but not the china purchased in 1952. I suppose it held an emotional bond for him. At the height of the mayhem, I stormed out the door and sought refuge at my best friend's mobile home – it was late – no lights – everyone asleep. I pounded hard against the door, knocked, knocked, knocked and knocked for an eternity – no one responded. I walked back slowly to the narrow rectangle on the favored lot not knowing what might be – circumstances now calmer. Perhaps the abuser and abused realized their dysfunction was close to full exposure. They momentarily put aside the absurd thrashing and bickering – broken china gone – asked where I'd been, didn't tell the truth – probably said walking. I speculated no one answered the door on purpose, my hand hurt – no one said anything about missing china the next time it was used – I possess only forty-five pieces.

One morning after a similar evening I remember my mother leaning in close to the bathroom mirror applying makeup to cover a bruise above her eye. Asked if she was okay – *"Yes, don't worry about it. I'm fine."* I knew she wasn't telling the truth. These occurrences are not easy to share because the scars of emotional pain and hurt triggered by spousal abuse never fade as real scars do, nor are they completely forgotten. The frightening circumstances didn't last – abuse eventually ended – alcoholism didn't. I believed the abuse and accusations toward my mother had a direct connection to his infidelity – loss of my best friend ended abuse. Didn't understand that aspect during real-time moments but later understood it to be the origin amplified by liquid spirits. The sacrifice of a friendship ultimately saved two marriages. Alcoholic indulgences triggered our threesome's darkest moments – compounded by lust and weakness of choice. As darkness engulfed and surrounded me, an internal voice sometimes spoke soothing unintelligible words of peace and freedom into the deepest portions of my soul. I listened attentively in the darkness and sometimes consoled.

Within darkness are faint glimmers of light. Peculiar and sadistic to say I enjoyed times when my father was physically ill. Obviously, times that stand in stark contrast to darkness – in sickness or taking medication, he didn't consume alcohol, at least not in excess. One time he started having nose bleeds – something I've never experienced – no DNA propensity. He was forced to seek a doctor because his condition worsened – he didn't understand alcohol consumption was a contributing factor. When he came home his nose was packed with gauze – necessitating he repack it often. An unpleasant sight, but for me so much more tolerable than the results of binge drinking. I talked to him – he talked to me – we laughed – enjoyed life and he was so much healthier overall. We didn't dismiss each other based on prior hurts or impending results. I clearly noticed a temporary alteration of circumstances – did my mother notice? She never spoke a word. More importantly, did my father notice a difference? He spoke nothing about it. Life was calmer, more peaceful, and conversational due to sickness – strange how sickness brought momentary light into darkness.

Darkness within family structures take on many facets – known as dysfunction in today's politically correct vernacular.

In reference to my family dysfunction, *darkness* strikes the right tone for describing diverse situations and trials – it's what I felt inside – darkness coupled with fear. I wanted it to end – not my life – but the constant upheaval appearing to never fade. I wondered, did the full implications of darkness apply to long-time friends Blanch and Ned Derris and their five children? At least from my perspective hope was on my side when comparing family dynamics. I didn't know the hidden fragments of their private lives. I would describe dysfunction in the Derris family as unstructured and happenstance. Nothing in the Derris family ever appeared in order or well put together – true minimalists at best.

We first met the Derris family on Maple Street in Madison when I was four and five – they lived next door. When my parents bought their new two-bedroom brick home on Shepherd Hills Drive – the Derris family purchased a home in a new development about the same time we did – we were all climbing the success ladder. Unfortunately, we only possessed our new brick home for one year. We then moved to the trailer park a few blocks from their developing neighborhood. The Derris family managed to keep their new home, but it didn't look new very long – they were not good housekeepers both inside and out. The inside of their house was sparse – nothing on the walls, not a lot of furniture. What they did possess was quickly damaged and worn due to five romping, jumping, and playing children. My home seemed well-organized and sane in comparison. In some ways I loved going to their house – no pressures, no restrictions – just pure unrestraint and wildness reigned throughout the house – I could let go of my perfectionism with unbridled abandonment while our parents partied late into the evening.

Blanch smiled a lot – revealing she didn't visit a dentist. Always happy go-lucky with simple surroundings and five uninhibited children. She never acted stressed about anything.

She and Ned both occasionally spanked one of the reckless five for pushing limits, but it was quickly over and never changed any unrestrained behavior. Lunch at the Derris house meant simple white bread and bologna with mayonnaise, possibly plain potato chips and white sugar sweet Kool-Aid. Nothing ever lavish or overdone, never cooked an extravagant meal like the Spann's or what we ate at my house on any given day.

My parents enjoyed partying at their house – Ned and Blanch were hearty beer drinkers – cheaper than whiskey. I witnessed numerous occasions the adults exchange partners dancing to Patsy Cline, Ray Price, and many other country music favorites. One evening as we departed their house returning to our mobile home, I was in the car with my cousin Bill waiting – my uncle must have been driving because my father was too drunk to drive – he walked out on the small concrete front porch – made a wide swing of his leg to one side thinking he was stepping onto a lower step below – instead he fell over into a shrub and landed on the ground. My cousin Bill and I witnessed, he laughed hysterically – I pretended – don't remember who assisted him to the car. The incident didn't seriously upset me; he wasn't driving and we had company, but hidden away deep inside I was hurt and saddened – suppressed my desire to yell then cry.

Never remember staying overnight at the Derris house – too disorganized and chaotic for me. I preferred our better food choices. What I liked was playing in and around their newly developing neighborhood. Mike was the second oldest and my same age, but I played with all the siblings. Jimmy the oldest, Jerry, then Philip, and Kelly was the youngest. We had a blast playing in and around the construction. Every new building site a huge pile of sand along with scrap 2x4 pieces of wood – lots of left-over brick – a perfect playground for reckless kids to create. We played for hours at some sites and never told to leave by workers. If we got too hot or a little bored a large stream was a couple of blocks away and we would go cool off in the water – again, reckless, sometimes innocent skinny-dipping, nonstop fun times.

Mike and I continued in the same schools, but he chose a different path of coping – addicted to smoking pot and other drugs. Perhaps he was deadening his darkest moments in life. His moments I knew nothing about, but we both knew how to hide, place our darkest moments in protected spaces until seepage, little by little in forms of depression, anger, or defiance. Mike found refuge and an abnormal comfort in being stoned. He didn't have loving grandparents providing solace and peace. Mike didn't have the expanse of Spanntown where unhappy circumstances could be misplaced for a weekend. He didn't have a space to himself behind a pocket door to reflect and ponder his future. Mike needed a quick fix, something to dull pain – quickly take him away from life as he knew it.

In high school when we crossed paths his face downcast, long hair unkempt and tousled, hiding from connection, he didn't notice me – a friend I once knew now recoiling into a life of addiction and suffering. Years later I heard Mike's younger brother Jerry was in a serious car accident as a teenager – ended up with lifelong injuries – won an injury claim lawsuit and was paid several thousand dollars. Our relationship with the Derris family ended and the lawsuit money squandered within a year or two. The family threw it all away with no regard for budget or saving. Perhaps Jerry's accident, Mike's drug addiction, coupled with unstructured dysfunction overall, plus darkness I didn't know, led them to darkness of a different form.

My mother and I reminisced about our friendship with the Derris family during her short stay in the *facility* before death. She wondered about her friend Blanch. I located her online obituary and shared – a rush of melancholy enveloped her face – looked off toward the window she thought was on an upper floor of the *rehabilitation facility* – she pondered a lost relationship – a friend she truly loved.

A manifestation of darkness is loss of innocence – another unintended casualty caused by poverty. After my parents lost their new brick home with a fireplace and full-size basement garage, poverty trapped my youth within adult circumstances before I was mentally competent to process – forced me into a cesspool I couldn't navigate. Little to no privacy in our limited space, every sound a body is capable of emitting or create is heard – even blinks. I despised every forced encounter with private commotions and expelled noises – longed for privacy. A tiny bathroom smashed between two bedrooms separated by pocket doors and paper-thin paneling never provided what I desired. What did my mother think and feel the first time she strolled through the dimly lit narrow rectangle? Ejected from a spacious dwelling made of brick is sickening perhaps – required to abandon dreams of a better life – privacy lost. She never expressed those feelings to me. Privacy no longer attainable for adulthood or childhood in the rectangle dwelling, and what immaturity didn't recognize, my parents suffered the same dilemma as I eventually suffered – probably more so. Based on my recollections, we rapidly descended into a state of impoverishment.

One late night after booze flowed freely for several hours my father stumbled out of bed to relieve himself. He was so pathetically inebriated he mistakenly thought the small built-in chest directly in front of the bed was a toilet. He managed to pull a drawer open on my former chest of drawers and let it rip. I was suddenly awakened by my mother screaming for him to stop. His reaction time much slower, but he eventually heeded her pleas and stopped emptying his bladder. Thankfully he had only three unsteady steps to the real toilet directly behind the thin paneled wall. I absorbed every sound and shuffle through my thin pocket door – remained silent and still while he emptied. A portion of me wanted to laugh but a bigger portion wanted to yell then cry. The next day my mother had unexpected laundry to wash – the incident never mentioned.

Fading innocence awakened every morning by bodily functions – how could I not be repulsed and highly tuned-in to private moments of others when so little buffered the space between us? Didn't like secret noises disturbing my brain and began to conceal my own – an arcane struggle for any child to bear. When younger I heard noises that I didn't understand – yelled, *"Stop making that noise!"* Sometimes the noise stopped, other times not – innocence seized again. During adolescence I perceived my parents probably hated my presence and treasured my absence – they needed a break too. Poverty magnified family issues and shaped our *love-hate* relationship, leading me to be imaginative and highly motivated to seek alternatives for a more tranquil future. Odd how forms of *darkness* can instigate resolve and drive.

Accepted

Acceptance by a father is critically important to social and emotional growth, self-worth, and overall stability as a male or female. I believe *masculinity*, however that is defined, is best conveyed by another male and hopefully for a guy it's his father, grandfather or close male relative – of course there are always exceptions. Other males as in peers convey masculinity – their acceptance can be equally as important as a father's. Unfortunately, I didn't experience healthy doses of acceptance by either one. Males desperately need other males. Political correctness arbiters might raise its collective antenna and strongly disagree with my *father* or *peer, male* to *male* premise. My initial response to a sentiment like that is simple: this is strictly my opinion based on personal experiences. A twisted form of masculinity was conveyed upon me by a totally perverted, immoral form – primarily pornography. Was that appropriate? No. My father remained self-absorbed and addicted to alcohol and pornography for the better part of his adult life. I'm describing a huge number of men during the decades of the 60's and 70's – the critical period of my adolescent growth and development. A large percentage of men in my father's generation were war veterans; they had numerous vices that served as coping mechanisms and never really understood or realized the level of pain and anguish inflicted upon so many children. The hurt and dysfunction heaped upon their families and especially their own children led to countless numbers of generational addictions, divorces, and overall dysfunction – statistics bear out this truth.

My parents somehow avoided divorce – perhaps *misery loves company* applied to them. Addiction and dysfunction were both alive and well in our home, though my father's two addictions superseded any addiction or dysfunction of my mother's. She was the typical wife of servitude – male dominated and weak – it was her duty to cook and clean – not ever his unless grilling. A trailer park version of *Mrs. Cleaver*. He insisted on a full meal every evening – we rarely ate out. Her alcohol consumption was minimal, and it was rare to see her intoxicated. On those rare occasions when both were intoxicated fireworks usually ensued over a variety of unresolved issues. Doors slammed, dishes deliberately broken, verbal and sometimes physical abuse, and always hateful words. I detested all of it and terribly resented every confrontation. In trailer life, children always have a front row seat.

Addiction and dysfunction are the root causes of why I never felt fully accepted by my father. Perhaps the discovery through Ancestry that he is not my biological father explains on a deeper level his behavior towards me even more – I simply don't know. What truth did he know when he married and she was five months pregnant? Did he think I was his child, or did he suspect I might not be? He was extremely distant – never attempted to include me in any type of father-son adventure – rarely just the two of us. Yes, I rode to the liquor store or grocery with him. Once I had my driver's license, he occasionally allowed me to keep his car, but I had to rise early, take him to work and pick him up. Never had a heart-to-heart, father-son conversation but for the attempt to tell me about the *birds and bees* – didn't go well, he was drunk

– the finger demonstration was embarrassing. He never encouraged me to pursue post high school education, that was all on me. I desired so much more from him – longed for it – but it never happened.

I internalized his rejection as nonacceptance – as if something was wrong with me. I ached to feel loved by him. I wanted to be told what a good son I was. I wanted to be honored for my good choices. I wanted to be recognized for my unique talents. He never verbalized any of those things. Perhaps I buried my anger when I buried him at just fifty-five. I felt cheated. I had opportunity to reconcile my anger and resentment toward my mother. As I've shared, I held her hands after telling her it was okay to go. I was at total peace without regrets after seeing to her needs for over twenty-five years. Not the same with my father. I did forgive him. Why grip anger and resentment – that nagging gets old. After a *spilling* he told me, *"It's highly probable you have suppressed feelings but outwardly it's unseen."* Perhaps that's the uneasy gnawing I feel when my emotions occasionally reach a boiling point, typically over something totally unrelated and often insignificant. Perhaps that explains the occasional unwarranted outbursts toward my wife. She's in close proximity most of the time, so it's just easier but not fair to her. She has said numerous times when we are in a heightened discussion, *"Why are you yelling?"* Old habits die hard.

During my father's funeral visitation, one of the proprietors of the meat packing business where he worked expressed condolences and shared something I didn't expect to hear. He said my father talked about my attending college seeking a degree and how proud he was that I became a professional teacher. Stunned is the best adjective but it also made me a little angry and more resentful toward him in a strange type of way. Here he was stretched out in a casket in the only suit coat and tie he owned; why did I feel this way and why did he never tell me? What prevented him from uttering those simple words? Why is it so important to me that I'm spilling my story at age sixty-three? Why can't I just say what the hell does it matter at this point and move beyond – way beyond?

My feelings about acceptance may also be rooted in not being accepted by other males in general. Every time a male didn't accept me at school feelings of anger surfaced and still surface to this day when I sense rejection. It's never been my nature to be very aggressive, but I swear, knocking the shit out of several male acquaintances from my past would feel very satisfying. Would it solve any unsettled issues with the father who raised me? Probably not. I'm glad to know he was actually proud of me. But what do I do to overcome this gnawing? It seems to have taken up residence somewhere deep within. Since I rarely felt accepted by male peers at school and especially not by my father, he suggested, *"Consider talking to your father and your biological father through letters or visit their graves, tell them how you feel about this issue – speak directly from the heart."* My wife said that might be an opportunity to be the most open and honest I've ever been about this particular subject – she's usually right.

In a gritty attempt to prove manhood and be accepted among a group of males I hoisted the heavy backpack through one arm and around to my backside, then the other arm with a sudden realization, heavier than I originally thought. A forced unspoken question – would my lower back hold out? It was about 4:00 pm and I knew we were pushing our luck to make it to the first camp site before dark – didn't happen. The incline path was narrow and rocky and became narrower as we slowly trekked upward. After a long mile or so on the incline it was clear my life could come to a tragic end if I took a misstep to the left. Although tempted to gaze, I avoided looking too long because it seemed my curiosity pulled in that direction – desperately wanted to view the depth – reasoning halted a dangerous desire. Manly?

Seven males slowly navigated several switchbacks as the incline steepened. By this point, about two hours into the climb I needed to pee. Do I just stop and say excuse me; I'll catch up? Wasn't sure about wilderness protocol for pee breaks on a narrow path. Seven guys from age seventeen to late-forties, wasn't a privacy issue because there was no one else so my better reasoning said take a break, but there was nowhere to step away. So, I spoke up and said I'm taking a quick break and will catch up. The other six guys were good with a quick break – so we all took a break not only to relieve bladders but give our backs a short respite. Took my water bottle out of the side pocket for a hasty drink and wondered where our water source would come from after eventually emptying bottles. This was my first wilderness hike. I didn't remember Mark talking about a water source – perhaps I had forgotten something. We were in northeastern Washington State walking north toward the Canadian border – no water fountains. What was I thinking? Dismissed the life sustaining question and hoisted the heavy backpack into position because I'm a man and this is what real men do – at least that was my thinking at that moment.

Mark and a few other guys had taken this similar wilderness hike before because Mark's parents lived in that area in the small town of Pateros near the base of Alta State Park and wilderness area – an area on the northeast side of Lake Chelan. Hearing conversations about their adventures intrigued me. Mark encouraged me to go on the next trip planned for July – it was mid-February when we first talked. Since a trip of this type was not in my comfort zone, I knew a lot of preplanning must occur. I requested a detailed briefing with Mark – so many questions – I needed answers. After hearing detailed descriptions of the trip, I committed myself –

count me in. I knew I must prepare physically which meant losing some weight and conditioning my body for the rugged terrain. I started walking with a weighted backpack in early March and continued until the trip. What I didn't realize was the difference in weight of the actual backpack for the real hike. Mark had a way of not sharing details – something I didn't fully understand until a mile or so into the hike. What else was there to discover that I didn't know or understand – a lot.

Light was fading fast as the narrow rocky path moved closer to my face as I leaned forward balancing the heaviness on my back. Suddenly I realized after being buried in my own thoughts for several minutes, it was completely dark. Time for flashlights – we paused, I looked up. The darkness seemed closer than ever; speckled with thousands of tiny glimmers, I thought of movies when people look into a dark sky and Hollywood simulates a star filled sky with more stars than the naked eye can actually see. But I was gazing at the real creation at its best – no man-made light interrupted the sparkly, celestial night sky – I beheld untarnished beauty. I remember walking what seemed like another two miles, probably less. The landscape leveled off a bit, and we were actually walking on a slight decline. Some relief, but I had to forcefully straighten my spine to now compensate for the change and equalize the weighty load.

The path was actually muddy in spots from rain earlier in the day and portions of the beaten, compacted soil pliable enough to leave boot prints. I had purchased new hiking boots that were extremely comfortable and waterproof – new thick hiking socks too. Mark and his brother from the area noticed another type of print in softer trampled soil – paw prints. Someone mentioned a mountain lion. I slowly processed the comment considering my options then decided it was best to dismiss the thought because I couldn't see anything around me but a star-studded sky and there were seven of us – a mountain lion would only eat one of us – one in seven isn't bad odds. I kept walking when I heard commotion several yards before me. No one was screaming – good sign but heard men talking. Then the animal was revealed – a large Rottweiler walked among us, sniffing our legs and wagging a stumpy tail. I was thrilled and relieved to see the dog and knew we were safe from any wild animals looking for a late-night snack. We had walked upon another campsite where a few men had already set up tents and were sitting by a small fire barely burning.

We continued our trek to what I hoped was another suitable campsite – I was growing tired of walking and the heavy load. Finally, around 10:00 pm we stopped. Of course, I had no idea where in the world I was other than somewhere in northeastern Washington State. We used our flashlights to assist one another in preparing what we needed for the overnight rest stop. Yes, I was going to sleep in a tent – first time since I was about eight or nine years old. Santa Claus brought me an army tent and we set it up in the yard next to my trailer. I'm not certain I ever stayed all night, but I do remember my best friend Andy or favorite cousin Bill being in the tent with me on several occasions. The small tent I borrowed from Mark was not going together well – it was late – we were tired. Mark's friend, about my age, said I could share his tent, but it was small – we barely managed to make it work. The tent was apparently over a dip, so when I finally positioned myself, it was like being sideways in a half-reclined recliner – not comfortable, but I was so sleepy it didn't really matter at that point. I thought about sleeping in the floorboard of Mr. Pigg's pickup truck at Kentucky Lake as a little boy. Also, mountain lions, bears, whatever crossed my mind was quickly absorbed by an overpowering desire to sleep.

Awakened to sunshine – finally seeing our surroundings –

majestic, snow-covered mountains in the distance – rolling hills immediately before us flanked by walls of layered rock. I was thrilled to take it all in from every direction as my eyes darted – nature's sheer beauty at its very best. We were all comfortable at this point in taking care of our personal needs, so that was no longer an issue for me. Once everyone was awake and out of tents, we discussed the day ahead and all it involved. I munched on a strawberry iced pop-tart and finished my water bottle. I finally asked about a water source and was told by the experienced hikers we would soon locate a fast-moving stream where the water was rushing over rocks – that water would be naturally purified. My mind thought about deer and bear pee but quickly learned to dismiss those concerns because it didn't seem to be important to anyone else.

Grabbed my roll of toilet tissue to head off and locate an appropriate spot. I was reminded not to go too far from camp. I was originally told we would never leave camp alone, but no one seemed interested in making my little excursion a double. I found what I thought was a good spot several yards away behind some low bushy growth. Looked for some downed trees because of what I had learned about these private moments on a wilderness hike. Scratched out a hole in the thick ground cover with my boot and took care of business – minor success. My private excursion was second nature to seasoned hikers, but not for me. I wanted to do things right and not be embarrassed by an inability to handle quotidian routines of daily life in the wilderness. I wanted *nature calling* to become routine, no big deal – it's life. Act like a man!

After returning to camp, I wanted to explore a bit more – the other guys were drinking coffee they had brewed over fire, but I wasn't interested because I didn't drink coffee. I walked to what appeared to be a pathway into an open field below the steep rock wall I spotted on an earlier *routine* excursion. I froze, struck by nature's beauty once again. A field covered in blooming wildflowers, scarlet paintbrush, lacy cow parsley, purple camas, Alpine lupines – imagined a beautiful bouquet of wildflowers but our masculine troop would not understand my creative inclinations. Thirty yards away a large boulder sat solitary, surrounded by perfect loveliness. I observed it all. The boulder looked as though I might be able to climb upon it for a little awestruck meditation – I did just that. Attempting to register the enormity, the silence overwhelmed my senses, deep breathing unpolluted air – only interrupted occasionally by a mountain bluebird or western meadowlark alerting me I invaded their private sanctuary. I didn't want to leave – peered again at the elevation of solid rock two hundred yards or so before me – scanned the magnificent floral blanket of soft hues at its feet – manly? Who cares? I thanked God for His beautiful creation – my feeble words fell short. I asked for guidance and safety for our hikers. Did not yet fully understand the unseen marvels Washington State had in store for my senses. We hoisted our slightly lighter backpacks onto our backsides and started the second day trek to another wilderness campsite.

During the next few miles, we hiked to a higher elevation – some elevations we reached were over 5000 feet. Typically, altitude sickness doesn't occur before 8000 feet unless someone is not well conditioned. None of us had experienced any breathing issues yet even though the elevation was gradually growing higher. We stopped along the way up at some beautiful, crystal-clear lakes. At one point we came to a fast runoff of water from a higher elevation where the snow was melting because it was early July. The water was super cold and appeared to be perfectly clean. We filled water bottles – gulped it down and filled again – the best tasting water I had ever consumed – deer and bear pee weren't even noticeable.

At one of the largest clear lakes, vestiges of winter had not been completely relinquished. Ice and snow still gripped shaded edges covering portions of the clear water below. The lake was so clear it looked deceivingly shallow because you could see the bottom scattered with boulders and timbers past. We fished, or I should clarify, they fished and I attempted to fish. We didn't catch any at this location but again, the beauty of the lake and surrounding mountains were so breathtakingly spectacular it didn't seem to matter. Nothing our human eyes gazed upon was manmade – every intricacy fashioned by nature.

We heard in the distance, from the far side of the lake, a continuous crunching sound. Someone said it might be a bear. To this point we had not seen any wild animals, and that was okay with me. Upon closer inspection we discovered the crunching sound was a tree that had fallen across a water fall of melting snow and ice. The runoff was pounding the tree against the thick undergrowth at the edge of the lake, creating a repetitive crunch. Relief for me. We arrived at our new campsite that had been abandoned for several days it appeared. Four neatly cut logs surrounded a crudely trenched firepit. The campsite was flat which made me think I wouldn't be sleeping in the awkward position like the evening before.

Mark was very quiet as he rested on one of the logs. He was concerned because his breathing was shallow and he suddenly felt fatigued – was our wilderness hike about to abruptly end? He and his brother discussed the options because they both knew he was experiencing signs of altitude sickness. Mark decided while he had a half day of sunlight left, he and his brother would go back to the trailhead and his brother would take him to his house. His brother would rejoin us the next morning. This meant we were going to be left alone in a remote area of wilderness in northeastern Washington State – how would we survive? But I did not want our journey to end. One semi-experienced hiker was still with us and the remaining four of us wanted to continue our manly adventure.

We sat up camp and gathered firewood for the evening. After Mark and his brother left, we decided to set out to locate a fishing area Mark and his brother had told us is close to our campsite. On the short hike to the lake, we walked through a lot of thick brush and trees. Suddenly we heard what seemed to be a sawing noise. After walking under and over several downed trees we walked upon two forest rangers hand sawing a tree to clear the path to the lake. They told us they had been working in the area all day to clear the path to the point where we met. They asked if we were good, and I was calmed by their authoritative presence – secretly wished they would camp close to us.

At the lake we all separated and fished alone around the large perimeter – it was huge. I stood on a naturally ossified wood debris portico just above the shallow water. The lake perfectly still – surrounded by majestic mountains to the north and west. I was glad to be fishing alone because I typically fumbled with my rod and hook, but I knew what to do. Silence saturated the entire area. After several attempts I finally got a nibble then a tug – a fish. I pulled my rod up and sure enough a fish was on the other end. Before thinking I broke the code of silence and yelled across the lake to my fellow fishermen, *"Look, I caught a fish!"* I immediately realized that was not the cool fisherman thing to do. A little embarrassed, I retreated back into myself and reinstated silence. I carefully strung my fish and tied it to a secure log and waited. I caught my dinner. Many years ago, trailer park friends Mr. and Mrs. Pigg taught me how to clean fish at Kentucky Lake. Mr. Pigg was a fisherman's fisherman – I reflected on those earnest memories.

The other guys caught enough fish for dinner, and we made our way back to camp. We cleaned and prepared our fish for dinner in the pristine, cold water of the stream close to camp. Cooking my fish over the fire, I attempted to deny the gutting and cleaning ritual, smell, and the fact I didn't have enough seasonings to disguise the *fresh* taste. I ate like a true outdoorsman and pretended to love my fish. I brought homemade trail mix and munched on it after the fish dinner. A blueberry iced pop tart restored my palate to a more satisfying place. It's unfortunate, but as I fully expected, my digestive system would be affected by the change in eating habits. An abrupt change in eating habits naturally changes other routines as well. Before dark I needed to take another *true outdoorsman* much-needed short hike alone and attempt to relieve my overdue system. I wanted to do it right this time, but this was not routine for me. A seasoned outdoorsman can deal with this issue as par for the course – very routine and they probably give little attention to it. I was damn well determined to do this right.

My brother-in-law, an avid outdoorsman, had described to me exactly how to do this in order to maximize results. I was unyielding to do it this time as he described. I knew going too far from camp was not advisable, so I scanned the area with a sharp eye and moved far enough away but stayed close enough to not get disoriented from camp. I found what I thought might be an ideal location – two downed trees separated by about a foot and a half – one slightly bigger than the other. I inspected the sight as my excitement and anticipation for success grew. Scanning the entire area, I looked for foreign invaders or unwanted guests – no signs of people or animals. Let's do this. I first tried positioning myself before removing clothes. The position of my gluteus maximus off the largest log appeared textbook with my feet positioned under the lower log in front of me for all-out leverage. Now the real deal. Debated for a brief moment whether to remove my shorts and underwear completely or risk an accident on my clothes. I couldn't walk back to camp naked holding soiled clothes – I'd be forever known as the laughingstock of our hiking troop.

Thought about bugs crawling on me once I got positioned but quickly dismissed that concern. Placed the roll of tissue on a small stub next to me – removed my lower clothes – used the shorts as a pad for my legs – carefully placed myself on the larger log – braced my feet under the lower log for maximum leverage. After a few strains the deed was done, realized I didn't dig out hole below my position on the larger log. Oh well, a minor breach of protocol no one would ever know. Gathered lots of broken pieces of brush and forest debris to cover my successful moment. I proudly walked back to camp like a true outdoorsman – fully dressed and accomplished, happy, content, pleased, ready for an evening of fireside banter with my fellow outdoorsmen – we were real men, and I was feeling it.

After waking up the third morning I was trusting Mark and his brother made it back okay but was equally concerned for Mark's brother locating us. We did what was now our regular morning routines. I decided it was time to clean up a little – it had been four days since I had showered, and I purposely didn't bring shaving supplies – facial scruff had increased each day. I walked down to the pristine stream and washed my face and hair – the water was too cold for a full bath. I returned to the tent and cleaned myself in other neglected areas with wet wipes. I felt cleaner and now ready for the day. I seriously doubt real outdoorsmen worry with these things, but I was a temporary outdoorsman. Mark's brother made it back about 9:30 am because he got an early start – so pleased for his return. I'm not sure we could have made it back to the original trailhead without him. He suggested we hike a few miles back toward the trailhead, take a few short side hikes along the way, then head back to the original trailhead and return to his house. He said some of us could bunk there, the others at his parents with Mark and we could leave early each morning for the remainder of the trip and do day hikes. We all agreed that sounded like a good plan. Food items we packed were already running low, and this way we could easily replenish each day and lighten our backpacks tremendously. Mark had fully recovered and was ready to hike again.

Mark's brother knew the area well, so he guided us to several interesting panoramas and landscapes. In one area we came across an abandoned log cabin that had fallen into disrepair – probably constructed over fifty years ago – perhaps longer. I imagined the many people that may have once occupied the now crumbling structure. In this particular area I immediately noticed the abundance of beautiful pines – unlike any I see in Tennessee – other than much smaller versions during Christmas. The vertical branching structures, pine, fir, and spruce completely dominated the landscape. If I had counted just within my immediate eyesight, I could have easily counted a thousand perfect Christmas trees. In one location we climbed an interesting rock formation in the middle of a large grove of fir and spruce – we could see for miles and miles. A thousand vertical branching structures framed by what appeared a Claude Monet impressionistic masterpiece of mountain peaks in various hues of grays and blues – highlighted with rays of sun – scattered white to remind us of winter's dominance all within nature's colossal canvas.

In another area we paused, reverently allowed our senses time to process a massive trough-shaped valley sculpted by glaciers now quilted by forest trees spread out between bordering walls of scoured rock. The force and power of nature is undeniably breathtaking. We were somewhere between the eastern border of the North Cascades and Western edge of Okanogan Highlands. Nature loudly boasted and bragged of its enduring beauty throughout the total hike. We all stared with undiminished awe – no adequate words. On the return to the trailhead, my eyes now captured everything that was cloaked in darkness a few days before. Magnificence overstimulated my senses – everything a picture-perfect postcard better than the one before it. Truthfully, photos serve as a frail substitute for expressing the exact story of an area like this. Throughout the return hike I was energized minute by minute – every moment beyond comparison. We finally arrived at what appeared to be a seventies hippie van – funky wall-to-wall orange shag carpet interior. I was suddenly disengaged from Monet and breathtaking awe – hello Jimi Hendrix, Purple Haze, and Woodstock.

We piled into the van and headed to Mark's brother's house. I assumed he had owned the van for many years because it was in very good shape. I wondered if he'd been part of the hippie subculture at one time and grew beyond it but wanted to keep a vestige from his past. I'm certain the van had seen and heard a lot of unconventional subculture behavior during years of rebellion. We arrived at a picturesque home nestled at the base of a gigantic rolling hill of apple orchards. We met his wife, and she was putting finishing touches on dinner – the smell enticed my taste buds and made me forget my little fish cooked over fire. After a delicious dinner of roast beef, roasted potatoes, carrots, and green beans we settled into cozy chairs and watched the movie *Gladiator* – another manly moment. The movie stimulated my emotions but most importantly should inspire integrity within every man – something all men desperately need.

I was assigned a downstairs bedroom and shared a bathroom with the father and son on our trip. Before going to bed, each took our turn in the shower – so appreciated the shower, something I take for granted, because we had been denied this usual luxury. The bed felt so good too – didn't worry about any bears or mountain lions visiting my bedside. After an early breakfast we all hopped into the hippie van and headed to a new trailhead. My excitement was knowing we would return to the comfortable bed that evening. It appeared we drove forever, but it was worth the long drive once we could see Canadian mountain ranges in the distance. Lots of snow banks still remained at the highest ranges we hiked. At one point I stepped onto what I thought was a solid snow bank. It had melted some below and didn't hold my weight – sank to almost my waist. I wasn't hurt, just slightly damp. We threw a few icy snowballs then hiked. The weather was perfectly clear that day with a high of seventy degrees – lunch a snack of sandwiches and chips.

On the long ride back to Pateros we stopped at a family-owned pizza restaurant in the middle of a small town. The building resembled an old western saloon. In the middle of Washington State, I ordered Hawaiian pizza – ham and pineapple – thick and delicious. The next day Mark suggested we visit Lake Chelan. It's a narrow fjord-like lake that is 80 km (50 miles) long. Chelan was the largest natural lake in the state until the completion of Lake Chelan Dam. We decided to take the Lady of the Lake ferry to Stehekin. Most of the lake ride we rode on the top deck and enjoyed fabulous views. High rocky cliffs that give the impression of coming straight out of the water bordered each side of the lake for miles – the water deep rich azure. Once we arrived in Stehekin we visited the lodge, snack and gift shop. I bought a new ball cap with Stehekin on it – liked the word Stehekin. On the trip back we got a reversed view of everything, and it was just as strikingly spectacular. Arriving back to Pateros we were starved, and all agreed the local McDonald's sounded delicious – admittedly, fake food can be delicious. A big mac and large fries, the first fast-food meal I had eaten since I started training for the hike. I was due a chemical splurge full of calories.

Pateros is a small town with a population of about 650 people. A lot of those people, including Mark's brother, are apple and cherry farmers or labor workers. Washington State grows more sweet cherries than any other state in the nation. Mark's brother took us to an apple processing and warehouse site. I didn't know until then how old some of the apples are once those are received in retail markets – apple shipments from Washington can be nine to twelve months old. Not so with cherries because a cherry is considered a soft fruit – the prime harvest time is June and July. I also wondered why Mark's brother wore knee high rubber boots in the apple orchards; he said those protect your legs from snake bites. Yikes, I didn't wish to take a walk in the orchards surrounding his house now.

For our last hike we walked a simple trail that started off paved then we had the option to take an unpaved offshoot. We chose the unpaved trail. At one point we were forced to take a detour due to some large trees that had recently fallen. We were unable to walk over or under the massive trees. This led us into some high brush that concerned me because of our earlier conversation about snakes. It was July – snakes are out during summer months. We didn't see any snakes – thank goodness. An uneventful last hike but nonetheless gorgeous. I reminisced marveling in Seattle when we ate lunch at an Arby's surrounded on one side by huge mountains. I treasured the final day because the same was true in every direction – rolling landscapes toward the ocean, snow covered mountain peaks north and east in the distance, serenity and quietness enthroned everywhere we hiked – even the uneventful.

As I reflected on my concluding adventure, I was proud of the fact I had endured and survived. I was proud of the fact my physical training paid off – never any breathing or lower back issues. I was proud to have hiked like a real outdoorsman – perhaps not as rugged as some. Drank the freshest, cleanest, and coldest untreated water I had ever drank before – no invading parasites – total success. Even though I observed the hike from a different perspective, I was fully accepted by this group of men. The literal end of my journey to Northeastern Washington State a bit anticlimactic I'll admit, except for my final gaze of wonder at Mount Rainer in the Cascade Range of the Pacific Southeast. The active stratovolcano is located in Mount Rainer National Park southeast of Seattle – a summit over 14,000 feet, I'm certain my only viewing will be the quick fly over as our plane banked eastward – that's okay because I was accepted.

In an earlier attempt to declare manliness I attached myself to my father's favorite college football team even though I was never a skilled athlete. I've often pondered why I sit and cheer for my favorite college team? It seems rather absurd at times the amount of time and effort I carve out of a busy schedule to support a college team. I do not know anyone on my favorite college team – not one soul – not one coach, one player, one assistant, one trainer, no one. But I'm willing to sit for hours, screaming, clapping, yelling, getting angry, sending happy and disgusted text messages to friends and relatives who are watching, acting as though life depends on my team winning. I don't consider myself as bad as I once was, but I still support my team wholeheartedly. I wear team colors and emblems the whole day and proudly go out into the public arena wearing the same – win or lose – at least I appear to be somewhat athletic.

Why do I do this? I truly enjoy the gameday hoopla until I stop and ponder the silly insanity of it all. But my pondering quickly subsides and I'm right back in my favorite chair, eating my favorite gameday foods hoping for another big win. I also seem to know the exact way each player should have executed a particular play once it fails. But I never seem to question the play when it's successful – just clap and yell as if the players can hear me. Aside from the real game I believe another game is being played out in my living room every football Saturday

– is it really all about endless captivation for my favorite team? The game demands my full, undivided attention until the very end – the grasp is tight. Perhaps a harmless tradition? Maybe. As he typically suggests, *"I should go a little deeper and explore those feelings."*

My Saturday sports attachment began when I was young. I have vivid memories of my inebriated father attempting to listen to his favorite team, now mine, on a small pink transistor radio. Occasionally, he hit it, sometimes shake it for better reception, often cussed, like that was going to help, and of course get angry when his team messed up. Something about him sitting there after several adult beverages, stooped toward a tiny pink transistor, eyes blinking slowly, attempting to discern an announcer's commentary, and allowing cigarette ashes to fall from his fingers seemed rather pitiful. But it was his captivated moment.

The memory elicits a deep sadness as I sit now and think of my captivated moments – ballgame day staging compared to his. He loved his team as I now love the same – over fifty years later. I continued the legacy but with a few changes. I watch the game on a large flat screen within the luxury of my home nestled in our wooded sanctuary – something he never experienced before his untimely death at fifty-five. I have perfect reception through my internet provider – something he never knew. I have delicious gameday foods – something he didn't experience. I proudly wear team colors all day, team socks and caps – items he never owned. I'm supporting the same team because I watched as he listened intently to a tiny pink transistor he could barely hear – for him, something special – same is true for me.

Why do I have all the gameday privileged benefits my father never knew? For one, I chose a different path of life and I suppose feelings of guilt occasionally creep in at times or perhaps deep down I really long to sit with my father, the man who raised me, or with the man I do not know. Wish I could reverse time and watch our favorite team together – cheer and yell, cuss a little over bad plays, clap a lot, and high five when we score. Something I will never do with either man. I intentionally created those moments with my daughter, minus cussing, passing on this legacy to her. She proudly supports the same team but with much less fanfare and in her own unique manner.

So, how much of my intent is seeking acceptance as a father? A pink transistor, meager at best, yet profoundly important because it branded my heart. I've now created the same for my daughter but with different elements – result the same – heart branding can last a lifetime. One of my favorite photos is a casual pose of my daughter and me decked out in gameday garb, she's about five years old, both of us holding up a number one finger smiling proudly for our winning team. That's precisely what I desired as a child and the most important reason I was intentional – even though my motivation was tainted by a desire to be accepted. I created prized moments so that when I'm no longer she will reflect on the cherished photo and revive a warm memory that began many years ago.

My father never had the privilege of attending at game at Neyland Stadium – I've attended several. My first time to attend a live game for my favorite team was after I married. My new life with Pam opened up all sorts of new possibilities I didn't have before. She was not necessarily a big fan but was good with going and supporting our team. We didn't really know the way to do it right, so we chose to ride a bus from the hotel to the stadium. It was fun but nothing like we would eventually experience. The main advantage to riding the bus was I didn't have to battle traffic from a throng of over one-hundred thousand people. The disadvantage is the fact you miss out on some of the gameday festivities all around campus. Campuses in the SEC are electrifying on home gamedays. We didn't realize this as novices. Even though game time was always a total blast win or lose, we missed a lot by riding the bus until a new tradition was introduced.

I was presented a new way when an older man from my big church asked if I would like to drive him to Knoxville for the game – everyone in his *orange and white* family had other plans. I said yes without hesitation. *Driving Mr. Terry.* I learned how to enjoy the whole campus, gameday experience from a real pro. Mr. Terry was a tried-and-true fan for life – his blood ran orange – he and his wife had an orange and white bathroom – checkerboard toilet seat. Once we arrived and parked in his designated space, we started his ritual trek across campus. He did the same things at the same time every game – he was totally focused and serious – I was totally captivated by the pageantry. I never again rode a bus from a hotel to the game. The apprentice was learning the traditions from a professional *Big Orange,* Volunteer fan.

First, we walked to the upstairs portion of the student center where he read the newspaper sports page and chatted with a few buddies doing the same as he – they appeared to perfectly execute every necessary move as he did. Next, we walked to the student theatre to check out *College Gameday* on the big screen and catch a few minutes of the first game of the day. After thirty minutes or so we left to walk to the Football Sports Center where all the memorabilia are displayed. We walked through slowly as if we might be viewing something sacred – learned later I was exactly correct. We were in a hallowed museum dedicated to Volunteer football history. The people filing through were obviously having a religious experience and so was I. We stayed the longest at the Sports Center, and before leaving we paused for a brief moment to gaze at the inside practice facility – a mini football field with checkerboard endzones and all. We couldn't go in but allowed only a brief peek – another *holy* moment.

It was now time to return to the crowded student center where excitement was building before the game and to eat. As we walked across campus, I observed a sea of orange and white – all true believers. Groups of people everywhere, every space occupied, all ages, tailgating, playing games – I could hardly take it all in. Inside the dining hall the lines were long, but we all had the same goal and happy anticipation awaiting us. We ate a small lunch because I didn't realize we would stop at Western Sizzlin' off interstate 40 – another part of the ritual routine if timing worked out on the trek home.

Our final destination – the Vol Walk then follow the band to the stadium. This was my favorite event of the day because the crowd was enormously electrified. I watched Mr. Terry as his Vols walked through the tight space left for them – he was mesmerized – people reaching out attempting to touch football royalty – it was a sight to behold, and I loved it. The band followed and they stopped often to fire up the crowd more than the previous time by playing "Rocky Top" and other well-known fight songs – I was overtaken by chills. We followed the band down the hill, and they stopped again to let the majorities do their thing before an adoring throng – all truly amazing. The band then played a melody of all the usual fight songs and headed to the stadium. We stopped at the outside radio show and listened to the commentators and phone calls from fans not at the game. I saw legendary broadcaster John Ward in person – couldn't wait to hear him say, *"GIVE – HIM – SIX!"*

Time to find our reserved seats. Once we were seated, I realized everyone around us knew each other because he sat in a sea of season ticket holders. The next big event is when the team and cheerleaders run through the power T created by the band as they play "Rocky Top" for the hundredth time. Being in a stadium with over one-hundred thousand screaming fans is surreal. I was gripped, seized by exuberant mayhem. I now knew the lay of the orange land – a pro and couldn't wait to do it all again. I had the privilege of driving Mr. Terry a few more times over the next two years, and we performed the exact same ritual each time. Being accepted by Mr. Terry didn't substitute for my father, but I truly appreciated all that he taught me. I thought about my father often as I reflected on the campus hoopla and rituals – what would he think about this experience? I think he would love it as I did.

My daughter was in fourth grade. She had a Tennessee notebook due at the end of the second semester. I wanted her to have some special memories to share in her notebook about our love for Tennessee Volunteer football. I decided we would go to the Arkansas game in Knoxville. The team was undefeated and playing very well. Just the two of us made the big trip to orange country. We left school on Friday and stayed overnight in Knoxville in order to get an early start. I knew the ritual and was going to share it all with my offspring. We did exactly what I had planned. Decked out in all orange and white we made our way around campus at every favorite spot and made pictures for the notebook. During the Vol Walk Caroline reached out and was high-fived by Peerless Price, and she met and posed for a photo with Courtney, a first-team varsity cheerleader, the daughter of a man Pam worked with at Peterbilt Motors.

The game brought more excitement than we anticipated and was a nail biter to the last few seconds. Rain peppered us throughout, but we were prepared with plastic ponchos. With only a minute and a few seconds remaining, the stadium was emptying out because we were behind with no hope because Arkansas had possession of the ball. With rain still steadily sprinkling us, Arkansas fumbled on a faulty snap and we recovered – a revised hope seized the moment. We couldn't believe it – could they pull this off? Within the next few quick plays, we were in the endzone and victory reigned. It was exhilarating. I'm so thankful we stayed to the very end. The volunteers went on to remain undefeated and win the National Championship over Florida State. Our team was almost tripped up by Razorbacks on a rainy night in Knoxville as we sat alone in the upper deck. We had the perfect view of the fumble that led to a national crown. A cherished memory for two generations – only wishing it could have been three.

Gameday joy and exuberance is not sustainable – teams lose – coaches fired and replaced – losing seasons come and go. The whole of my life cannot be framed by a football team and its record. Proper perspective is vital. College football endorphins captivate and entangle me in their trivial web. Nothing like getting a heavy dose of endorphins when your team wins the big game or better yet, a National Championship. I've been intoxicated by sports endorphins many times – it's tantalizing. After several years a crucial reality was spoken without audible words – life doesn't stay balanced by winning or losing – acceptance does not depend on the people around you. An acknowledgement of this fact was necessary if I actually desired a proper perspective regarding acceptance.

Why do I stake so much joy on immature athletes barely removed from high school – on a leather ball touching or crossing a goal line – on winning even though at times we lose? Or on whether I can prove my manliness by hiking in Northeastern Washington State. Proper perspective is a heavy truth that strips away much of the hoopla that honestly has no meaning whatsoever. So, win or lose, accepted or not, I must learn to be satisfied – there is no other choice – even though winning and being accepted is always more enjoyable in the moment. Perhaps my father understood better than me because he wasn't bothered or distracted by hoopla. He seemed satisfied as long as the tiny pink transistor worked properly – and of course if his team won.

Most of my misguided assumptions about males within my sphere hinged on me not being accepted as an equal, Tim is one of the rare exceptions. Tim fully embraced who I was during our time together and he understood my targeted mission to right all the wrongs within the halls of Christian education. He likewise attempted a similar task in his *pastoral* setting. I met Tim through his wife Polly, a PreK assistant at Southeastern Christian Academy. I knew immediately after meeting Polly she was much smarter than her job required – she also carried the burden of being a preacher's wife – a role she appeared to manage with great ease. Tim, with his commanding laugh that could be heard above loud chatter in a crowded room, wasn't shy about sharing his opinions or concerns on a variety of topics. He certainly portrayed more confidence than me, but I never thought he came across as a know it all – I admired the confidence he exuded.

Tim and I likely forged a bond due to Polly sharing my *radical* vision for SCA, that type of focus was right up Tim's alley. He seemed to thrive on living his preacher status on the edge, and I liked that quality in him. Many times, his encouragement gave me the impetus to move forward on initiatives I sometimes doubted and what others viewed as controversial. We started meeting regularly for lunch, and I opened up about my struggles in righting the ship I was commandeering. What I immediately sensed from Tim was full acceptance. We were both in positions of leadership, but he didn't seem to have the amount of baggage I had which often hindered me from moving forward. Without fail, he always prayed for me regarding my mission and work at SCA – his prayers were real and meant the world to me.

He invited me to a collective prayer gathering of local pastors he helped organize. He likewise fully accepted these

God-fearing pastors from a variety of denominations as brothers in Christ – even though he was surrounded, as I was, by *Christians* that didn't accept these people as brothers – several in our *tribe* didn't act as though they understood the true meaning of *in Christ*. I was impressed by Tim's acceptance and his attitude also stirred me to begin a move in the same direction. I knew my meeting with this bunch of holy characters would not sit well with the powers that be, but I did it anyway. I found these men to be open and highly respectful to the ideas of everyone in attendance. The stirring in me was something bigger than I realized at the time, and I knew it felt right – not closed-minded, rigid, fearful of considering another view point. I hungered for more.

Tim became a close confidant – someone I could *spill my guts* to and not be judged – it felt good too. We had many deep spiritual discussions but also exchanged hilarious banter about our stations in life and the craziness that surrounded both of our callings. Tim was the lead minister at a local church and battled similar issues within a fairly conservative doctrine of beliefs and dogma. Although Tim was far beyond my understanding and openness, he continually challenged my long-held beliefs without ever damaging our relationship. I desperately needed a trusted male friend and Tim fit that category perfectly.

When my mother died an immediate thought was to ask Tim if he would perform her graveside eulogy. He never met my mother but graciously agreed to do it. I didn't have another *holy* person to ask that I felt comfortable trusting with her last *big moment* – I wanted the eulogy to be a special tribute. My mother had always said she was a believer. Throughout her adult span she pretended to be Southern Baptist – a family heritage she held in her heart but didn't practice outwardly. The only living Southern Baptist pastor she knew was her brother in Texas – an option I did not wish to ponder.

I shared with Tim an odd statement she spoke on the day of her death. I arrived at the hospital for a second visit and asked how she was feeling. *"I feel like the last rose of summer."* Where did that poetic phrase come from? I had never heard my mother use that phrase nor did she ever wax poetic. She didn't read books and especially not poetry. Did she somehow know Thomas Moore's 1805 poem from somewhere in her past? Perhaps her mother used the phrase. She loved growing flowers until she was no longer able, but I remain baffled by the elegant last exclamation of fading rose consciousness. Tim used the elegant phrase as a theme for her eulogy. Everything he spoke about the *last rose* touched my heart in the brief moments as he stood next to her white coffin with soft touches of pink on every angle – most importantly, his words avowed her last moment in the spotlight. I'm constantly amazed and mystified by the intricate weaving of lives and how at just the precise moment certain people enter your world and provide exactly what you need – my experience for numerous junctures of life. The very reason he was able to deliver as I knew he would, Tim perfectly understood and without condition accepted me.

A small vase with a beautiful single red rose was positioned in the center of my executive desk – no card, just vase and rose. I had returned to my office after a few bereavement days. Pondering the rose, my thoughts regressed to a feeble declaration: *"I feel like the last rose of summer."* I turned and walked to my administrative assistant's station and inquired. I should have known; she had lovingly positioned the multi-petaled crimson bloom because a few days earlier she attended the quiet graveside memorial framed in robin-egg blue with lite touches of cool, wispy cirrus. Touched by her gesture of supreme thoughtfulness, my heart swelled with emotion. I still have the rose, now encased in glass next to a photo of my mother and father in wedding clothes. Special administrative assistants are unique in this way. Though there were several differences regarding our world Christian views, she fully accepted me, never once disrespected my views or position of authority. In fact, she was totally loyal in an over-the-top manner – allegiance I struggled to embrace. For numerous years, hearts at SCA were touched on a deeper level, as I was, by her thoughtful gestures – how lucky to be one of her several recipients. Whenever acceptance was extended, regardless of gender, it never really mattered to me; my longing to be accepted is rooted in a form of disjointed maternal and paternal conditional love.

Motivation

Perfectionism fueled motivation to achieve something different than my parents. A naïve imagined world became the major player and hopeful ticket out of forced dysfunction and poverty. Artistic enterprises protected me from reality – while I waited to hear from Hollywood. Apprehended by intrinsic motivation born from dysfunction was not the only guiding force that led to certain choices. What about providence? I believe in a Higher Power – a Supreme Being, God. Do I struggle with doubt? Yes. Do I have moments of unbelief? Yes. I believe everything my eyes perceive and the microscopic unseen is created – a Master Designer – Creator. I do not believe the intricacies of this world and universe occurred through a big bang – intricate design has a Maker – as do my artistic endeavors. Power and desire of human conscience to overcome enormous obstacles have been present since the Garden. But whether I believe in a higher power or not, I can't deny the power and desire of human conscience effort. Partnering human facets with Divine may be the best way to succeed, overcome, and triumph. How much is providence? I believe every person, event, sorrow, and brief encounter shaped who I am. When episodes occurred, I wasn't typically thinking in terms of being shaped but reflection leads me to see and know significance and life changing manifestations that followed – or were those episodes simply providence?

A modest example I've not been able to explain is why I didn't take up smoking. Nearly everyone in my young life smoked – I detested it. What drove the strict stance? Why did I not experiment? I don't have clear answers to those questions. Why not inebriation? Alcohol consumption was widely accepted in my family but in another family – boundaries set by religiously conservative viewpoints – found myself straddling a *moral fence* for years. Zero tolerance the accepted norm in one family – indulgence accepted in another. I married zero tolerance but knew Jesus was the premium Spiritual vintner of his day. His first miracle supplied a wedding feast with gallons after everyone consumed all the choice drink. His mother told them, *"Do what he tells you."* His purpose not a statement about alcohol usage or irresponsible drinking. I believe Jesus intervened to avoid a shameful moment for the host family but more importantly to demonstrate Divine power, open up his public ministry and his ability to create perfection from something imperfect – the same way he recreates a willing, open heart.

Thankfully I'm no longer under stringent conservative overreach and no longer believe social drinking is sinful. I'm in my sixth decade and remain loyal to a vow – a vow not to become intoxicated. Not seeking a badge of honor – just humbly asking questions, attempting to understand the accurate source of my motivation – no clear answers – providential perhaps. He suggested I likely gleaned several positive traits from my paternity source. *"Have you considered what those positive traits might be? Perhaps you should."* I again pondered his suggestion on the drive home then made a list.

Raphael said during our one-time face-to-face he always sensed he was probably adopted. What factors led him to wonder? Why did his adoptive parents not tell him? Perhaps they didn't want him to find his birth mother – perhaps they feared he would reject them – perhaps they knew her – perhaps it was all prearranged by his family? Answers neither of us will likely ever discover. It would be satisfying if both of us knew the full story; instead we remain curious and can only speculate. What motivated my brother to succeed as a trained chef? He managed to graduate from Duke University with an engineering degree due to the external motivation of parents – most likely more so from a father who was an attorney. Raphael was obviously driven enough to challenge his father and convince him that being a trained culinary chef was a better route for him – the choice paying huge dividends.

Raphael likely loved or possibly hated certain aspects of his privileged life. He told me when his mother decided she wanted a new house his father would tell her to find what she wanted or a property and he would take care of it. Raphael shared that when his parents hosted large parties, he remembered country music stars attending and the mayor of Nashville. My parents enjoyed good times and parties with friends and neighbors, though not something I necessarily desired. As a teenager Raphael served as a valet for party goers – I knew nothing of valet parking. Did these events and people motivate Raphael to succeed at life pursuits? I assume those events molded him as mine molded me – although two very different stories unfolded. Most of my drive and motivation grew out of unconventional rebellion – for Raphael, I do not know his true source – and I continue to question mine.

Mr. and Mrs. Pigg lived in the trailer park and formed a friendship with my parents. They were one of many examples of lifestyles I did not desire, although they held a place of odd affection in my heart and mind. The older couple lived in a small blue travel trailer and from the outside it appeared you could not stand upright. Both were chain smokers, and he was an alcoholic carpenter also suffering with emphysema. Mrs.

Pigg fussed and argued with her husband constantly – language coarse at times and it didn't seem to matter who was present. I recall Mr. Pigg driving me to an original McDonald's in Madison in his white Ford pickup truck – large golden arches from the front to the back – had a coupon for free food. My mother apparently asked because it was a regular workday – she didn't drive. The outing was a short respite for Mr. Pigg away from nagging – I had pretended to be sick – a break for my mother too.

One evening during a visit in their tiny rectangle Mr. Pigg suffered a serious breathing episode and fell to the floor gasping. I thought he was dying. His wife attempted to assist, and he finally regained his breath – a scary moment for everyone. I wondered why she didn't call an ambulance. On several occasions my mother and I rode with the Pigg's to Kentucky lake where Mr. Pigg loved to fish from his small boat with a single engine. He steered the little boat from the back; the front rose off the water as he zipped to favorite fishing areas. A few miles before our camping destination at Richland Creek, sat a small tavern shack – a ritual stop to stock up on beer and consume a couple of beers before the fishing began.

Don't recall an official name for the tavern; the weather-beaten shack's front porch had large stones for steps. The rickety shack rested on stacked rocks instead of concrete blocks like my trailer – I could see underneath both. Mr. Pigg referred to the tavern as *Eggs,* named for another favorite of his – boiled pickled eggs – a large jar sat on the bar and looked gross. The wobbly door squeaked loudly; wide-planked floors uneven – could see through holes in the oiled planks in certain places. A strong stench of alcohol and tobacco melded with oiled wood bathed us – every surface slightly damp to the touch and the odor didn't fade until hours later. A juke box sat in the corner. I asked for a dime to play The Foundations' *"Build Me Up Buttercup,"* a favorite song, while I drank a bottle of ice-cold Coca-Cola from the bright red non-alcoholic cooler – my treat usually included barbeque chips – ignored the beer drinking. Went outside sometimes to walk around, watch cars speeding by wondering where they were headed. Considering my general disposition at the time, I'm a little surprised I didn't protest the stop at *Eggs*.

Mr. Pigg built his own camper on the back of his pick-up truck bed. I rode in the hand-built camper section before seatbelts – an alcoholic driver with emphysema – it was hot with little ventilation. I didn't consider how the homemade camper was attached, too young to ponder safety issues – my mother should have but obviously didn't. One evening at Kentucky lake my mother slept on the front seat of his truck, I slept on the floorboard – the hump in the middle was terribly uncomfortable. Somehow though, the whole camping event was fun for me – fishing, playing around the lake, preparing our own food. Mrs. Pigg showed me how to clean freshly caught fish – I thought it was a messy job but managed to assist.

My father wasn't there if we went on Thursday or early Friday morning, but his plan was to come after work on Friday. When my family visited Kentucky Lake, where Mr. and Mrs. Pigg camped, we sometimes rented a tiny concrete block, dirty stuccoed, flat roofed cabin at Richland Creek – a musty smelling one-bedroom, small kitchen, roadside type bathroom with a rusty molded shower. Nothing appeared clean, faucet water tasted corroded, I wouldn't drink it – amenities less than desirable even for a trailer park kid – much worse than my narrow rectangle, but I relished the freedom and picturesque lakeside view.

My cousins Janice, Little Bill and their parents rented a real lakeside cabin at Trails End, an area on the other side of the lake. They had access to a swimming pool and small restaurant – we would visit if we were there at the same time.

We used the narrow curvy road that led to Trails End, but my cousins used their boat to connect. We eventually stayed some at Trails End with my cousins – always wondered if my uncle Bill paid the fees. One evening my cousin Bill stayed with me at Richland Creek during an annual fish fry. We had full access to all the free cold drinks we wanted – consumed an insane number of carbonated drinks that evening. Perhaps we were dehydrated, more likely mimicking adult habits.

Mr. Pigg continued his love for fishing but deteriorating health issues eventually caught up with him and he died a few years later. His wife had no income or savings – her only choice was a move to Selma, Alabama where a daughter and son lived – she rented a government subsidized apartment just as my mother did after my father's untimely death. Since my aunt and uncle also moved to Selma, my mother eagerly reconnected with Mrs. Pigg during Selma visits. I remember the sparsely decorated apartment, speckled grey tiled floor, paint chipping on the metal framed windows, still chain smoking – but her home was larger than the tiny trailer. My mother and Mrs. Pigg held a special bond and were especially delighted to reconnect. I found joy in observing the sweetness of their reunions, the cheerfulness in their voices – similar souls fused together by similar destinies. My strange fondness for Mr. and Mrs. Pigg was born from their acceptance of me, what seemed like a willingness to include me, show me things parents didn't, simple attentiveness – McDonald's, Coca-Cola at *Eggs*, cleaning fish. The lives of diverse people unintentionally brought into my presence formulated different forms of internal motivation. I firmly believe *sane* and *crazy* circumstances inadvertently created yearnings to seek similar and alternate paths. My stubbornness and a pompous attitude combined to steer me away from undesirable outcomes.

Five People

Everything I accomplished as a professional educator, I believe, is directly connected to my formative years of development. Moments when I chose to intervene as a child, assert myself in an attempt to remedy situations, those traveled the journey into adulthood – catapulted professional endeavors – but all born of dysfunction. Hands down, the key for me – choices – choices by far the most impactful and those altered circumstances. But I needed outside people too, people to step in when I was young, administer essentials – grandparents supported to a degree but remained on the periphery – never fully understanding my plight but acted intuitively. I'm thankful other people throughout the journey stepped in knowingly and unknowingly to construct pathways and restore breaches.

People come and go. People show up at pivotal times. Certain people in my life managed to leave indelible impressions – altering my whole life progression. These people succeeded in tapping into my deepest core of emotion, and most often not even aware of the influence they possessed, nor did they necessarily set out to accomplish any great task toward that end. Nevertheless, extraordinary individuals went about their mission totally unconscious of the power they possessed to inspire a sense of meaning and hope, boldness and courage, resilience and determination, moving me forward in spite of monumental obstacles. The majority of these people were never conscious of the obstacles I faced but simply acted instinctively.

I hold vivid remembrances of five people that crossed paths of my growth and development, making indelible impressions – most totally unaware, some purposeful, some for use of my talents, but all five highly intuitive and watchful. These people hold distinct positions in my personal improvement and progression as a human being. They instinctively sensed something – they seemed to know what I didn't know at the time of our association. While I can point to scores of other people, I'm exceedingly indebted to these five because they answered the call of their position and influence in life at the precise time it was most needed. These people used their power to make a difference for me, offer opportunity and alter the course of my life at appropriate moments. The five people are in order based on the time frame of influence and change on the trajectory of my life. First, sixth-grade teacher, Rebecca Ramsay. Second is minister Dr. Jim Mankin. Third is private school principal Nila Sherrill. Fourth is principal Michael Jordan, and fifth is basketball coach and private school president Ronnie Sarver.

Rebecca Ramsay entered my life as my second sixth grade teacher when I most needed her. My first sixth grade teacher, Betty Everett, was located in the portable classroom next door. Our principal walked in a few weeks after school started and said he needed five students to move to the other sixth classroom to balance numbers. He asked if there were any volunteers – my hand shot up. Not exactly sure why because I liked Mrs. Everett. She glared at me like she had been completely rejected – my hand a little too quick. Four other classmates volunteered, and we moved our desks that day. Ms. Ramsay was likely only twenty-two and it was her first year to teach – didn't matter to me. She was young, very pretty, and artistic. She conducted class in traditional ways for reading, math, and the typical core subjects.

When she was feeling creative a whole different dynamic permeated our classroom. Desks moved aside allowed the floor to be converted into an artistic palette from which magic blossomed. In October we made scarecrows. I remember the straw and burlap and being confident in my ability to create the perfect scarecrow. During our study of ancient Egypt, Ms. Ramsay teased that her mother was bringing something very special to our classroom. I happened to be sitting next to the window when she arrived in a station wagon weighted down with wet bricks. Desks pushed aside, each student got a wet brick to fashion a relic of ancient Egyptian art – I chose high-end and created a sphinx – wanted to impress Ms. Ramsay and she loved it. Our artistic palette was covered with smeared wet brick clay. Cleanup lasted longer than our creative activities, but I never sensed our teacher was stressed.

Another time I recall using colored chalk to create an entire prehistoric rain forest mural on the chalkboard. Ann was the other student artist assisting me with the mural – Ms. Ramsay raved with pleasure. I described previously the book report project she made a big deal over when I presented it to the class – a profound moment for me – asked me to walk among the class to share it up close. For an end-of-year project, we performed a play, *The Cross Princess*, in Shakespearean style. Boys performed female parts which is Shakespearean and girls the male parts – she slightly adjusted historical fact to include everyone. Ms. Ramsay was young and pushed established norms, and we loved her for doing it. Three boys auditioned for the lead role including me and somehow, I got it. After a few weeks of practice and memorizing lines, I stood center stage in a red satin dress and blond wig – the curtain opened. My first action was to stomp my foot, cross my arms in disgust, and yell opening lines. I think I must have channeled anger and frustration with home life into the role – a cathartic moment for certain. Only my mother witnessed the lead role. These are heartfelt memories I recall from Ms. Ramsay. But most importantly, her unbridled support and attention soothed my world – and she didn't even know it.

Close to the end of our sixth-grade journey with Ms. Ramsay, we were offered another opportunity to select from a variety of interesting end-of-year projects – my teacher now well-known for her innovative ideas. I don't recall the broader purpose but knew immediately what I wanted – read a book to a first-grade class and guide students in an activity related to the book. I was all in and totally committed to being *teacher for an hour.* I chose *Where the Wild Things Are,* by Maurice Sendak. I remember being so excited with anticipation. I read the whole book to the class, then guided the students to draw and color a picture of something they had been afraid of during the night – thought of my own personal fears but shared nothing. Several students shared their drawings, and I assumed my first shot at teaching real students went fairly well, thanks to Ms. Ramsay – a seed planted. My emotional health flourished in her classroom between 8:30 am and 3:00 pm. Although my grades left much to be desired. No one at home really cared; life away from sixth grade and Ms. Ramsay slowly descended into a hellish nightmare most evenings – but I suffered alone and never told anyone.

In seventh-grade I returned to her classroom late one afternoon hoping to reconnect because I wanted her to know. She was alone at her desk; the moment felt awkward, but she welcomed me with her usual exuberance. Again, I was fully accepted and embraced. We talked briefly and I probably lied about how I was doing. My life at the time a living hell but being in her presence returned me, if only for a brief moment, to a tranquil supportive classroom time that warmed a hurting soul. It was my last time to see her until our paths crossed twenty-five or so years later. I had opportunity to tell her what she meant to me and did for me during a very difficult period of life. My hand shot up that day in Mrs. Everett's room for a reason. Ms. Ramsay's caring, intuitive spirit and support inspired me to eventually pursue a teaching career. Rebecca Ramsay was placed in my life at a pivotal moment – a necessary moment.

Dr. Jim Mankin was our new minister at the big church. I was a college student upon his arrival, and he was assigned the young adult class for mid-week Bible study in addition to Sunday preaching. His first night to teach he stood at the door to greet each class member. As we shook hands, I introduced myself as *Jim Morris.* My name acquainted me to what I would come to learn as his unique trademark, he enthusiastically responded without hesitation, *"Two Jim's, we are like precious stones!"* He had a way of immediately drawing people into his world with a personal, engaging quip. He cared deeply and never forgot a name, perhaps mine a little easier.

I thought he had a striking resemblance to a middle-aged Winston Churchill – without the cigar. Even his mannerisms were similar – using his fist to make a point, contorting his face with a variety of expressions, sometimes even his stride just like Churchill. Jim Mankin could have easily won an Oscar for a portrayal of the British Prime Minister. He had a huge heart for people and cherished those connections. As our relationship grew, he asked me to be his driver to some small country towns where he was invited as guest speaker. These religious gatherings were called *Gospel Meetings.* My favorite part, the homecooked dinner before the meeting – the driver was considered a special guest too. On our drive to the destination the conversation was limited because he often studied his lesson. On our return home we had lots of meaningful conversations about family and life issues in general. Jim Mankin was never without words. Once he knew someone a little and identified the uniqueness of their personality, he spoke words of affirmation and encouragement into that person – he did that to me on numerous occasions. He seemed to know just what to say at just the right time.

I visited his church office several times and marveled at the abundance of books he possessed – we talked about many of those books. He inspired me to read more, introduced me to authors I didn't know and broadened my thinking. At the time he was working on his Doctorate in Theology. For one portion of his thesis, he needed creative techniques and strategies to engage children in Bible study. He asked my advice since I was teaching in the children's department at our big church. After completing two years at Vol State, I applied to Lipscomb College. Dr. Mankin is the reason I was accepted. He wrote a letter of recommendation which convinced important people I was worthy of consideration – though, living up to his glowing recommendation created an underlying fear I might fail and let him down.

Mr. Mankin was thrilled when I proposed to my girlfriend Pam. We knew he would perform our wedding ceremony and he did. He did not ask us to do any pre-martial counseling. It was not the vogue thing to do at that time. He and his wife Delores did invite us to lunch on a few occasions. I think it was their way to speak into us the importance of family and marriage permanence. One to one conversation with him aided me to clearly see I wanted a marriage like the Mankin's – they modeled marriage perfectly without words.

Two weeks before the wedding I was scheduled to attend a Bible teacher's workshop in Abilene, Texas. Jim Mankin the featured speaker. A week before departure I finished my last week of summer camp work. I awoke on the last day with a huge knot in my jaw due to an abscessed tooth. I had no dental care during my twenty-five years with parents and no insurance. Jim was notified by someone, and he arranged for a dentist from our church to see me immediately. Of course, I couldn't travel to Texas with an abscess. The dentist made his diagnosis and put me on a strong antibiotic to kill infection. He said after the wedding he would see me again and start the process of correcting my teeth. The dentist made no mention of any costs. In less than a week I was scheduled to ride a bus to Texas. Jim was flying – a perk for a lead minister and featured speaker. He called me and said he had arranged for me to fly out with him instead of riding the bus, thinking it would be easier and more comfortable considering my current condition. Again, good conversations as we flew, and he spoke into me with his unique style.

I traveled back to Nashville on the bus with the regular folks since all swelling had subsided and only one week until the wedding. Jim's only marriage advice directed to me was simple but far reaching. He told me, "*Always place Pam on a pedestal.*" I knew it was figurative language meaning to treat her with high respect and dignity. When I told the groomsmen, they turned it into something more nefarious as one would expect horny groomsmen to do. When I walked out of the side room with Jim and the best man the processional music was loud. Each groomsman, to my surprise, had placed a raisin on a tooth and smiled as they walked to their position – appeared as though each groomsman had lost a tooth. Pondering *missing teeth*, I flashed back to a moment after the rehearsal dinner at our new house, an unexpected surprise concocted by the best man and groomsmen – but I behaved myself in spite of it.

After the wedding and honeymoon my relationship with Jim Mankin now included a new partner. On the wall of our den, we have two beautiful framed pictures given to us from the Mankins for our wedding gift. When I look at those gifts, I think of the fond association with such loving and caring people and the privilege of knowing them. After about six years Jim Mankin was released from his duties at our big church to make way for another shiny new minister – he had done nothing wrong. I didn't fully understand, and I know his wife and children were deeply hurt by the decision. Jim held his head high and was totally gracious about it all. I was impressed – another lesson he spoke into my soul I've attempted to mimic. I regret not traveling to visit him at his next landing spot in Abilene, Texas where he preached, served and died of cancer. My deepest regret is not flying to Texas for his final tribute and burial. I spoke with his widow Delores. Jim Mankin's positive disposition and style of reaching into people served me well. I will always be grateful for his profound influence. Dr. Jim Mankin was placed in my life at a pivotal moment – a necessary moment.

Nila Sherrill was a career educator, religiously conservative, and highly opinionated on a variety of issues, never hesitating to share her sentiments. When she was in the room, she made her presence obvious. Her teaching career started at Amqui Elementary before moving to a Christian school in the same community – two schools that played a significant role in my life as well. I met Mrs. Sherrill at the big church where she was highly respected for her teaching expertise and was often gossiped about behind the scenes because of her abrupt comments and manner of approaching others. She projected the impression of being able to intimidate a lot of people but not me – we bonded quickly. One interesting characteristic was her mannerisms in how she conveyed information and especially when she was speaking to just one person. Stepping into a person's personal space is the best way to describe it. As she spoke, the other person often felt compelled to slowly back up providing more distance – topic of discussion didn't matter. She conveyed information like no one else. The subject might have been a simple grocery store outing, but she told it as if lives were at stake. It was her unique style, and I was never bothered by this but many people, especially other women were intimidated. She taught a ladies' Bible class for many years.

Mrs. Sherrill learned of my artistic ability through our work together at the big church. At the time she was teaching third grade at a private Christian school and asked me to stop in to see her one afternoon. She shared big news. She had been selected the new elementary principal. She wanted me to create a personalized design on document portfolios purchased for each elementary teacher. I agreed to do it and was paid for my artistic work. This started a tradition she continued for several years. Each year she chose a different novelty item to personalize until I started my teaching career.

Flossie Mize, a first-grade teacher who secretly smoked, also employed my artistic ability. She had reached the age where she didn't particularly desire to be as creative with her classroom décor, so she allowed me to create her bulletin boards during the time I was attending Vol State Community College. Mrs. Sherrill called one morning and asked if I could substitute. I excitedly agreed and hurried to the school. My first time to substitute was for Flossie Mize, I was already very familiar and comfortable in her classroom. I never saw her smoking, but her classroom closet was the giveaway where she kept a sweater and coat. I continued to substitute for several different teachers when I had free days from college classes. I loved the experiences of being in different classrooms. Mrs. Sherrill spoke often of me coming to her Christian school fulltime – appreciated her trust in my ability and how she instilled hope for my future.

Upon graduating from Lipscomb College principal Sherrill did not have a teaching vacancy. I was officially hired in Metro Nashville Public Schools and started my teaching career

October 1, 1984. It was sixth grade, in a portable, at Neely's Bend Elementary, Michael Jordan the principal – a lot more about him to come. I naturally continued my association with Nila Sherrill because both of us attended the same big church. We would have numerous discussions about experiences in public education and she regularly offered advice, even when I didn't ask for it. After eleven years in public education, I was a bit weary and ready for something different. As I detailed earlier, a good friend told me of a potential vacancy at the private school and it was my favorite grade level. I applied for the job and she hired me. Nila Sherrill was now my new official principal. I was thrilled to start a new chapter in my teaching career under the tutelage of Mrs. Sherrill – learning her bark was worse than her bite. We worked well together.

During the next two years as a sixth-grade teacher, I was able to complete a Master's Degree in Educational Leadership and was credentialed to be a principal. The Christian school superintendent talked to me often about leadership possibilities, and I knew Mrs. Sherrill was approaching retirement. She often told me privately she wanted me to replace her, but it was not her decision. In a totally unexpected turn of events, I was offered a principal's position at Southeastern Christian Academy on the far south end of Nashville. I accepted the offer and dreaded telling Mrs. Sherrill. She was most gracious and happy for my advancement but seemed a bit disappointed. We talked regularly my first year as principal and she helped me through some sticky discipline issues. Toward the end of the year, I was told Mrs. Sherrill was retiring so I applied for the position. The interview went extremely well. I was very comfortable with the superintendent because we had worked closely for two years. I left the interview confident the job was mine. Little did I know another plan was being engineered by someone with all the power. I waited several weeks anticipating a call that never came. I finally received a short, generic response stating the decision was made to move in a different direction. Why such a cold letter from someone that talked so openly about my leadership potential? Within a few days truth was revealed. The president's daughter, who was teaching first grade, was appointed elementary principal. At that time, she held a master's degree in curriculum, not educational leadership. I happily remained at SCA thirteen more years.

Nila Sherrill was diagnosed with cancer and underwent treatments for several years. Her health slowly declined, but she steadfastly fought the disease in her typical *face-to-face* manner, determined to win. We stayed in contact, and she was thrilled to continue her support of my efforts in leadership at SCA and in my eventual return to public education at Amqui Elementary where she began her teaching career. She reminded me regularly it was her desire for me to follow in her footsteps as principal. The irony is palpable; I followed her by going to the school where she began her illustrious career. I still marvel at the numerous connections throughout my professional journey. During this same time period my wife and I grew increasingly discontented with the big church. It was not a faith crisis but driven by pointless church dogma. Nila Sherrill knew of our discontent and in her typical manner conveyed her conservative stance. When we finally decided to leave for a newly established church, she was very troubled by our decision. A part of me did not wish to disappoint her because I highly respected her opinions, solicited or not. Her health began to decline more rapidly and finally reached the point of hospice care at home. She lost a hard-fought battle. I did not visit during the final weeks of life because I didn't wish to upset her since I knew she was unhappy with our church decision. During her celebration of life service, I felt another deep regret – not visiting. Nila Sherrill was placed in my life at a pivotal moment – a necessary moment.

My first principal as a teacher, Michael Jordan, in an odd type of way was as dedicated to his craft of leadership as famous basketball superstar Michael Jordan was to his. Mr. Jordan is tenacious and persistent in obtaining and achieving what he wants. He is a first-class showman – a boaster – a namedropper – and sometimes braggadocious, but all in a good way making those around him feel as if it was all for the advancement of everyone involved. When in fact, he typically pushed his advancement too. Somehow those of us within his reach did not feel used or degraded by his intentionality because he graciously rewarded everyone with lots of acclamations and praise. I know he worried the stew out of the director of elementary education until he finally got a yes on hiring me. I know this because others in the district had been substituting for many months and some for years. The problem for them was not pedagogy, they didn't have Michael Jordan advocating as I did. I was young and naïve – had no say in the matter – allowed the system to play out as it did. I was blessed to have someone quite persuasive pulling strings for me but didn't see or comprehend the bigger picture of where Mr. Jordan's intentionality would take me. He projected confidence in my abilities to be something much greater than I imagined.

On the first Monday morning as a new sixth grade teacher, Mr. Jordan walked into my classroom I thought to officially greet and welcome me to his school. Instead, he walked in and immediately eyeballed everything I had created for the room. He looked carefully at each bulletin board and what I had placed on the paneled walls of the portable room. It all met his lauding approval. Nothing was said about teacher manuals, necessary supplies, or most important – the curriculum. OCD made everything perfect because I had converted the portable room into a model classroom with all the hand-crafted artwork and meticulously constructed bulletin boards. His tenacious persistence paid off. Throughout the school year as seasons changed so did room décor – always perused by the forever watchful eyes of Mr. Jordan.

He used me often for other school projects requiring a creative touch, and I was happy to assist. I recall very few serious discussions about curriculum or teaching strategies with the exception of one formal observation. Those discussions and his eye for detail focused more on patterns of teacher words and movement within the room. I remember him stating I used an *"okay, alright"* pattern of speech. Probably due to a little nervousness, but I was determined to never use those words again during a direct teaching lesson or formal observation. In the end, his eye for detail grew my teaching professionalism.

Two weeks before the summer break of my first year, Mr. Jordan announced he had been promoted to director of Elementary Education – he was leaving for the district office. Mike Jordan was also a member at the big church I attended, so we continued our relationship for the remainder of my time in public education and beyond. Mr. Jordan urged me to pursue a master's degree in leadership, but I wasn't ready. He also tried unsuccessfully on numerous occasions to persuade me to join teacher associations. He loved being involved politically, but more so for the relationships with people and for big events. He tried another angle by having me design the logo for the leadership association he was immersed in. I did it – finally joined but only paid dues. I eventually stopped because I didn't enjoy the big events that seemed mostly political. After Mr. Jordan retired from public education he moved to a private Christian school as middle school principal. I worked at another private Christian school, so once again we had something in common, spoke often about our work and the unique challenges within those environments.

On a more personal level, Mike Jordan and wife Mabel

were gracious hosts and so kind to my family. Aside from the school bond we had a close bond as families, Mike and Mabel loved our daughter Caroline and for many years treated her like a grandchild. We visited often, ate in their home and they never forgot our daughter's birthday. To this day both Mike and Mabel never fail to inquire about Caroline and her well-being, as well as ours. They are truly some of the kindest and giving people I know. Mabel is wonderfully suited for Mike because she seems to bring a calm spirit to his over-the-top flamboyance. Don't get me wrong, it's always present but Mabel adds a little peace to the crest of the wave. I obtained my first teaching position due to Michael Jordan. I'm truly grateful for his unwavering persistence. Michael Jordan was placed in my life at a pivotal moment – a necessary moment.

Ronnie Sarver, a fairly unassuming presence unless coaching basketball – and that he did with unbridled tenacity. Once again, I met this person at the big church where he was teaching a young adult class. I observed his coaching style at a Christian school where he coached high school varsity boys. His style was to run the coaching box, squat, jump, flail arms, yell as most coaches do, and challenge the referee's missed and sometimes correct calls. Highly animated might be another good description for his style. This style earned him a chance at a state championship. The coach and boys gave it their best shot but lost the top trophy – a disappointing loss to say the least. I attended that particular game at Middle Tennessee State University because of my loose association with the school and elementary principal Nila Sherrill. He finally won that state championship title by way of his son at Southeastern Christian Academy – not as coach but as school president and most importantly father. I watched with delight as he and his wife embraced their championship son and his team.

Ronnie Sarver left the coaching position to become the head at Fellowship Christian School. His coaching career ended but not his love for the game. He and his wife Shearon are known for attending as many basketball games as they can fit into their hectic schedule, and that doesn't include their love for Kentucky Wildcat basketball. During this period, we parted ways and basically had no direct relationship. He and his family decided to attend another church, so I rarely saw him. After his successful tenure at Fellowship, he moved to Southeastern Christian Academy as their new head of school – his title president.

Throughout his tenure at Southeastern he battled the board of directors. He attempted to broaden their horizons on many business issues. His relationship with the board could best be described as shaky. He had enough support to maintain a yearly contract renewal, but one touchy issue was his desire to see change within the administrative ranks. For too many years the board had accepted mediocre efforts from principals of each branch of the school. The board's strongest exertion focused on the priority of maintaining strict conservative viewpoints on all issues pertaining to the school's spiritual dictates. The newly hired elementary principal announced she was going through a divorce. Based on board policy her employment would be terminated because the board refused to hire anyone divorced, previously divorced, or married to a divorced person. Ronnie Sarver was looking for a new elementary principal.

I was in the process of completing a Master's degree at Trevecca Nazarene University. In my cohort was a former player of Ronnie Sarver's completing his Master's but had no interest in pursuing a principal's position. He told me Coach Sarver was searching for an elementary principal. All of his former players fondly referred to him as *"Coach Sarver"* or simply *"Coach."* He urged me to check it out. As I detailed earlier, Ronnie Sarver hired me as the new elementary principal. The new role opened my eyes to behind the scenes politicking that often occurs in small bureaucracies like our private school. In a school like SCA, everyone knows everyone and usually knows too much. The school was dominated by overly strict, religiously conservative people attempting to preserve a 1973 mindset – the founding year of the school. This attitude was not blatantly visible unless the outdated status quo was challenged. Ronnie Sarver was not a strict conservative but respectful of the board's wishes, he faithfully upheld all religiously based dictates. He was not shy in challenging the board when he thought it was necessary to uphold and maintain the integrity of the school. I witnessed him doing so on several occasions. He shared with me numerous times how he was tremendously troubled by the incompetent bumbling antics of a few good men serving on the board. Some of the men served only in name and several rarely contributed financially. There were notable exceptions – several board members during my tenure gave liberally of their financial resources – Don, Burch, David, Harry, Jim and Sam to name a few – and never desired or sought any public recognition for their generosity. Ronnie Sarver focused most of his energies on the business and financial workings of the institution. During his time as president SCA had its largest student enrollment numbers.

During the interview conversation he talked about the need for a comprehensive teacher evaluation process. He said the school was sorely lacking in this area and inquired of my interest. He hit the bullseye and didn't realize how thrilled I was to hear his desire for the school. I was more than eager to assist in creating a process for teacher evaluations. I asked what was in place and he said nothing. I also didn't realize that no teacher evaluations were occurring in any branch of the school. After my official hiring process was finalized, I immediately worked on developing a plan. I shared the plan with Sarver, and he seemed pleased. He was given copies, and

I assumed he shared those with the other two principals – if he did, they chose to ignore it. I instituted the plan during the first pre-service staff development and started formal observations shortly after school began. This was an area I know Ronnie Sarver wanted to mandate for the other principals – I was enthusiastic, but the other two principals were not interested.

My responsibility was the elementary school, so I didn't mention the process during administrative meetings unless it was necessary. The other two principals simply ignored those issues even when we spoke of it. I quickly learned of the inequities regarding how the other administrators conducted themselves. It was best for me to mind my business and let the other two branches do what they do. Tensions between the board and Ronnie Sarver were growing, and by early spring of my second year two allies on the board had cracks in their overall support. The vote to renew his contract for another year fell short of a majority and he was finished at SCA. He was completing his seventh or eighth year as president. Within a week of the vote a board member asked me of my interest in the top job. I immediately told him two years as elementary school principal did not qualify me with enough experience to consider the top position. The board hired the high school principal as the new president.

Ronnie Sarver seemed miffed by the decision but hurriedly moved forward in a new direction – he left the school in excellent financial shape. A few persnickety board members the root cause – but a little hardheadedness on both sides likely contributed. What I know for certain: Ronnie Sarver is a good man but needed to replace a few *starters* with more capable *players* – just like he did as *Coach*. He knew what to do but couldn't quite get everyone to *play* their best *game* and execute well – nor could I. My association with Ronnie Sarver continued outside of school, and his wife chose to remain a pre-school teacher at the school. I admired her for doing so – not easy considering how a few friends on the board spitefully turned on her husband. I obtained my first administrator position due to Ronnie Sarver. He told me I was one of the best administrators he had ever worked with. *Coach* Sarver was placed in my life at a pivotal moment – a necessary moment.

Five influential people allowed providence to play out and light within their souls to shine brightly. When I was fortunate enough to be in the glow of their presence, the warmth these people exuded shaped me because they slowly and steadily guided me along beneficial paths. They constructed metaphorical bridges by which I was able to walk across – connecting me with people and resources that were once unreachable. Even though I may have resisted at times gentle nudges and prodding and challenged motives, I was forever enriched and made to be a better product of myself. They added value and worth to my daily walk – pushed me to go beyond what I thought I might achieve. I'm certain there are many other people they touched with their brightness, intensity, and bridges – others who would echo similar scenarios. The five people were by no means random connections – not by chance or sheer luck. The five people answered a providential calling, both unknowingly and knowingly. Their determination to influence and encourage was achieved; for that I am continually grateful. Without any doubt, each person was placed in my life at pivotal moments – necessary moments.

Is Raphael able to point to five influential people in his life? Likely he can, perhaps more, but those people probably served very different purposes because his lifestyle was opposite of mine. Raphael and I viewed life through totally dissimilar lenses. Habits and perceptions of comprehending his environment would not be the same as mine. Unfortunately, I can only speculate how he viewed the influences upon his formative years. It's fair to say his parents instilled within him a drive to succeed financially even though he was blessed with a financial cushion I did not possess. Raphael could have easily chosen to squander his privilege using it for personal indulgences and destructive behavior. Instead, he obviously placed controls and limitations on his privilege, made wise business decisions, functioned with diligence, married, raised four children, and reaped financial gain and security created by those choices. By the world's standards he is considered a highly successful business entrepreneur. He has taken greater financial risks than most people are ever capable of doing. Perhaps his financial cushion assisted in those efforts – again, speculation. What I know, we are similar in many ways, but the paths by which we achieved our goals in life were vastly different. It would be fascinating to know the when, where, and what influential people were placed in Raphael's life at pivotal moments – necessary moments.

Reckoning

Numerous life events and circumstances I witnessed are not shared, and I've heard many rumors that are unverifiable. My story could have revealed several living family members, friends and situations I do not wish to disparage. I don't believe anything illegal or criminal occurred, but do I really know? I was never physically or sexually abused by anyone in my family or by acquaintances – at least to my knowledge. I was fortunate to have a father that didn't physically abuse me, although our relationship was layered with thorny complexities. The most visible manifestations were his alcoholism and resulting neglect. He didn't deliberately neglect me – addiction dominated his life instead, concern for my overall welfare and future was not his priority. Perhaps the prevalence of his pornography in our narrow rectangle might be considered incidental abuse, perhaps a more correct description is blatant thoughtlessness. Emotional neglect could loosely apply, but then I could be accused of being a whining, spoiled only child – truth be told the title probably fits. I do know many questionable things occurred around me, but I was not aware of most of those specific occurrences during childhood and young adulthood. I know many people have horrendous stories regarding their past, many of which involve levels of poverty and dysfunction I never experienced. References to poverty and dysfunction are only relative to my life story.

Numerous studies demonstrate how children with a significant person or people in their lives like grandparents or someone that cares deeply for their well-being, chances for the child's success in life are much greater. Thankfully, those people existed in my life. Both sets of grandparents unknowingly modeled rhythms of life which highly attracted me. Under their tutelage I felt security and love rarely felt in my home. I watched grandparents with eagle vision, carefully registering everything in my brain I liked and dismissing portions I didn't. As previously stated, home life teetered on uncertainty, was precarious in many ways and simply didn't provide the sanctuary I desired or needed.

At times I was extremely rude and ungrateful toward my parents – raised an only child automatically enabled me the right to be *spoiled*. Of course, to some degree I own the title by virtue of unshared spaces, attention when I got it, and sole possession of limited personal things. Although expertly obedient, my ears never received affirming conversation from parents regarding compliant behavior. As a teenager I never caused my parents a moment of emotional pain or worry. Fully trained directly and indirectly I definitely possessed the ability to be a first-class *hell-raiser* or *rebel without a cause*. Instead, I chose to be the *elder brother*, not the *prodigal*, and persisted in my pompous perfectionism.

On numerous occasions I remember wanting to leave everything about my life all behind, literally walk out, leave my home – tell grandparents truth, the whole truth, live with one of them but didn't. Thinking back, they had to know my home was less than desirable – not what it should be – both sets surely suspected something didn't exactly add up. My mother transferred enough of her paranoid, unfounded fears, and denial onto me that I endured the discomfort – kept family secrets well protected. Somehow, I tolerated our psychosis until age twenty-five when a new life adventure was initiated. Packed all my emotional baggage and headed off – all firmly rooted deep within. And there's good news, alcohol abuse didn't move to my new life adventure, nor domestic abuse, child neglect or pornography. Terminating family destroying compulsions and problems with a resolve and motivated determination is a good thing, but recollections die hard and refuse to let go – faint transmissions and temptations loiter.

Compassion for my mother was unlike my love for her. I loved her because she was my mother, though not out of obligation – she sacrificed for me in her own unique way – cooked – washed clothes – loved irritably. Deeper compassion developed throughout my lifetime because I witnessed firsthand the wounds from her sufferings and misfortunes. Abruptly widowed at sixty-four, I immediately knew she would literally not survive her calamity without constant guidance and direct management. I'm at a loss to fully explain the actual cause of my mother's inability to operate on her own – she didn't seem to grasp certain basic concepts and functions of ordinary life. It troubles me to state this truth. Perhaps her family knew this truth well but didn't know how to appropriately relate – this may have created her sense of inferiority. Perhaps it explains her desire to use physical qualities to attract attention – especially from men. I know my grandmother seemed to favor my mother, but I know she disapproved of her lifestyle choices. There were moments when I witnessed my grandmother appearing very protective of her third child. My mother was the sibling that visited longer and more often – both seemed comforted by each other's company. Perhaps the truth of my mother's circumstances drew parent and child closer.

I'm searching for truth by way of a DNA paternity source. I've wondered if the unions that bore two sons were based on mutual love or something less desirable? At this juncture locked and sealed silence seems to be the barrier. In all honesty, does it matter at this point – poor decisions are carried out every day without considering consequences – a commonality we all share. I've hesitated at times to expose the hard-hitting truths of my parents' choices, how they chose to live day-to-day. Of course, it's true not all was problematic or troublesome. I can point to many pleasurable moments. Unfortunately, time was not on my side to develop the same deep level of empathy for the man who raised me as it was for my mother. I've wondered how our lives would have played out if death had not snatched him at fifty-five. Even though it's not easy to outline or expose my life in descriptions that are suitable or comfortable for sharing, my not so ordinary story is factual and unfolding. After the fourth *spilling of guts*, he asked a question that baffled me – attempted to make up quick answers to the two-part question and move beyond but I didn't. He asked me to ponder the question and return with my resolutions.

It pains me not to know my real bloodline – my DNA given name. It pains me when I look at my daughter and see a beautiful genetic smile I do not recognize and connect to someone. What's next? What do I do with the DNA information I hold? How do I reconcile the fact I have real family members out there I do not know? I want to know more details – more truth. I do not wish for this to end at this juncture. Realizing there is a strong possibility the real truth of my paternity may never be revealed, it's possible as other DNA results become available, I may discover additional and perhaps closely connected family. Will they be as eager as I am to make connections? I hope yes. I've shared everything I can conceivably share on the DNA website in hopes someone will recognize a name, date, event, or connection.

Believing that life events happen for particular reasons and that people are brought together for specific purposes, I know this search cannot be left to chance. How one responds to unexpected life events is a personal choice. My choice is to be as open as possible to whomever and wherever this may lead. At the same time, recognizing how tremendously blessed I am to have weathered the storms of my young life. In the midst of the storms, decisions were made that led to life altering consequences. The trajectory of my life could have taken so many wrong turns. I'm grateful it didn't, but my heart strings remain tied to a past – one never truly severs all connections to the past – my past and present are with me every day, every waking moment. Every time I see the numerous names in my DNA lineage, I see my past but I also see potential future. Perhaps a potential future that will interweave one day with new people or just a single person to add another piece to the puzzle to aid in shaping and molding me into the individual I am becoming.

I hesitated several times but finally gathered enough courage and inner strength of mind to conquer one half of the assignment he recommended – the second half I didn't know where to start – funny when an educator is the one on the other end of an assignment – not knowing what to do. The following is the letter I wrote to the father that raised me – our reckoning finally occurred in a silent city.

Dear Father:

I wish Pam and I had given more attention to your impending heart failure the day you died but we just didn't know. I must say, dying on Father's Day was a hell of a day to die! When we got into the car, we knew something wasn't right but dismissed it. Would you have listened to us if we had asked how you were feeling? Probably not. I honestly didn't grieve your death because my entire attention turned toward my mother. You know how needy she was and how she depended on you for everything. It all eventually worked out for her, but your untimely death wasn't easy, and my life immediately became more stressful.

When I was a child and adolescent, I longed for and desired your undivided attention, but your alcohol consumption didn't allow you to give me what I wanted and desperately needed. I resented it terribly. Here's something amazing, I've never abused alcohol – never! I do enjoy drinking occasionally but I've never been drunk because I made a vow; I didn't want to be like you. I don't say that to hurt you – just raw truth. I hated all holidays most years and especially during the turbulent years of adolescence. Why did you think overindulging in alcohol was a good thing? Why didn't you see how much it was hurting our relationship? Here's more good news, I forgave you a long time ago, but I may be harboring resentment. I think it goes back to your sudden death and how you left me to do everything for my mother. I'm unsure about those deepest feelings toward you and how bouts of gloominess and especially around holidays are probably connected. I'm attempting to sort through those feelings with the help of an objective listener.

I have a theory, perhaps you were deeply wounded emotionally during childhood. You never told me anything about your childhood. Perhaps you were deeply wounded by fear and uncertainty during your time in Korea. You never told me anything about your time in the war other than you served as an airplane mechanic. Perhaps you resented the fact my mother was five months pregnant, possibly with someone else's baby, or perhaps you assumed I was your child. You never said anything about this to me – not one word. Did you ever think I might not be your biological child? If you did, did you know my biological father? Perhaps my mother never told you and led you to believe I was your child. As you knew well, she lied a lot about many things. I discovered through something called DNA you are not my biological father. DNA are microscopic molecules carrying our genetic codes for reproduction and growth. Sorry for the mini science lesson, but I'm connected genetically to the Millard family of Murfreesboro. There are two Millard bothers within a year or two of my mother's age. One of the bothers worked at the VA where she worked. Of course, both are deceased. I may never know the true source of my paternity.

Here's a shocker, did you know I have a brother eighteen months older than me? Nile Tenpenny drove his sister to Kentucky to have the baby she named Jack, and he was immediately adopted and grew up in Belle Meade. I think his oldest child looks like you in your Korean service photo. His middle child looks like my mother and his other two resemble the Tenpenny family. I realize you may have never known this or perhaps he is your child. I'm thinking it's very possible the two of you were involved, she got pregnant and y'all broke up. You later got back together, she got pregnant a second time then you married when she was five months pregnant – why the wait? Something else you never spoke about. This portion of my story is a whole different dimension I struggle to find ways to resolve. I'm not certain I'll ever know truth. I asked my mother about it, but she would never tell me. When she died, I knew truth may have died with her.

There are so many layers of dysfunction to dissect. I feel like our relationship was cheated because I never had opportunity to reconcile our relationship as I did with my mother. I took good care of her for the remainder of her life. I was with her when she died – it was a sweet moment, but no truth before her last breath. Perhaps you may have told me if we had had more time together. I was about to confront you about drinking on the job – yes, I knew you were doing it because I spied on you one day.

But you died before I was able to confront the issue. By the way, you never had opportunity to meet your granddaughter, Caroline. She's a beautiful young lady and possesses the best qualities of Pam and me.

Before ending, I must ask about the pornography. Why so much? Why was it so readily available? Surely you didn't think I wouldn't be curious – not snoop when y'all were out. All kids are curious about things pertaining to human anatomy. I saw too much before I was mentally and physically ready for it. It warped some of my thinking about sexual matters and relationships. Fortunately, I didn't act out with other people based on my newfound knowledge. Some of the images are still clearly chiseled in my mind. I never heard you say anything about it except for the time you told me one of your bosses had lots of pornography including films. You called him a hypocrite because he was a deacon in his church. I wondered why you shared that with me but didn't ask. My exposure to your pornography as a pre-teen created lots of conflict within my mind that I still find troubling. I wish it were possible to erase it all from my memory.

I do not wish this letter to be all negative, although my experiences as a child, pre-teen, adolescent, and young adult primarily fall in a negative column, I have many fond memories I attribute to you. Always providing the best cuts of meat was something I loved and still love to this day. I'm an excellent griller due to you. The little sacrifices you made on my behalf I truly appreciated but never told you. One of my best experiences was the time you offered $500 toward the diamond for Pam's engagement ring. You loved Pam because you knew she loved me. Both my mother and you prepared a delicious rehearsal dinner in our new home where Pam had lived only one week. Both of you created a wonderful memory. You respected Pam's parents and my friends by not *drinking that day – thank you! And here's a little nugget of truth, my first night with Pam was our honeymoon night. I didn't wish to repeat history.*

I wish our relationship could have been different – more positive – more father son togetherness. I wish we had had more years to know one another and I help you overcome addictions. I could have asked you all those questions regarding my paternity. But I thank you for doing the best you could do. Allow me to say it again, I forgive you for all the dysfunction caused by your addictions. May you rest in peace!

Standing between two rectangle grave markers bearing names of my parents, a letter written to my father in hand – I read aloud. Used proper inflection for certain phrases and words, and when I mentioned my mother, I glanced to the left at her grave marker as if she was listening. My voice lowered when on the other side of a new chain link fence that replaced the stone wall, an elderly lady walked her black English bulldog for a potty break. I glanced at her, she glanced at me, I wanted to yell, *Go back in the house; stop spoiling my private moment.* Looked back at my letter without pause and thought how the ordinariness of life has a way of balancing solemn moments. I finished reading with little emotion – paused briefly to inhale and exhale fresh morning air – peered across the peaceful setting, manicured grass wintered brown by cold. Decided to walk the access road back to my vehicle instead of navigating the multitude of flat rectangular grave markers of unknown fathers, mothers, brothers, sisters, cousins, and friends. I steered slowly through the crowded silent city back to the main entrance.

The persistent gnawing subsided and contented calm engulfed all senses. I shared the completed part of my assignment later that day – he listened and stressed, *"Do not underestimate the impact and meaning of that moment."* The

English Bulldog briefly crossed my mind, but I pondered more seriously my unknown biological father buried somewhere. Would I one day read a letter to him about hopes and dreams of what could have been? Perhaps time and truth will eventually answer that question.

I've derived from reflections and remembrances an underlying truth that my life has been a series of poor and rich sagas all rolled into one bundle. I've experienced life as poor and rich, highs and lows, successes and failures – and after the first twenty-five a highly satisfying and comfortable life. A secret sibling discovered his birth family – a brother I don't truly know remains an enigma. I may be depending too much on the accuracy and power of DNA to unravel this mystery. DNA bonds parent with child, sibling with sibling, distant relative to relative, frees the mistakenly incarcerated and much more, but will DNA answer my numerous questions? No clear answers yet, but I eagerly invite more defining DNA moments.

Acknowledging my existence as a series of tiny life sagas, mostly typical, some not so typical, I wrestled hard out of struggle for something different and ultimately found my *remnant of Eden* – but it hasn't removed a desire to know my past, my brother, his family, our extended family. A desire overpoweringly as real as that day in Shoney's. So, I ask the same two questions. Who am I? What's my real name? Surely my story and longing for truth doesn't end.

Emptied

Choices shaped past, present, and future for one privileged and one underprivileged – different pathways but destined for eerily similar outcomes. Fate eventually converged two brothers – one searching, one questioning. If wealth had dropped upon my circumstances early the potential for overindulgence could have taken its due course – a likely disaster. On the flip side, wealth for another was common-place, everyday life. If wealth had suddenly been removed, he may have experienced a similar childhood as mine – possible catastrophe. How did our adult lives end up eerily similar? The answer may rest in dissimilar beginnings and lives tendered by dissimilar sets of parents. A thousand threads of destiny determined by parental choices – but ultimately, choices fell on two siblings, and we altered our circumstances – two uniquely *woven tapestries* both charting paths of success and fulfillment.

Choices to participate or not participate in the follies and absurdities of youth, pursuing dreams through higher education, which determined specific careers, marrying wisely chosen partners and choosing to remain married shaped us and is still shaping. I believe a multitude of insignificant occurrences indeed mattered – hundreds upon hundreds of tiny moments with no meaning for anyone else enabled my character and determination to develop. Storytime with a retired teacher on a concrete patio, sweet taste of cold watermelon on a sweltering summer day, bold enough to plead with linemen to have electricity in working order before *The Wizard of Oz*, hooking a snake instead of fish in a moss-covered cow pond, building child-like dams with all the seriousness of an engineer, standing in the front door coveting expensive vehicles, unknown drivers taking short cuts through a pauperized neighborhood, walking to high school and a scam college because I didn't own transportation – embarrassed by what others thought, hours awake in bed imagining a future different than what engulfed me – significant? Yes.

Nine different *houses* – dappled with a variety of *hues* – but I wanted my one fantasy *house of four seasons*. Instead, flawed houses on Spanntown Road, Campbell Road, Old Hickory Boulevard, Maple Street, Shepherd Hills Drive, Monticello Avenue, Forest Park Road, Harris Street, Idlewild Avenue. Twenty-five years of four seasons all reverberated with forms of dysfunction – occasionally balanced by satisfying moments of insignificance, seemingly buffering hits, scrapes, and multiple scars of disappointment, but I survived. Perhaps it's not possible to walk away from twenty-five years of imposed dysfunction clean and completely unaffected. I suppose there's comfort knowing it's okay to be a little messed up emotionally because everyone carries *baggage,* hauling it from one place then to another. Author and illustrator Roger Duvoisin captured a little boy's budding creativity, not only with a house the family fell in love with nestled among tall trees, he captivated artistic sensibilities with his use of a color wheel – blending red, yellow, and blue creating each season of color.

The book intrigued me because four family members wanted each side of the house painted a different color for each season, the childlike fantasy allure for me. But I had no understanding of the deeper meaning in elementary school – how the ingenious father arrived at a winning trifecta of negotiation, education, and thrift with his family solving a color dilemma – teaching his children an important lesson. In the end the family ended up in a beautifully painted house. I wish my family had functioned in that manner when I was a child, but would my story still be a tale of *flawed houses?* As in most storybooks of my generation, everyone lived *happily ever after*, and that's what I desired with every ounce of my being. By a curious coincidence, I ended up in a beautiful house nestled among tall trees just like the storybook family – *little did I know.* The first night in our new home an old owl unexpectedly swooped across the Venetian window just outside our living room. I think the old owl was letting us know we invaded its territory. We often hear mysterious hoots in the night when our nocturnal friends search for vermin. And by another coincidence of little importance, the old storybook owl that once occupied the abandoned structure, returned to the tall trees surrounding the newly painted, renovated house – to live among the family – surely *happily ever after.*

After six weeks I remained conflicted, unable to articulate why I needed to know – no second letter yet, an incomplete assignment for now. All my paths ultimately led to a life of fulfillment – then why the void? He ended the final hour of *spilling my guts* with a simple question – *"What have you learned?"* Thought about Dorothy being asked the same by the Scarecrow in the city of Oz before clicking ruby slippers together. But I didn't have an insightful response as she did. Thought about my deepest thoughts and inner conflicts shared for the first time with a trusted male coming to an end. The only thought I could muster, *"I remain uncertain how to reconcile this desire to know my paternity source."*

For every spilling, he sat and I sat on opposite couches. Time really did fly. With another slenderest of grin and this time a heartier nod of confirmation he initiated the wrap up, *"I believe some angels were working overtime."* He may have borrowed the phrase from Luke Combs being the huge music fan he is, but that's alright with me. He again paused briefly – in silence glanced at notes – pen gently tapping the notebook while gathering thoughts – tap, tap, tap. I waited patiently. He proposed with calm, simple words a poignant perspective – a thoughtful discerning of my paternal and sibling dilemma I had not considered. *"You do know there is dog shit in the green grass on the other side of the fence, you just can't see it!"*

On the drive home I pondered his comment. My interpretation – I needed a poignant perspective, first to remind me be careful what I seek and where I step, second, that my life cannot be viewed through the lens of fantasy – a default mindset I sometimes languish in but don't like to admit. Truth is, all houses, including mine nestled among tall trees are flawed when occupied by people. I just *can't see it.*

I was emptied – though a chasm and longing persist, a forever hunger to hear...

Yours is the Earth and everything that's in it,
And—which is more—you'll be a Man, my son!

Dedication

My first published book and perhaps my only book, I dedicate to *super glue* – a perfect description of my wife and best friend. I use the term *super glue* because she is undeniably the glue that consistently holds our relationship together. Allow a quick clarification, we have never been at a point of separating or ending our relationship – not anywhere near. However, as in all relationships we've experienced our share of disagreements. I'm by far the most difficult to live with, and she knows this to be true. She married a bundle of dysfunctional attributes, but I do a pretty good job disguising those most of the time. Her steady persistence in being the most stable presence in our relationship has assisted me the most. When we first married, I held serious doubts deep within that I might not live up to her expectations and mine, but never breathed a word about those uncertainties. What I did instead likely worse, I allowed those insecurities to seep into conversations, into everyday actions, and in my disgust for certain things – all while she remained steady as a rock. Her stability and financial means in the beginning got me through college; I was motivated, though doubted my ability to finish well. Her salary supported us well during those early years, and a generous gift from her grandparents allowed us to purchase the three-bedroom brick home as newlyweds – a privilege I had not experienced since first grade.

Her spiritual astuteness and dedication to faith the first several years together, although rigid at times, kept me pointed in the right direction – eventually aiding me to solidify my personal faith. My immaturity focused on our financial means, and I unwisely desired a higher standard of living through material possessions. Vehicles and clothes my primary weakness but thankfully we never experienced any financial short falls or repossessions. I'm lucky in that she is not a clothes person, not a jewelry person, buys cheap makeup, not fond of shopping in general. She finally admitted money I spent on flowers was not necessary – much prefers expenditures on eating out. She's simple, an easy person in that regard – I'm lucky and do not consistently honor her for that huge portion of her character. Her spiritual fervor and commitment to faith grows with every passing day – she inspires me to maintain my spiritual quest for renewal.

My purpose in writing this dedication is to simply honor her. I am sincerely grateful for her enduring my many hours of typing and retyping, constant revisions, lots of doubts, listening to me read aloud a story she had basically lived. It is difficult for me to find exact words to adequately express how fortunate and blessed I am to have her in my life. She knows I despise wordy greeting cards and sappy phrases, so I'll be cautious with words. What I honestly love is her steadiness of character, her ability to welcome others into her life with open arms hospitality – a trait I consistently resist, and her eternal patience. Pam lovingly brought our daughter into this world, and she thankfully possesses her mother's most prized qualities. Even our dogs recognize what I'm describing – both chose Pam as their favorite human. She's my favorite human too, and I honor her with this memoir. She doesn't hold a prominent spot in the story because I avoided writing our love story. A unique type of naivety and innocence infuses her soul, and the dysfunction narrative I chose just doesn't fit well with her character, though, I could not have told the story without her. From the deepest heart level, I thank her for being the *super glue* I've always needed and for being that which holds our lives together.

Dear Readers,

A sincere thank you for enduring my stream of consciousness, or should I say, spilling my guts.

About Atmosphere Press

Atmosphere Press is an independent, full-service publisher for excellent books in all genres and for all audiences. Learn more about what we do at atmospherepress.com.

We encourage you to check out some of Atmosphere's latest releases, which are available at Amazon.com and via order from your local bookstore:

Twisted Silver Spoons, a novel by Karen M. Wicks

Queen of Crows, a novel by S.L. Wilton

The Summer Festival is Murder, a novel by Jill M. Lyon

The Past We Step Into, stories by Richard Scharine

The Museum of an Extinct Race, a novel by Jonathan Hale Rosen

Swimming with the Angels, a novel by Colin Kersey

Island of Dead Gods, a novel by Verena Mahlow

Cloakers, a novel by Alexandra Lapointe

Twins Daze, a novel by Jerry Petersen

Embargo on Hope, a novel by Justin Doyle

Abaddon Illusion, a novel by Lindsey Bakken

Blackland: A Utopian Novel, by Richard A. Jones

The Jesus Nut, a novel by John Prather

The Embers of Tradition, a novel by Chukwudum Okeke

Saints and Martyrs: A Novel, by Aaron Roe

When I Am Ashes, a novel by Amber Rose

Grace, a novel by Nancy Allen

Shifted, a novel by KristaLyn A. Vetovich

About the Author

James Morris is a thirty-seven-year career educator and school administrator. He first pursued fashion merchandizing and design before returning to his original career desire completing a Bachelor's in elementary education. He taught in both public  and private schools before earning his Master's in Administrative Leadership. His first role as principal then president landed him in a private school. James returned to his roots in a large urban public elementary school with a 96% poverty rate. His debut published work is a memoir. James lives with his wife of thirty-eight years in rural Davidson County, north of Nashville, Tennessee.

Rachel Allison Photography

Made in the USA
Coppell, TX
29 December 2021

70272466R00198